starting out:
king's ind

JOHN EMMS

EVERYMAN CHESS

www.everymanchess.com

First published in 2005 by Gloucester Publishers plc (formerly
Everyman Publishers plc), Northburgh House, 10 Northburgh Street,
London EC1V 0AT

British Library Cataloguing-in-Publication Data
A catalogue record for this book is available from the British Library.

ISBN 978 1 85744 394 3

Distributed in North America by The Globe Pequot Press, P.O Box 480,
246 Goose Lane, Guilford, CT 06437-0480.

All other sales enquiries should be directed to Everyman Chess,
Northburgh House, 10 Northburgh Street, London EC1V 0AT
tel: 020 7253 7887 fax: 020 7490 3708
email: info@everymanchess.com; website: www.everymanchess.com

EVERYMAN CHESS SERIES (formerly Cadogan Chess)
Chief advisor: Byron Jacobs
Commissioning editor: John Emms
Assistant editor: Richard Palliser

Typeset and edited by First Rank Publishing, Brighton.
Cover design by Horatio Monteverde.
Printed and bound in the US.

Contents

Bibliography

Books

Attacking with 1 e4, John Emms (Everyman 2001)
Beating the Anti-Sicilians, Joe Gallagher (Batsford 1995)
Encyclopaedia of Chess Openings Volume B (Sahovski Informator)
Encyclopaedia of Chess Openings Volume C (Sahovski Informator)
How to Play the King's Indian Attack, Angus Dunnington, (Batsford 1993)
Nunn's Chess Openings, John Nunn, Graham Burgess, John Emms and Joe Gallagher (Everyman 1999)
Opening Preparation, Mark Dvoretsky and Artur Yusupov (Batsford 1994)
Play the Caro-Kann, Egon Varnusz (Everyman 1991)
Play the French 2nd edition, John Watson (Everyman 1996)
Play the French 3rd edition, John Watson (Everyman 2003)
Sicilians: A Guide for Black, Dorian Rogozenko (Gambit 2003)
The Complete French, Lev Psakhis (Batsford 1992)
The Ultimate King's Indian Attack, Angus Dunnington, (Batsford 1998)

Periodicals and Databases

Chess Informants 1-92
ChessBase Magazine
Chesspublishing.com
New In Chess Yearbooks 1-75
Mega Corr 3
Mega Database 2005
The Week in Chess 1-559

Introduction

What is the King's Indian Attack?

The King's Indian Attack (KIA) is a universal system of development for White rather than a specific opening variation. It is characterised by the moves Nf3, g2-g3, Bg2, 0-0, d2-d3, Nbd2 and e2-e4 **(Diagram 1)**.

Diagram 1
The KIA formation

The Attraction of the KIA

I was first lured to the KIA in my teens, and for a few years I played nothing else with the white pieces. One of the major selling points of the KIA is that White can play the same system of development against virtually any black set-up. Another positive is that there is much more emphasis on the understanding of ideas within the system than the need to learn theory – perfect for someone who has neither the time nor the inclination to memorise numerous different opening variations (i.e. me when I was in my teens!). The KIA is very easy to play and is an excellent weapon around which you can base an opening repertoire.

A Brief History of the KIA

The KIA first became prominent throughout in the 1950s and 1960s, when some of the world's leading players, including Fischer, Botvinnik and Smyslov, added it to their opening armouries. The KIA became a particularly popular set-up against the French Defence, as many players were enticed by White's attractive attacking possibilities against Black's castled king. Games such as the following certainly did its reputation no harm:

Game 1
□ **E.Vasiukov** ■ **W.Uhlmann**
Lasker Memorial, Berlin 1962

1 e4 e6 2 d3 d5 3 Nd2 Nf6 4 Ngf3 c5 5 g3 Nc6 6 Bg2 Be7 7 0-0 0-0 8 Re1 Qc7 9 Qe2 b5 10 e5 Nd7 11 Nf1 a5 12 h4 (Diagram 2)

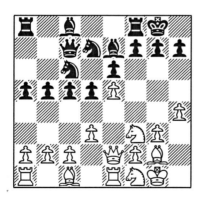
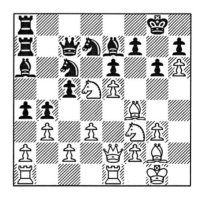

Diagram 2 (B)
An attack in progress

Diagram 3 (B)
18 Ne3xd5!!

White already has the makings of a powerful kingside attack. For 12

Bf4 see Game 5 in Chapter 1.

12...b4 13 Bf4 Ba6 14 Ne3 a4 15 b3 Ra7 16 h5 Rfa8 17 h6 g6 18 Nxd5!! (Diagram 3)

In Chapter 1 we learn that this particular sacrifice is not an uncommon weapon for White.

18...exd5 19 e6 Qd8 20 exf7+ Kh8

20...Kf8 loses to 21 Ng5! Bxg5 22 Bxg5 Qxg5 23 Qe8+, while 20...Kxf7 21 Qe6+ Kf8 22 Ng5! Bxg5 23 Bd6+ Be7 24 Bxd5 also leads to mate.

21 Ne5 Ncxe5 22 Qxe5+! Bf6

Or 22...Nxe5 23 Bxe5+ Bf6 24 Bxf6+ Qxf6 25 Re8+ and mate follows.

23 Qe8+ Nf8 24 Be5! Qb6 25 Bxd5 Rc8 26 Be6

26 Re3! followed by Rf3 would have finished Black off immediately.

26...Bxe5 27 Bxc8 Bd6 28 Bxa6 Rxa6 29 bxa4 Ra7 30 Re6 Qc7 31 Rae1 c4 32 Rxd6! Qxd6 33 Re6 1-0

After 33...Qc5 34 d4! Black's queen cannot stay protecting the knight on f8. A devastating performance by White against one of the world's leading experts of the French.

More recently the KIA has risen in popularity due in no small part to the efforts of the brilliant Russian grandmaster Alexander Morozevich, who has injected some new ideas from White's point of view. A small selection of grandmasters amongst many others who have also contributed to its theory include Vaganian, Aronian, Ljubojevic, Bologan, Glek and Kaidanov.

Choosing a KIA Repertoire

A KIA repertoire can be formed in two quite different ways. The traditional way of playing the KIA is via a flank opening where White usually plays 1 Nf3 followed by g2-g3, Bg2, 0-0, d2-d3, Nbd2 and then e2-e4. Playing in this manner, White can employ the KIA against virtually any set-up that Black chooses to adopt, and this is the way favoured by grandmasters such as Vaganian and Aronian.

The more modern way of using the KIA is to integrate it as part of a complete repertoire with 1 e4, as recommended by the renowned chess trainer Mark Dvoretsky, and taken up by the likes of Morozevich, Bologan and Glek. You'll discover in this book that playing with 1 e4, the KIA is more effective against certain defences than it is against others. I suspect most chess players starting out with 1 e4 play this move because they enjoy the 'Open Games' after 1 e4 e5, where they can employ the Ruy Lopez, the Italian Game, the Scotch or a number of different gambits. By using the KIA against other black defences to 1 e4, the White player can still get pleasure from playing Open Games without having to learn all the theory of the main lines of the French and Sicilian Defences.

The KIA can be played against most defences to 1 e4, the only real exception being the Scandinavian (1...d5); it is most popular against the French and certain lines of the Sicilian. In this book I've indulged a bit more in these lines because the theory is relatively more developed and I've found that the positions are very rich in ideas for both players.

About this Book

As part of Everyman Chess's *Starting Out* guide, this book is primarily aimed at players who have little or no experience in the KIA and who wish to master the basics. In each section I've begun with an introduction to the variation in question, and it's here I have tried my best to cover as many eventualities as possible, while pointing out different move orders and tricks.

In the illustrative games I have tried to explain the middlegame strategies adopted by both White and Black. These games have been selected more for their entertainment and instructional value than their theoretical relevance (not that the KIA is very theoretical in any case).

Even though this book will probably be more attractive (I hope!) to those playing the White side of the KIA, I've intended no particular bias for either side, and throughout I've suggested possible repertoires for both White and Black players.

Finally, the best of luck in all your KIA adventures!

John Emms
Kent
August 2005

Chapter One

KIA Versus the French

Introduction

If we're simply looking at openings stemming from the move 1 e4, there's certainly an argument to suggest that the KIA is at its most effective when employed against the French Defence. The point is that Black is already committed to the move ...e7-e6 even though as you'll see, in many lines of the KIA he would prefer his e-pawn to be on either e5 or even e7!

Many world-class players have used the KIA as a weapon against the French. Bobby Fischer turned to it when he was having trouble proving any advantage in the main lines of the French, and you'll find a few gems from him in the notes. More recently Alexander Morozevich, who has won over many supporters with his direct attacking style, has injected some new ideas into it.

The First Few Moves

1 e4 e6 2 d3! (Diagram 1)

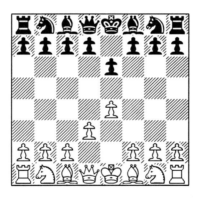
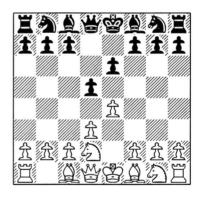

Diagram 1 (B)
2 d3 – crucial

Diagram 2 (B)
3 Nd2 – blocking the d-file

 TIP: It's absolutely vital to play this move before doing anything else.

The point is that after Black plays ...d7-d5, there's always the option for him to capture on e4. White wants to be able to recapture with the d3-pawn, thus maintaining a pawn on e4, but he also wants to keep the queens on the board. So 2 g3, for example, while being one of the crucial moves of the KIA system, is inaccurate here due to 2...d5!. Now after 3 d3 White doesn't have time to play Nd2; Black can play 3...dxe4! 4 dxe4 Qxd1+ 5 Kxd1, which is certainly not what White is looking for in the KIA!

2...d5

The whole point behind Black's first move. Just as White builds his game plan around the strongpoint of e4, Black builds his around d5.

3 Nd2! (Diagram 2)

Just in time! Now if Black captures on e4 White can happily recapture with the pawn and the queens stay on the board.

 NOTE: The other way that White avoids a queen swap is with the move 3 Qe2 – we'll look at this a bit later.

3...c5

The most ambitious move. Given that White has forgone the possibility of playing d2-d4, Black takes the opportunity to grab as much space in the centre as possible. I'll cover alternatives later in the chapter.

4 Ngf3

This is the normal move here, but White can also delay the development of the g1-knight and get on with the kingside fianchetto with 4 g3!?. Following, say, 4...Nc6 5 Bg2 Nf6 most players choose 6 Ngf3, reaching the main line, but there's also the option of lunging forward with the f-pawn: 6 f4!? Be7 7 Ngf3 0-0 8 0-0 b5 9 e5 Nd7 reaches a position that is similar to one of the main lines of the KIA except that White's pawn is on f4 instead of f2. On f4 it gives good support to the e5-pawn, but what probably puts KIA players off this f2-f4 advance is that, when the d2-knight moves, the c1-bishop is still blocked by the f4-pawn. Even so, 4 g3 is certainly worth bearing in mind.

4...Nc6 (Diagram 3)

The most flexible move. Black develops his queen's knight to its most aggressive square but remains uncommitted (for one more move at least) over his piece formation on the kingside.

4...Nf6 will probably transpose to a variation considered later on, but there is an independent line worth mentioning in 5 g3 b6 6 Bg2 dxe4!?

7 dxe4 Ba6!?, Black's bishop taking the a6-f1 diagonal and temporarily preventing White from castling. White can utilise the long h1-a8 diagonal with 8 e5! Nd5 9 c4! Nb4 10 0-0 when Black probably has nothing better than 10...Bb7 In the game A.Morozevich-A.Kogan, London 1994 the KIA expert continued strongly with 11 b3! (11 a3?! Nd3!, forcing an exchange of the c1-bishop, was Black's idea) 11...N8c6 (now 11...Nd3 can be met by 12 Ba3! followed by Qe2 and Rad1, when the d3-knight's future is very uncertain) 12 Bb2 Qc7 13 a3! Nd3 14 Bc3! 0-0-0 15 Qe2 Be7 16 Rfd1 and White was doing well. The knight on d3 looks active but in fact it's a pain for Black; it has no retreat squares and requires constant protection.

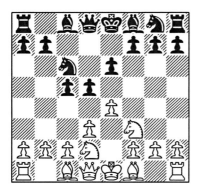

Diagram 3 (W)
Keeping options open

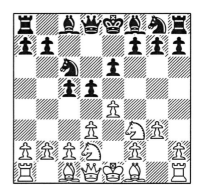

Diagram 4 (B)
Shaping up

5 g3! (Diagram 4)

The KIA development scheme is beginning to fall into shape – White is preparing Bg2 and 0-0. The bishop is much more effectively placed on g2 than it would be on e2. For a start it gives good protection to White's castled king. Secondly, it can greatly influence the game down the long h1-a8 diagonal. If the knight on f3 moves, the bishop on g2 adds pressure to the tension-filled centre (the e4-pawn against d5). One further point is that on e2 the bishop would hinder the queen's path to the kingside; with the bishop on g2 White only has to move the f3-knight before the queen can swing into action via g4 or h5.

Now Black must decide how to develop his kingside pieces; we will take a look at each approach in turn: 5...Nf6, 5...g6 and 5...Bd6.

It's also worth mentioning a couple of lines where Black exchanges on e4 and tries for a swift ...b7-b6 and ...Ba6:

a) 5...dxe4?! 6 dxe4 b6!? 7 c3!? (holding back on Bg2) 7...Nf6 and now White can demonstrate a problem with a very early ...dxe4 by playing 8 Bb5!. Now in the game G.Tringov-Y.Porat, Amsterdam 1964 Black soon got into trouble after 8...Bb7 9 Qa4! Qc7 10 Ne5! and following 10...Rc8 11 Qxa7! Bd6 12 Bxc6+ Bxc6 13 Qxc7 Rxc7 14 Nxc6 Rxc6 White was a clear pawn to the good. Black should probably settle for 8...Bd7, but this was hardly the intention when playing 6...b6.

 NOTE: White's bishop isn't always fianchettoed!

b) A more precise way for Black to play the same plan is with 5...b6!? 6 Bg2 and only now 6...dxe4 7 dxe4 Ba6!. White normally blocks out the bishop with 8 c4 at a cost of granting an outpost for Black on d4. Black can follow up with ...Qd7, ...0-0-0 etc, while White castles short and plays b2-b3 with Bb2, or perhaps aim for a2-a3 and b2-b4. White can also opt to keep the long diagonal open with 7 Nxe4 Bb7 8 0-0 Be7 (preparing ...Nf6) and here I think 9 b3 followed by Bb2 makes most sense.

The Traditional Main Line with 5...Nf6

1 e4 e6 2 d3 d5 3 Nd2 c5 4 Ngf3 Nc6 5 g3 Nf6 (Diagram 5)

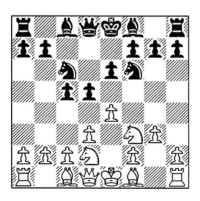

Diagram 5 (W)
Classical development

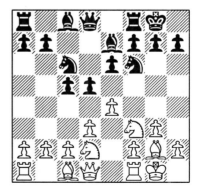

Diagram 6 (W)
Castling into it?

Black develops 'classically', that is he puts his knight on its best square where it has most influence on the centre. Of course Black has to bear in mind that White has the option of attacking this knight at some point with e4-e5. The variation beginning with 5...Nf6 is regarded as the traditional main line of the KIA French, and it is still very popular at all levels.

6 Bg2

Sensible play – White decides to finish kingside development and get the king into safety before commencing any aggressive action.

> WARNING: White must not get too excited early on. The impetuous 6 e5? forces the knight to retreat, but following 6...Nd7! 7 Qe2 Qc7! White cannot provide enough support to e5 and simply loses a crucial pawn. Here we see the value of Black's early ...c7-c5 – White is in no position to play d3-d4.

6...Be7!

With the knight on f6, this is the safest place for the bishop. There's a temptation to develop more 'actively' with 6...Bd6, but then Black always has to be wary of the pawn fork e4-e5. For example, 7 0-0 0-0 and now 8 Re1! immediately threatens to win a piece with e4-e5. Black can prevent this with 8...Qc7, but then 9 Qe2!, renewing the danger, is a bit annoying.

7 0-0 0-0 (Diagram 6)

Castling kingside is by far Black's most popular move here. However, given that White hopes to launch an assault on this side of the board, it's unsurprising that some Black players are nervous of committing their king so early. The flexible 7...b6!?, keeping the option open of castling queenside, is discussed in Games 2-3.

8 Re1!

The rook is very well placed on this square as it supports the intended e4-e5 advance.

> NOTE: 8 Re1 is what virtually everyone plays, but in all likelihood the immediate 8 e5 Nd7 9 Re1 will come to pretty much the same thing.

8...b5!

With his king 'safely' tucked away, Black begins his counterplay in aggressive style. It makes sense to attack on the queenside because this is the part of the board where Black holds a major advantage – space.

 TIP: It's always easier to attack in sectors where you have more space.

8...b5 is what those in 'the know' play here, but it's worth checking out some other plausible options.

a) 8...Qc7 covers the e5-square and following 9 e5 Nd7 White must protect the pawn with 10 Qe2 – see Game 5.

b) 8...b6 is a more restrained version of the text move – see Game 4.

c) 8...dxe4 9 dxe4 **(Diagram 7)** simplifies the position in the centre, but this exchange almost always helps White more than Black.

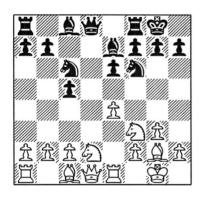 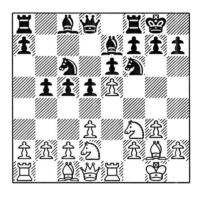

Diagram 7 (B)	Diagram 8 (B)
A central trade helps White	The push comes

 NOTE: Following an exchange on e4, White has more presence in the centre than Black, and after e4-e5 he gains access to the important e4-square, which effectively becomes an outpost.

A couple of examples:

c1) 9...b6 10 e5 Nd7 (10...Nd5 11 Ne4 Ndb4 12 Nd6 Bxd6 13 exd6 Bb7 14 c4 Qd7 15 a3 Na6 16 Bf4 looks good for White – the passed d-pawn is a real thorn in Black's side) 11 Ne4 (11 Nd4! cxd4 12 Bxc6 Rb8 13 Nb3 also looks good for White) 11...Ba6 12 Bf4 b5 13 c3 and White was better in T.Petrosian-I.Kan, Moscow 1955. The game continued 13...Qb6 14 Qc2 Rfd8 15 h4! Nf8 16 h5 Rac8?! (16...h6) 17 h6! and

White's attack on the kingside was far more effective than Black's on the other wing.

c2) 9...e5 (a radical move which prevents e4-e5 but at the same time weakens the d5-square) 10 c3 h6 11 Nc4! Qxd1 (after 11...Qc7 White should play 12 Ne3) 12 Rxd1 Nxe4 13 Nfxe5 Nxe5 14 Nxe5 and White had a big endgame plus in the game B.Badea-V.Danilov, Bucharest 1998. In particular the bishop on g2 is a very strong piece.

9 e5! (Diagram 8)

White has been building up to play this move for quite a while and finally it arrives. It's worth mentioning a couple of points here:

1) The pawn on e5 forces Black to move his f6-knight from its ideal defensive post. This will leave Black's kingside seriously lacking in minor piece protection – something that White will hope to exploit

2) With e4-e5 White has closed the centre – there is no longer any tension there. This leaves both sides free to concentrate their efforts on the flanks: White on kingside and Black on the queenside.

White could change tack completely by playing 9 exd5 exd5, but this approach isn't really in the spirit of this particular KIA line. Why deny yourself the chance of an automatic attack against the black king?

9...Nd7

The move played by the vast majority of players – Black keeps an eye on the e5-pawn. However, 9...Ne8!?, though seldom played, isn't a bad alternative. After say 10 Nf1 b4 the knight can join the queenside action via c7 and b5.

I can only find one example of the move 9...Ng4!? on my database, which seems to imply that there's something drastically wrong with it. However, despite the fact that the e5-pawn is well enough protected so White can simply push the knight back with 10 h3 Nh6, the knight isn't so poorly placed here because it has f5 in its sights. White can prevent this with 11 g4, but 11...f6 12 exf6 gxf6, while obviously carrying some risk, doesn't look disastrous for Black. Food for thought.

10 Nf1

A typical cog in White's plan of a kingside attack. The bishop on c1 is released and the f1-knight can join the action with Ne3-g4 or, after h2-h4, Nh2-g4.

10...a5 (Diagram 9)

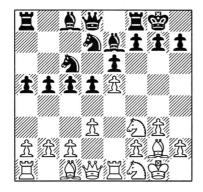
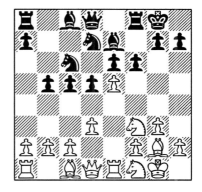

Diagram 9 (W)
Four pawns abreast

Diagram 10 (W)
Challenging the spearhead

Continuing the queenside demonstration. The four pawns abreast on the fourth rank now look quite impressive, if not yet particularly threatening.

Black players overly nervous of White's forthcoming kingside assault should either:

1) Not play this variation! (or)

2) Consider fighting back against White's e5-stroingpoint with 10...f6!? **(Diagram 10)**. White has no way of maintaining his pawn spearhead in the centre, and following 11 exf6 Nxf6 Black has some breathing space on the kingside and is unlikely to be checkmated inside 20 moves. The flipside is that Black is forced to accept a couple of weaknesses: the pawn on e6 is backward and vulnerable to attack down the half-open e-file, and White may be able to make use of the outpost on e5. For example, 12 Bf4! Bd6 13 Ne5 Nxe5 14 Bxe5 Bxe5 15 Rxe5 Qb6 16 Qe2 Bd7 17 Bh3! saw White making use of both factors in the game E.Bricard-R.Poulenard, Chanac 1989.

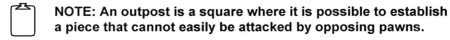

NOTE: An outpost is a square where it is possible to establish a piece that cannot easily be attacked by opposing pawns.

A possible improvement Black could try 11...Bxf6!?, the tactical point being that the greedy 12 Rxe6? sees the rook trapped after 12...Nde5!.

Strategies

Going back to the position in Diagram 9, White's pawn wedge on e5 undoubtedly acts as a catalyst for a kingside attack. As I've mentioned before, it gives White an enormous amount of space to manoeuvre behind on the kingside and it deprives Black, in particular a black knight, the use of the f6-square.

White's general plan of attack includes some or all of the following:

1) h2-h4 to give White the possibility of placing a minor piece on g5 – perhaps Ng5 followed by Qh5.

2) Nf1-h2-g4 or Nf1-e3-g4, placing this knight in the same vicinity as Black's king.

3) h4-h5-h6, creating a weakness in Black's kingside pawn structure. Black can prevent this by playing ...h7-h6 himself, but then he must be wary of sacrifices on h6.

4) Bf4 and perhaps Qe2, adding further support to the e5-pawn.

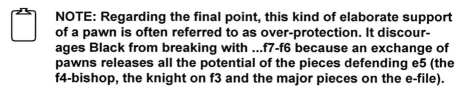 **NOTE: Regarding the final point, this kind of elaborate support of a pawn is often referred to as over-protection. It discourages Black from breaking with ...f7-f6 because an exchange of pawns releases all the potential of the pieces defending e5 (the f4-bishop, the knight on f3 and the major pieces on the e-file).**

It's quite easy to see how Black could be facing a potentially lethal attack. However, he can console himself with the fact that he has no pawn weaknesses on the kingside at the moment, so White has to work quite hard before can break through. While White slowly builds up, Black will be trying to create as much havoc as possible on the queenside, where undoubtedly he has the advantage. Black's pawns are already quite far advanced, and Black's plan involves a quick push of the a- and b-pawns in order to provoke a weakness in White's camp. If White is forced to deal with threats on the queenside, his own kingside attack may well lose momentum. See Game 6 for further details.

Statistics

White has scored 57% in over 3600 games against 5...Nf6. The percentage stays the same if we only take games from the position after 9...Nd7, and here it's worth pointing out that the draw ratio is quite low at 26%. Black has scored better when he has delayed castling with 7...b6 – a respectable 50% in over 1000 games.

Game 2
□ **A.Nazarov** ■ **V.Yandemirov**
Azov 1991

---

1 e4 e6 2 d3 d5 3 Nd2 c5 4 Ngf3 Nc6 5 g3 Nf6 6 Bg2 Be7 7 0-0 b6

An attractive choice for Black players wishing to keep their options open as to which side to eventually castle.

8 Re1 Bb7 9 e5

Playing in the same style as the main line. The next game covers the more flexible 9 c3.

9...Nd7 10 Nf1

Again continuing as if Black were going to castle short.

White has an enticing alternative in the shape of 10 c4!?, nibbling at Black's d5-pawn. The point is that after the natural-looking 10...d4 White may be able to make use of the newly created outpost on e4. For example, 11 h4 Qc7 12 Ne4! is a good pseudo pawn sacrifice: 12...Ncxe5 13 Nxe5 Nxe5 (or 13...Qxe5 14 Nxc5! Qxc5 15 Bxb7 giving White the advantage of the bishop pair) 14 Bf4 0-0 15 Qh5 f6 (15...f5?? loses to 16 Bxe5! Qxe5 17 Ng5) 16 Ng5! fxg5 17 Bxe5 Qd7 18 hxg5 Bxg2 19 Kxg2 and White had a nice position in M.Jadoul-W.Kruszynski, Copenhagen 1988 – there's the possibility of Rh1 in the air. In all likelihood, Black should probably refrain from playing the tempting 10...d4 in favour of 10...Nb4!?. Following 11 cxd5 Bxd5!? 12 Ne4!? (H.Ree-J.Vogel, Leeuwarden 1974) once again White has use of the e4-square but at least Black's pieces are quite active.

10...g5!? (Diagram 11)

Note that ...g7-g5 is only a realistic possibility because Black's king hasn't committed itself to kingside castling; with the king on g8 this advance would be risky at best.

The inconsistent 10...0-0?! would merely justify White's previous play and actually transposes to Game 4. However, 10...Qc7!?, further pressuring e5 and preparing long castling, is an attractive alternative: 11 Bf4 0-0-0 12 h4! (the battle now centres on whether or not Black can prepare ...g7-g5) 12...h6 13 Qd2 Rdg8! and now 14 c3 g5! 15 hxg5 hxg5

16 Nxg5 Bxg5 17 Bxg5 Ncxe5 18 Bf4 d4! is an illustration of how suddenly Black can obtain a kingside initiative. Instead White should slow down Black's play with 14 h5!; a few games have continued 14...g5 15 hxg6 Rxg6 with unclear play, while Black could also consider going 'all in' with 15...fxg6 16 Bxh6 g5 17 Bxg5 Ndxe5.

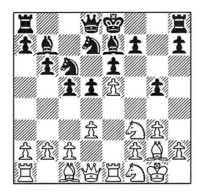

Diagram 11 (W)	Diagram 12 (W)
Lurching forward	h-file action

> NOTE: The pawn lunge ...g7-g5 is quite typical for a position like this. Black is preparing ...g5-g4 to undermine White's support of e5.

11 g4?

It's understandable that White wanted to eliminate the possibility of ...g5-g4, but after this move Black's counterplay is assured. White played with more imagination in the game R.Schlenker-V.Raicevic, Linz 1980 and was rewarded with an extra pawn in the ending after 11 Ne3! h5 12 c4 d4 13 Nd5! exd5 14 cxd5 g4 (or 14...Nb4 15 d6 Bf8 16 e6! and White crashes through) 15 dxc6 Bxc6 16 e6! fxe6 17 Nxd4! Bxg2 18 Nxe6 Bf3! 19 Nxd8 Bxd1 20 Nc6 Rh7 21 Bg5 Bf3 22 Nxe7 Kf7 23 Bh4. The line 11...Ndxe5!? 12 Nxe5 Nxe5 13 Nxd5 Bxd5 14 Rxe5 Bxg2 15 Kxg2 Bf6 16 Re4 is also slightly better for White because Black's king has no really safe place to hide.

11...h5! 12 h3

12 gxh5? g4! 13 N3d2 Ndxe5 is obviously undesirable for White.

12...hxg4 13 hxg4 Qc7 14 Qe2 0-0-0 15 c3 Rdg8! (Diagram 12)

Black has excellent counterplay on the kingside. This position has actually occurred quite a few times in practice, and it's quite revealing that White has only managed to score an appalling 17%.

16 Bd2 Kb8

Black has more than one good approach here: 16...Nf8 17 b4 Ng6 18 b5 Nd8 19 d4 f5! 20 exf6 Bxf6 21 Ng3 Nf4! 22 Qf1 Qh7 was also very promising for Black in R.Laven-S.Kindermann, Bundesliga 1983.

17 Rab1 d4! 18 Ng3 Rh4!! (Diagram 13)

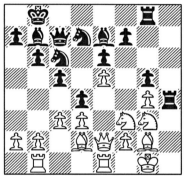

Diagram 13 (W)
18...Rh8-h4!

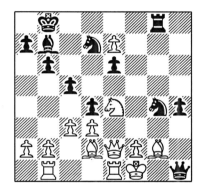

Diagram 14 (W)
Take my queen!

This exchange sacrifice, opening the g-file and netting the e5-pawn, is very effective here.

19 Nxh4 gxh4 20 Ne4 Ncxe5

Suddenly there are all sorts of threats, including...Nxg4, ...Rxg4 and ...f7-f5.

21 g5 f5 22 f4?

Giving up without much of a fight. 22 gxf6 is more resilient, when Black can either recapture with 22...Nxf6 or play the tricky 22...Ng4!?. Now Peter Horn points out that 23 fxe7? is met delightfully by 23...Qh2+! 24 Kf1 Qh1+!! (Diagram 14) 25 Bxh1 Nh2 mate!.

Instead White must play 23 f4, even if Black's initiative remains threatening after 23...Ndxf6.

22...fxe4 23 dxe4

Now Black is winning comfortably, but after 23 fxe5 e3! 24 Bxb7 Qxb7 25 Bc1 Nxe5 White isn't going to survive for long.

23...d3 24 Qh5 Nc4 25 Qf7 Rf8 26 Qxe7 Nxd2 27 g6 Qxf4 28 g7 Rg8 29 Rf1 Nxf1 30 Rxf1 Qg3 31 Rf8+ Nxf8 32 gxf8Q+ Rxf8 33 Qxf8+ Bc8 34 Qh6 d2! 35 Qxd2 h3 0-1

A model game for Black in the 7...b6 line.

Game 3
☐ **S.Gonzalez de la Torre** ■ **J.Pomes Marcet**
Ortigueira 2002

1 e4 e6 2 d3 d5 3 Nd2 c5 4 Ngf3 Nc6 5 g3 Nf6 6 Bg2 Be7 7 0-0 b6 8 Re1 Bb7 9 c3!?

A more flexible option than 9 e5. White keeps the tension in the centre and begins play on the queenside in anticipation of Black's long castling.

9...Qc7 10 a3 (Diagram 15)

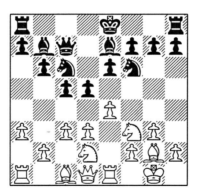 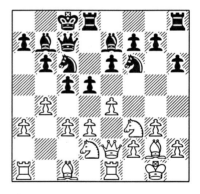

Diagram 15 (B)
Limbering up on the queenside

Diagram 16 (B)
Starting queenside operations

Another move dissuading Black from castling queenside – now b2-b4 is in the air.

10...0-0-0

Despite White's previous two moves, Black goes ahead with castling long, but there are certainly alternatives to this:

a) After 10...0-0 White reverts back to the 'old plan' by closing the centre: 11 e5! Nd7 12 d4 cxd4 13 cxd4 (a2-a3 has proved useful in preventing ...Nb4) 13...Na5 14 Nf1 Rfc8 (preparing ...Qc2) 15 b4! Nc4 16 h4 b5 17 Ng5! and White had some initiative on the kingside in L.Psakhis-D.Paunovic, Minsk 1986.

b) 10...dxe4!? 11 dxe4 is interesting. As we've seen before, this exchange in the centre usually makes little sense for Black – White's e4-e5 has more impact now as the e4-square will become available. On the other hand, White's a2-a3 and c2-c3 are not particularly useful if Black castles kingside. One possible continuation is 11...Rd8 12 Qe2 0-0 13 e5 Nd7 14 h4 and here in A.Fedorov-G.Kuzmin, Nikolaev 1993 Black came up with a refined plan in 14...Qb8! 15 h5 Qa8!, when he was ready to contest the long diagonal. The game continuation is worthy of note: 16 Bh3?! Na5! 17 Nh2 c4! 18 Qg4 Kh8 19 Nxc4? f5! 20 Qf4 (or 20 exf6 Nxf6 21 Qxe6 Bc8!) 20...Nb3 21 Rb1 Ndc5 22 Bf1 Be4 and White was in trouble.

11 Qe2 h6

Black plans to get going on the kingside with ...g7-g5.

12 b4! (Diagram 16) 12...c4!?

Mixing things up in the centre. 12...g5 is the obvious alternative, and this has been played quite a few times. However, I believe more in White's attack than Black's: 13 bxc5 Bxc5 14 Nb3 Be7 15 exd5 Nxd5 16 Bb2 g4 17 Nfd4 h5 18 c4 Nf6 19 Nb5 Qd7 20 d4 (J.Fries Nielsen-P.Cramling, Copenhagen 1982) is one reason why – d4-d5 may well blast Black's position completely open.

13 dxc4!?

Preparing an imaginative and surprisingly strong queen sacrifice. That said, the straightforward 13 exd5 also looks promising for White, e.g. 13...cxd3 14 Qxd3 Nxd5 15 Qc2 Bf6 16 Bb2 Kb8 17 c4! Bxb2 18 Qxb2 Nf6 19 c5! when Black will have long-term problems with his king, L.Psakhis-A.Nikitin, Berlin 1991.

13...dxe4 14 Nxe4 Nxe4 15 Qxe4 Nxb4

So that was Black's idea. But what is White's?

16 Qxb7+!! (Diagram 17)

Oh, I see!

16...Qxb7 17 axb4

White has only two minor pieces for the queen, but the bishop on g2 is a monster, the rook on a1 is seeing plenty of action ahead, and Black's king and queen are very much in the firing line.

17...Bf6 18 Nd4 Qc7 19 Bf4

19 Nc6! may be even stronger, for example 19...Bxc3 20 Bf4! e5 21 Bh3+ Rd7 22 Nxe5 Bxe5 23 Bxe5 Qb7 24 Bg2! with a neat queen trap.

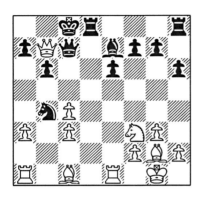

Diagram 17 (B)	Diagram 18 (B)
Not another queen sac?	Tricky for Black

19...e5 20 Nc6! (Diagram 18) 20...exf4?

20...a5 is the only chance, even if White still has a number of promising continuations: simply 21 Be3 or even 21 bxa5!? exf4 22 a6.

21 Nxa7+ Qxa7

After 21...Kb8 22 Nb5 Black is forced to give up his queen due to the threat of Ra8 mate.

22 Rxa7 fxg3

22...Bxc3? allows White to set up a mating net with 23 Bh3+! Kb8 24 Ree7 followed by Reb7.

23 hxg3 Rhe8?

This loses immediately, although to be fair Black was already in big trouble.

24 Ra8+ 1-0

24...Kd7 25 Bh3+ wins more material. A very nice game by White; I believe that the plan with 9 c3 and 10 a3 is more troublesome for Black than 9 e5.

Game 4
☐ **M.Dvoretsky** ■ **Y.Damsky**
Moscow 1970

---

1 e4 e6 2 d3 d5 3 Nd2 c5 4 Ngf3 Nc6 5 g3 Nf6 6 Bg2 Be7 7 0-0 0-0 8 Re1 b6 (Diagram 19)

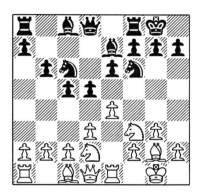 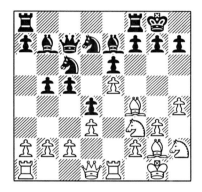

Diagram 19 (W)	**Diagram 20 (W)**
8...b6 – too tentative?	Too accommodating

> NOTE: A KIA player is likely to face ...b7-b6 quite often because it looks quite natural for Black to fianchetto his c8-bishop.

The move ...b7-b6 doesn't really work very well in conjunction with short castling. Often in the cause of queenside counterplay Black ends up playing ...b6-b5 in any case, essentially leaving him a tempo down over ...b7-b5 lines.

9 e5! Nd7 10 Nf1 Bb7 11 h4 Qc7?!

Another plausible move, attacking the e5-pawn, but this actually only helps White. Black should swallow his pride and continue with 11...b5!.

12 Bf4!

> NOTE: With White's bishop and Black's queen being on the same diagonal, this presents White with some tactical opportunities. In this game they are based around a possible Nf6+.

12...b5 13 N1h2 d4? (Diagram 20)

 WARNING: Black must always be very careful before playing ...d5-d4 as it offers White the crucial e4-square to use as a launch pad for his pieces.

It was already a very good version of the typical position for White, but after this error White's attack assumes decisive proportions. It's understandable that Black wanted to open the long diagonal for his bishop, and now ...Nb6-d5 is also a possibility, but the decision to give up the e4-square should never be taken lightly.

14 Ng5!

From here on White doesn't take a single step backwards.

14...h6

Black can eliminate the knight directly with 14...Bxg5, but after 15 hxg5! White has a ready-made plan of attack with Qh5, Ng4 and Be4!, making good use of e4.

15 Qh5! hxg5

Ignoring the knight on g5 doesn't help, e.g. 15...Nb4 16 Ng4! Nxc2 17 Nxh6+! gxh6 18 Qxh6 Bxg5 19 Qxg5+ Kh7 20 Qh5+ Kg8 21 Bh6 and Black will be mated.

16 hxg5 Rfb8 17 Ng4

Now Nf6+ is in the air, as well as the possibility of a mating attack down the h-file with Be4, Kg2 and Rh1.

17...Nf8 18 Nf6+! (Diagram 21)

Black was probably beginning to regret his 11th move by now! 18...gxf6 loses to 19 exf6! e5 20 Qh6 Ne6 21 Be4! followed by Qh7+ and Qh8 mate.

18...Bxf6 19 exf6! e5 20 Bd5 Re8

After 20...Rd8 White uses the h-file option: 21 Kg2! Nb8 22 Rh1! Bxd5+ 23 f3 Ng6 24 Qh7+ Kf8 25 Qh8+! Nxh8 26 Rxh8 mate! **(Diagram 22)**. Mark Dvoretsky gives the nice line 20...exf4 21 Re7!! (using the theme of interference) 21...Nxe7 22 Bxf7 mate.

21 g6! Nd8 22 gxf7+ 1-0

After 22...Nxf7 23 Qg5 g6 24 Qh6 Ne6 25 Bxe6 it's Qg7 mate next move. A demonstration of how frightening White's kingside attack can become if Black commits one or two seemingly minor mistakes.

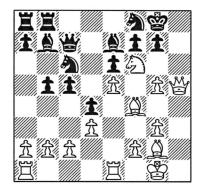

Diagram 21 (B)
The knight sinks into f6

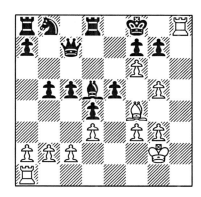

Diagram 22 (B)
Mate!

NOTE: White has the better practical chances in this line and in many other KIA variations. Because White is often attacking Black's king whereas Black attacks on the queenside, inaccurate defence is likely to have more serious repercussions for Black than for White.

Game 5
☐ **S.Yuferov** ■ **V.Zakharov**
Moscow 1995

1 Nf3 d5 2 g3 c5 3 Bg2 Nc6 4 0-0 Nf6 5 d3 e6 6 Nbd2 Be7 7 e4

This move order will be discussed in a bit more detail later on.

7...0-0 8 Re1 Qc7

Covering the e5-square for the second time. The idea of this move is to force White into playing Qe2 to defend the e5-pawn.

9 e5

By far the most popular choice, but if White wishes to avoid Black's possibility in the following note, he should consider delaying the advance and playing 9 Qe2!?. I can't see anything better for Black than to begin operations on the queenside (probably with 9...b5) after which White transposes back into normal lines with 10 e5.

9...Nd7

9...Ne8?! makes no sense now that the c7-square is no longer available, but the active 9...Ng4!? is certainly playable. White is forced to protect e5 with 10 Qe2, after which 10...f6! 11 exf6 Bxf6 changes the nature of the position; Black has active pieces and more space than usual, but in return he has been forced to weaken his pawn structure.

10 Qe2

This is forced. Were his d2-knight already on f1, White wouldn't hesitate to play the more effective Bf4, as we saw in the previous game.

10...b5 11 Nf1 a5 12 Bf4 (Diagram 23)

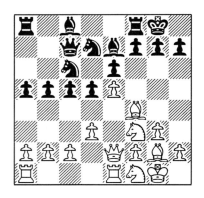

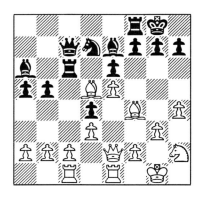

Diagram 23 (B)
12...a4 or 12...Nd4?

Diagram 24 (B)
Bg2xd5!

12...a4

One way to try to exploit the position of White's queen is with 12...Nd4!? 13 Nxd4 cxd4, which presents Black with an avenue of attack down the half-open c-file. On the other hand, Black must be wary of the possibility of his d4-pawn becoming vulnerable. The game R.Fischer-U.Geller, Nathanya 1968 is a wonderful demonstration of how the legendary American utilised the KIA to great effect: 14 h4 Ra6! (planning ...Rc6) 15 Nh2! (as well as going to g4, the knight may simply pressure the d4-pawn from f3) 15...Rc6 16 Rac1 Ba6? (Black should prevent White's next move with 16...Qb6!) 17 Bxd5! **(Diagram 24)**.

This is a typical KIA breakthrough, again exploiting the position of

Black's queen on c7. The game continued 17...exd5 18 e6 Qd8 19 exd7 Re6! 20 Qg4! f5 (20...Qxd7 21 Be5 wins the d4-pawn) 21 Qh5 Qxd7 22 Nf3 g6 23 Qh6 Bf6 24 Rxe6 Qxe6 25 Be5!! (brilliant positional play; the natural-looking 25 Re1?? allows Black to escape with a draw by playing 25...Qxe1+!! 26 Nxe1 Bg7! 27 Qg5 Bf6! 28 Qh6 Bg7 when White cannot escape the repetition) 25...Bxe5 26 Re1 f4 27 Rxe5 Qd7 28 h5! fxg3 29 hxg6!! gxf2+ (or 29...Rxf3 30 Re8+!! Qxe8 31 Qxh7+ Kf8 32 g7+ Ke7 33 g8Q+) 30 Kxf2 hxg6 31 Qxg6+ Qg7! 32 Rg5! Rf7 and Black resigned on account of 33 Qh6, pinning and winning. Notice how the bishop on a6 was a spectator throughout, and a vulnerable one at that.

13 a3!

Preventing Black from playing ...a4-a3 in this line of the KIA was Fischer's patent – see the next game for more details.

13...b4 14 h4 bxa3 15 bxa3 Ba6 16 h5

Planning to probe for dark-squared weaknesses with h5-h6. Black now faces the difficult decision whether or not to prevent this possibility with 16...h6!?. The downside of this move is that it could allow a future sacrifice on h6 or a possible breakthrough with g3-g4-g5.

16...Rfb8 17 h6 g6 18 Ne3 Nd4?

Falling for a devastating trick; after 18...Nb6! 19 Ng4 Nd4 there's still everything to play for.

19 Nxd4 cxd4 20 Nxd5!! (Diagram 25)

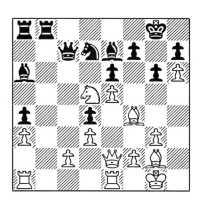

Diagram 25 (B)
Sacrificing on d5 again?

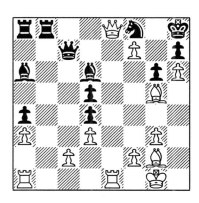

Diagram 26 (B)
In a mating net

TIP: With White's bishop on f4 and Black's queen on c7, both players must always watch out for possible sacrifices on d5. In this particular position it is instantly decisive.

20...Qc5

The equivalent of resignation, as Black loses a considerable amount of material. 20...exd5 is critical, but 21 e6! wins. For example, 21...Bd6 22 exf7+ Kh8 (22...Kf8 23 Qe6! Bxf4 24 Qe7 mate) 23 Qe8+! Nf8 24 Bg5! **(Diagram 26)** and there is no good defence to Bf6 mate; or 21...Qd8 22 exf7+ Kf8 23 Bc7!.

21 Nxe7+ Qxe7 22 Bxa8 Rxa8 23 Qe4 Rd8 24 Qxd4 1-0

Game 6
☐ **G.Kaidanov** ■ **F.Nijboer**
Elista Olympiad 1998

---

1 e4 c5 2 Nf3 e6 3 d3 Nc6 4 g3

The game begins with a Sicilian move order but after Black's next move we're back into the French.

4...d5 5 Nbd2 Nf6 6 Bg2 Be7 7 0-0 b5 8 Re1 0-0 9 e5 Nd7 10 Nf1 a5 11 h4 b4 12 Bf4

The usual move here, but White can also leave the bishop at home on c1, only going to f4 if Black commits his queen to c7 (as in Game 4). For example, 12 N1h2 Ba6 13 Ng4 a4 and now, as well as 14 Bf4, White can consider offering an exchange of dark-squared bishops with 14 Bg5, or play 14 h5 or 14 a3.

12...a4 13 a3! (Diagram 27)

TIP: Preventing Black from playing ...a4-a3 is usually a good idea in this line.

Chess principles hammer home the message that you should never make an unforced pawn move on the side of the board where you are weaker. However, this paradoxical idea, the invention of Bobby Fischer's, must be the exception that proves the rule.

If Black gets his a-pawn to a3 he seems to obtain more counterplay, e.g. 13 N1h2 a3! 14 b3! (naturally White is reluctant to open the position on the queenside) 14...Ba6 15 Ng5 Nd4! (illustrating an advantage of playing ...a4-a3: White no longer has the option of c2-c3 so this knight is invulnerable on this powerful square) 16 Rc1 Rc8 17 Qh5 h6 18 Nh3 and now in O.Dolzhikova-V.Malakhatko, Kiev 2000 Black struck back on the kingside with 18...f6!. Following 19 exf6 Nxf6 20 Qg6 Qe8! 21 Qxe8 Rfxe8 Black can be very happy with his active position, while in the game the sacrifice 19 Bxh6 Nxe5! 20 Rxe5 fxe5 21 Qg6 Rf7 didn't quite work. Notice the importance of Black's d4-knight in these variations.

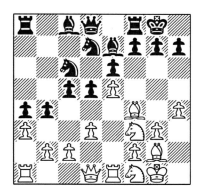

Diagram 27 (B)
Stop right there!

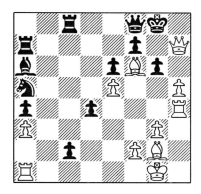

Diagram 28 (B)
Fischer on the KIA

13...Ba6!

The stem game in this line, R.Fischer-L.Myagmarsuren, Sousse 1967, is worth giving in full because the finish is quite beautiful: 13...bxa3 14 bxa3 Na5? (the knight does little here; Black should continue with 14...Ba6) 15 Ne3 Ba6 16 Bh3 d4 17 Nf1! (another paradoxical move; 17 Ng4 looks more natural but White doesn't want to block the queen's route to the kingside) 17...Nb6 18 Ng5 Nd5 19 Bd2 Bxg5 20 Bxg5 Qd7 21 Qh5 Rfc8 22 Nd2 Nc3 23 Bf6! Qe8 (or 23...gxf6 24 exf6 Kh8 25 Nf3 Nd5 26 Qh6! Rg8 27 Ne5 Qc7 28 Bg2! and there is no good defence to Be4) 24 Ne4 g6 25 Qg5 Nxe4 26 Rxe4 c4 27 h5! cxd3 28 Rh4! Ra7 (28...dxc2 29 hxg6 fxg6 30 Rxh7! mates after 30...Kxh7 31 Qh4+ Kg8 32 Qh8+ Kf7 33 Qg7) 29 Bg2!! dxc2 30 Qh6 Qf8 31 Qxh7+!! **(Diagram 28)** and Black threw in the towel on account of 31...Kxh7 32 hxg6+ Kxg6 33 Be4. Not a bad advertisement for the KIA!

14 N1h2

White can win a pawn with 14 axb4?! cxb4 15 Rxa4, but Black's counterplay on the queenside following 15...Nc5 16 Ra1 b3! seems well worth the investment.

14...c4!?

Continuing with real ambition, striving to open the queenside as quickly as possible. In contrast, White tries to block things up.

15 d4! c3! 16 bxc3 bxc3 17 Ng5 Nb6?

Black must chase away the g5-knight while he has the chance: 17...h6! 18 Qh5? is an unsound sacrifice, with 18...hxg5 19 hxg5 Nxd4 20 Ng4 Be2! putting an end to White's fun. Instead White must be content with 18 Nh3, intending Qh5, after which Black can try 18 ...Rb8 intending ...Rb2, or 18...Qb6 hitting d4.

18 Qh5! Bxg5

It's too late for 18...h6 as now White can ignore the threat: 19 Ng4! hxg5 (otherwise Nxh6+ is coming) 20 hxg5 g6 (or 20...Nxd4 21 Nf6+! gxf6 22 gxf6 Bxf6 23 exf6 Qxf6 24 Be5 and White wins) 21 Qh6 Nxd4 22 Nf6+ Bxf6 23 gxf6 Nf5 24 Qh3 (Kaidanov) is winning for White due to the idea of g3-g4, for example 24...Nd7 25 g4 Nd6 26 Qh6! Ne8 27 Re3! Nexf6 28 Rh3 **(Diagram 29)**.

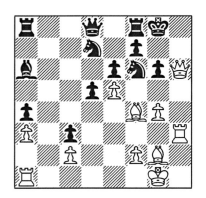

Diagram 29 (B)
Carnage down the h-file.

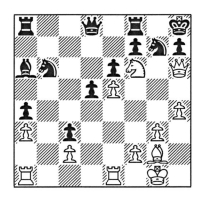

Diagram 30 (B)
Game over

19 Bxg5 Qe8 20 Bf6! Nxd4?

20...gxf6 is tougher, but Kaidanov's 21 Ng4 Nd7 22 Bxd5! exd5 23 exf6 Kh8 24 Rxe8 Raxe8 25 Qxd5 Ncb8 is still clearly better for White.

21 Ng4

Threatening 22 Qg5 Nf5 23 Nh6+!.

21...Nf5 22 Qg5! Kh8 23 Bxg7+! Nxg7 24 Nf6 Qd8 25 Qh6 (Diagram 30)

It's the end – Black must give up his queen to avoid mate.

25...Qxf6 26 Qxf6 Rae8 27 g4 Nd7 28 Qf4 Bc4 29 h5 Rc8 30 Rab1 f5 31 exf6 1-0

Perhaps more than anything this game illustrates how difficult Black's position is to play in practice, even for a strong grandmaster like Friso Nijboer.

Black Plays 5...g6

1 e4 e6 2 d3 d5 3 Nd2 c5 4 Ngf3 Nc6 5 g3 g6 (Diagram 31)

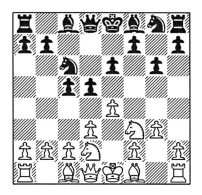
Diagram 31 (W)
Black fianchettoes too

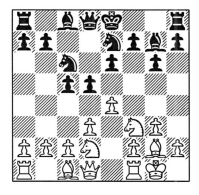
Diagram 32 (W)
A typical black set-up

5...g6 is an ambitious move which I would say is more popular with grandmasters than at club level. There are a couple of good reasons for developing this way: firstly, Black's fianchettoed bishop controls the vital e5-sqare and thus puts pressure on White's spearheading pawn if and when it arrives there; secondly, the bishop also provides protection to Black's king if it castles short. The only real problem with ...g7-g6 is that it does weaken the dark squares on the kingside, and White can always hope to take advantage of this later on.

6 Bg2 Bg7 7 0-0 Nge7 (Diagram 32)

This is the most common move here. The knight sits well on e7: it neither blocks the g7-bishop nor encourages White to play e4-e5. However, it's noticeable that a few grandmasters have recently been trying out 7...Nf6!?. When compared to the ...Nf6/...Be7 variation, the value of the fianchettoed bishop is illustrated in the line 8 Re1 0-0 9 e5? Nd7, when the e5-pawn simply drops off the board. If White wishes to advance in the centre he needs to show a bit more finesse with 8 c3 0-0 9 e5 Nd7 after which the e5-pawn can be protected with 10 d4. Even so, Black can assure himself of sufficient counterplay by immediately attacking the front of White's pawn chain: 10...f6! 11 exf6 Bxf6 12 dxc5 Nxc5 13 Nb3 Nxb3 14 Qxb3 Na5 15 Qd1 e5 (V.Iordachescu-I.Glek, Porto San Giorgio 2001). In view of this, White should consider holding back on e4-e5 with the non-committal 9 Re1.

White can also opt for a completely different approach with 8 exd5!?. Now 8...exd5 9 Re1+! is a bit awkward for Black, so 9...Nxd5 is the main choice. This line used to be considered dubious due to the energetic 9 Nb3 (9 Ne4!?) 9...b6 10 c4 Nde7 11 d4, but in fact 11...Ba6! seems fine for Black.

8 Re1

As against 7...Nf6, White also has the option of 8 exd5!? here. With the knight blocking the e-file Black can safely play 8...exd5, but then comes the surprising 9 d4!?. I believe this was the invention of the well-known Russian trainer Mark Dvoretsky, who has injected quite a few ideas into the KIA. White offers a pawn to mess up Black's structure. If this pawn can be regained then White usually keeps an advantage, but that's quite a big 'if'. The continuation 9...cxd4 10 Nb3 Qb6 11 Bf4 0-0 12 Bd6 d3! 13 c3! Bf5 has been seen more than once in practice – I suspect that Black's doing okay here.

 NOTE: When compared to the ...Nf6/...Be7 lines, the possibility of exd5 must be taken much more seriously.

8...b6

It's more common for Black to delay kingside castling in this line, although

8...0-0 is certainly possible (see Game 7).

9 c3 (Diagram 33)

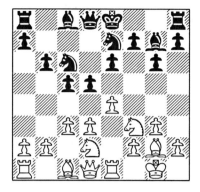

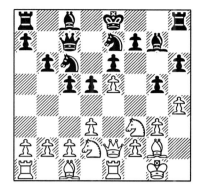

Diagram 33 (B)
White plays c2-c3

Diagram 34 (W)
Swooping for the e5-pawn

We've already seen the idea of c2-c3 in the note to Black's seventh move. It's useful in that in some lines White is ready to play e4-e5 quickly followed by d3-d4. On the other hand, Black can try to benefit from the fact that the d3-pawn is now vulnerable. Alternatively:

a) 9 exd5!? is covered in Game 8.

b) 9 e5?! is premature as White hasn't made enough provisions for this advance: 9...Qc7! 10 Qe2 and now Black plays 10...h6!, preparing ...g6-g5 after which ...Ng6 and ...g5-g4 will be real possibilities. Following 11 h4 Black can still play 11...g5! **(Diagram 34)**.

Now after 12 hxg5 hxg5 13 Nxg5 Qxe5 14 Qxe5 Bxe5 (Dvoretsky) Black can be happy with trading a wing pawn for White's e5-pawn.

 WARNING: In this line White must be especially careful before advancing in the centre with e4-e5. The pawn can easily become vulnerable to a quick attack.

c) Sometimes White throws in 9 h4!? here, which is a dual purpose move: firstly, it prepares e4-e5 because it prevents ...g6-g5; secondly, White has the possibility of probing Black's structure with h4-h5. Black often replies to 9 h4 with 9...h6!, preparing to meet 10 h5?! not with the positionally horrible 10...gxh5 (this would be grim even if White couldn't win the pawn back immediately with 11 Nh4) but with 10...g5!.

9...a5!?

Black has quite a few different options here, but it's this outwardly strange move that's currently number one in the popularity stakes. One of its ideas is to gain space on the queenside with ...a5-a4 (and possibly ...a4-a3). Another point is that the light-squared bishop prefers to sit behind a pawn if it goes to a6 – it's then protected by the rook and invulnerable to Qa4 attacks.

Alternatives include the following:

a) 9...0-0 is covered in Game 9.

b) 9...Bb7 10 e5!? (White can also hold back on this advance by playing useful moves such as Qe2 and h2-h4) 10...g5!? (again the critical response to an early e4-e5; 10...Qc7 11 d4! demonstrates the point of 9 c3) 11 Nxg5 (what else?) 11...Nxe5 12 Ndf3 N5g6 13 d4 h6 14 Nh3 and White is a bit better because Black's king won't be completely safe wherever it decides to go, L.Yurtaev-B.Gulko, Moscow 1994.

c) 9...Ba6!? **(Diagram 35)**, immediately hitting the tender d3-pawn, is perhaps Black's most visually enticing move.

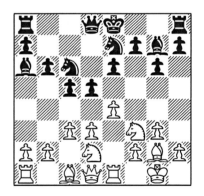

Diagram 35 (W)
Attacking the d3-pawn

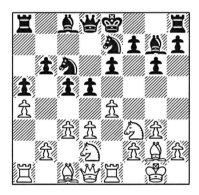

Diagram 36 (B)
...a7-a5 met by a2-a4

Now 10 Qa4!? is very tricky, the point being that 10...Bxd3? 11 exd5! puts Black in big trouble, e.g. 11...b5 12 Qa6! Nb8 13 Qb7!. However, following the calm 10...Bb7! it's not clear whether the white queen is any better on a4 than it would be on d1. White can also play 10 Bf1!?, which is not as passive as it looks. 10...0-0 11 e5! h6 12 h4! Qc7 13 Qa4

Bc8 14 d4 was better for White in D.Minic-S.Marjanovic, Bar 1980.

10 a4! (Diagram 36)

Preventing Black's queenside expansion plans and gaining the b5-square as a possible outpost. See Game 10 for further details.

Strategies

As far as I can see, White has two distinct plans here:

1) The advance e4-e5 followed by typical moves such as Nf1, h2-h4, Bf4, N1h2-g4 etc. This plan is more likely to work if Black quickly commits his king to the kingside.

2) The exchange exd5. If Black recaptures with ...Nxd5, White gets a juicy outpost on c4 for his knight. If Black recaptures with ...exd5 White often plays Nb3 followed by d3-d4, trying to induce a weakness in Black's pawn formation. If Black reacts to d3-d4 with ...c5-c4, White will retreat the knight and then nibble at Black's structure with b2-b3.

The main plus points of Black's position is that his pieces are well coordinated and he has a fair amount of space. If White is not careful Black may get the opportunity to cramp his opponent with ...d5-d4 and ...e6-e5. In general White will want to avoid this by meeting ...e6-e5 with exd5, and ...d5-d4 by e4-e5.

Statistics

Taking the 'starting position' after 7...Nge7, Black has scored an excellent 51% in just over 2000 games, although his results are probably enhanced by a higher average rating (as I mentioned earlier, 5...g6 is a particular favourite amongst stronger players). It's also worth pointing out that 8...b6 has scored quite a bit better than 8...0-0 (52% against 44%). It's not necessarily a stronger move, but perhaps just easier to play in practice.

Game 7
□ C.Nanu ■ I.Puscas
Baile Tusnad 1999

1 e4 e6 2 d3 d5 3 Nd2 c5 4 Ngf3 Nc6 5 g3 g6 6 Bg2 Bg7 7 0-0 Nge7 8 Re1 0-0 (Diagram 37)

This natural move has been condemned by at least one KIA expert. I don't thinks it's that bad, but I have to admit that Black must play carefully to avoid drifting into a passive position where White has an automatic attack on the king.

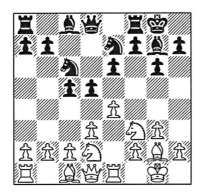

Diagram 37 (W)
Dvoretsky doesn't like this

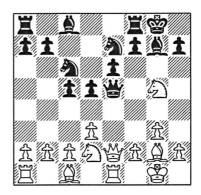

Diagram 38 (W)
Forcing off the queens

9 h4!?

The immediate 9 e5 is tempting, but Black can meet this move in typical fashion with 9...Qc7! 10 Qe2 g5!. It's true that this lunge is often much more risky when Black has committed his king to the kingside, but after 11 Nxg5 Qxe5 **(Diagram 38)** Black gets away with it because a queen exchange is forced due to the threat to g5.

 NOTE: With the queens off the board, Black's kingside weaknesses become less important and his extra central pawn is not to be sniffed at.

9...h6

If Black wishes to avoid White playing e4-e5 at any cost, then the move to play is 9...e5!? when 10 exd5 Nxd5 leads to a type of reversed King's Indian position we'll see more of in Chapter 4.

10 e5

White should remember that 10 h5? is met by 10...g5!, but if he wishes to delay e4-e5 then 10 Qe2 isn't a bad move.

10...Qc7

A critical alternative for Black here is 10...f6!? (I suspect 10...f5 comes to the same thing as if White doesn't capture en passant Black's king-side is difficult to breach) 11 exf6 Rxf6, which has been played by some strong players. For example, 12 Nb3 (planning Bf4) 12...Qd6! 13 d4 (13 Bf4 Rxf4! 14 gxf4 Bxb2 gives Black excellent compensation for the exchange) 13...cxd4 14 Nfxd4 e5 15 Nb5. French GM Joel Lautier assesses this double-edged position as slightly better for White, which is probably true, but White must play accurately to bear this assessment out. Following 15...Qd8 I like 16 c4, e.g. 16...Qb6!? 17 Be3 d4 18 Bd2 Be6 19 Nd6 Raf8 20 Ne4 R6f7 21 Nbc5 Bf5 22 b4!.

11 Qe2 g5?

Following the same antidote to 9 e5 but, as we'll see, the inclusion of h2-h4 and ...h7-h6 makes a crucial difference.

The kind of problems Black can face with passive play is illustrated well in the game M.Dvoretsky-A.Feuerstein, Parsippany 2000, which continued 11...b6?! 12 Nf1! d4 13 N1h2 Kh7 14 Ng4 Nd5. Here I like the look of 15 h5! because 15...g5? 16 Bxg5! hxg5 17 Nxg5+ Kg8 18 Qe4 f5 19 exf6 Nxf6 20 Qg6 is winning for White. Instead maybe Black should free his position with 11...f6 with play similar to the previous note.

12 hxg5 hxg5 13 Nxg5 Qxe5

Forcing the exchange of queens, right?

14 Nde4!! (Diagram 39)

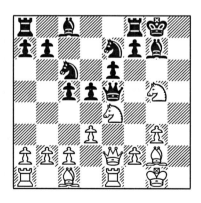 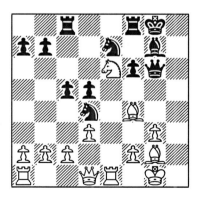

Diagram 39 (B)
14 Nde4!!

Diagram 40 (B)
Reset the pieces!

Apparently not. The point is that 14...dxe4? loses to 15 Qh5! Qf5 16 Bxe4.

14...Nd4

Now 15 Qh5? Qf5! defended for Black in C.Nanu-V.Iordachescu, Calimanesti 1999. However, Nanu has a second bite at the cherry.

15 Qd1!

Calmly done. Black still cannot capture on e4, as 15...dxe4 loses to 16 Qh5! Qf5 17 Bxe4. Also, 15...Nxc2 goes down after 16 Bf4! Qf5 17 Nd6.

15...f6 16 Bf4! Qf5 17 Nd6! Qg6 18 Nxc8 Raxc8 19 Nxe6 (Diagram 40)

And that's pretty much that. White has won a crucial pawn and Black's position falls apart. The game goes on for a while but Black could have resigned a lot sooner.

19...Rfe8 20 Nc7 Bh6 21 Nxe8 Rxe8 22 Bxh6 Qxh6 23 c3 Ndc6 24 Bxd5+ Kf8 25 Bxc6 bxc6 26 Re6 Rd8 27 Qf3 Kf7 28 Rae1 Rd7 29 Rxe7+

There are numerous other ways to win, but two extra pawns in a pawn ending are usually good enough.

29...Rxe7 30 Rxe7+ Kxe7 31 Qe3+ Qxe3 32 fxe3 1-0

In conclusion, 8...0-0 is playable but Black must play very precisely, otherwise he can easily end up in big trouble.

Game 8
☐ **S.Solomon** ■ **G.Szuveges**
Suncoast 1999

1 e4 e6 2 d3 d5 3 Nd2 c5 4 Ngf3 Nc6 5 g3 g6 6 Bg2 Bg7 7 0-0 Nge7 8 Re1 b6 9 exd5!?

A departure from the usual plan of e4-e5. In contrast to that push, this exchange in the centre is far more direct, with White attempting to exploit Black's unfinished development and the long h1-a8 diagonal.

9...Nxd5

White's idea after 9...exd5 is to play 10 d4! à la Dvoretsky. Now 10...cxd4?! 11 Nb3 Bg4 12 Bg5 0-0 13 Bxe7 Nxe7 14 Nbxd4 is pleasant for White due to Black's isolated d-pawn, while 10...c4 should be answered by 11 Ne5! preparing to meet 11...Nxd4 with 12 Ndxc4!.

The move 10...Bf5!?, threatening ...Nb4, can lead to huge complications after 11 c4!. In *Attacking with 1 e4* my main line was 11...Nb4!? 12 cxd5! Nc2 13 d6! Qxd6 14 Nh4! Nxe1 15 Nxf5 Nxf5 16 Bxa8 Nd3 17 Qe2+ Kd7 18 dxc5 Nxc5 19 Ne4 Nxe4 20 Bxe4 when Black is in some trouble. The safest continuation for Black is probably 10...0-0 11 dxc5 bxc5 12 Nb3 and now either 12...c4 or 12...Qb6 13 c3 limits White's advantage to a minimum.

10 d4!? (Diagram 41)

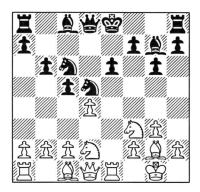

Diagram 41 (B)
Playing the 'unplayable'

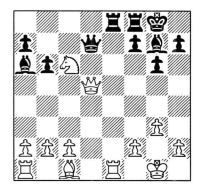

Diagram 42 (B)
Leaving the queen en prise

At first sight this advance in the centre looks unplayable because Black has d4 covered three times, but it's actually a very dangerous move for Black to face.

10...cxd4

10...Nxd4 11 Nxd4 Bxd4? 12 Nb3 leaves Black in some trouble.

11 Nb3 Bb7

11...0-0 12 Nbxd4 Nxd4 13 Nxd4 Ba6 prevents c2-c4 and may be a stronger way for Black to play. It's true that White can now win a pawn with 14 Nc6!? Qd7 15 Bxd5 exd5 16 Qxd5!, meeting 16...Qxd5 with 17 Ne7+. However, Black has a remarkable resource in 16...Rae8! **(Diagram 42)** as suggested by Horn. Perhaps the best that White can do is allow a cute perpetual after 17 Qxd7 Rxe1+ 18 Kg2 Bf1+ 19 Kf3 Be2+, with 20 Kf4? being more foolish than brave after 20...Bh6+ 21 Ke4 Bg4+!.

12 Nfxd4 Nxd4 13 Nxd4 Rc8

Black had to prevent c2-c4, but now White has a strong sacrifice.

14 Rxe6+! fxe6?

At first sight this recapture looks forced, but in fact Black has an incredible resource in 14...Ne7! (Horn). This surprisingly calm retreat, allowing Bxb7 but exploiting the pin on the d-file, is not as bad as it looks: in *Attacking with 1 e4* the analysis ran 15 Bxb7 fxe6 16 Be3! (16 Bxc8?! Bxd4 threatens ...Bxf2+) 16...Rc4 17 Nxe6 Qxd1+ 18 Rxd1 Bxb2 19 Rd8+ Kf7 20 Ng5+ Kg7 21 Ne6+ with a draw by perpetual check. However, after looking at this a second time (with the aid of a more modern computer!), I like White's compensation for the exchange after 17 c3!, especially since 17...e5? 18 Ne6! Qxd1+ 19 Rxd1 Bf6 20 Ba6! leaves Black without a good move, 20...Re4 running into 21 Rd8+ Kf7 22 Rxh8 Bxh8 23 Ng5+.

15 Nxe6 (Diagram 43)

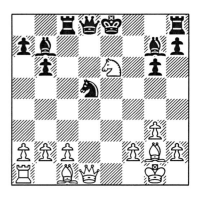

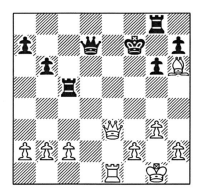

Diagram 43 (B)
Winning back some material

Diagram 44 (W)
Déjà vu?

The point: due to the fork against d8 and g7, and the attack on d5, Black's queen is overloaded and White picks up a minor piece to go with his two pawns. Given that Black's king is out in the open, the rook sacrifice is looking like a good investment.

15...Qd7 16 Nxg7+ Qxg7

16...Kf7 17 Bh6 Rhd8 18 Qe2 was also very nice for White in J.Howell-

P.Soln, Bled 1995.

17 Bxd5 Bxd5 18 Qxd5 Qd7 19 Qe5+ Kf7 20 Bh6!

Threatening Qg7+.

20...Rhg8 21 Re1 Rc5 22 Qf4+ Qf5 23 Qe3 Qd7 (Diagram 44) 24 Qf3+

Unbelievably, or perhaps not so given the vast number of games on databases these days, up to 23...Qd7 this had all been seen before (in the game V.Komliakov-V.Moskalenko, Noyabrsk 1995). So it could have simply been a case of White doing his homework well.

24...Rf5 25 Rd1! Qe7?

The endgame after 25...Rxf3 26 Rxd7+ Ke6 27 Rxa7 is depressing, but I guess that's still Black's best chance to scrape something from the game. After 25...Qe7?, however, White has a forced win.

26 Qb3+ Qe6 27 Rd7+! Kf6 28 Qc3+ Re5 29 Qd4!

Black cannot deal with the twin threats of f2-f4 and Rd6.

29...g5 30 Rd6 Ke7 31 Rxe6+ Kxe6 32 Qc4+ Rd5 33 Qe4+ Re5 34 Qxh7 1-0

Game 9
☐ **S.Berry** ■ **A.Gershon**
Dresden 2003

---

1 e4 e6 2 d3 d5 3 Nd2 c5 4 Ngf3 Nc6 5 g3 g6 6 Bg2 Bg7 7 0-0 Nge7 8 Re1 b6 9 c3 0-0 10 e5!?

This is the move that 10...0-0 encourages, but Black can still hit out with ...g6-g5. If White wishes to avoid the following complications he can opt for something like 10 h4 or 10 Qe2.

10...Qc7 11 Qe2

11 d4 cxd4 12 cxd4 Nb4! gives Black play based on ...Nc2 and ...Qc2.

11...g5!

Again the critical move.

> **NOTE: There's certainly some risk involved in playing ...g6-g5, but if Black plays 'quietly' there's an even greater risk of slowly getting squashed on the kingside after h2-h4, Nf1, Bf4 and N1h2-g4 etc.**

12 Nxg5 Qxe5

Now if White exchanges queens, Black will be very happy, but...

13 Nde4!? (Diagram 45)

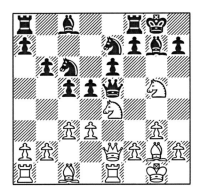

Diagram 45 (B)	**Diagram 46 (B)**
Seen this before?	Black must be precise

This move again! We've already seen how well it worked in Game 7, but here the presence of the h-pawns surely helps Black's defence. On the other hand, the extra move ...b7-b6 gives Black some problems down the long diagonal.

13...dxe4!?

Black is certainly not forced to accept the sacrifice, but let's see what White's got in store.

14 Qh5?

Erring immediately. The way to go is 14 Bf4! Qf6 (14...Qd5?? loses to 15 Bxe4 Qd8 16 Bxh7+ Kh8 17 Qh5) when both 15 Bxe4!? e5 16 Bxh7+ Kh8 17 Qh5 Bg4! 18 Qxg4 exf4 19 Be4 and 15 Nxh7!? Kxh7 16 Bxe4+ Ng6 17 Qh5+ Kg8 18 Bg5 Qe5 19 Bxc6 Qb8! lead to very unclear positions.

14...h6 15 Bf4 Qf6 16 Bxe4 e5! 17 Nh7 Qd6 18 Bg5! (Diagram 46) 18...Rd8!

Not falling for 18...hxg5? 19 Nf6+! and Qh7 mate, or 18...Re8? 19 Nf6+! Bxf6 20 Qxh6.

19 Bxe7

Now following 19 Nf6+ Bxf6 20 Qxh6 Bxg5 Black's queen is defended by the d8-rook.

19...Qxe7! 20 Bxc6 Bb7 21 Bxb7 Qxb7

The fireworks have ended and White is actually a pawn ahead. Unfortunately for him, his knight on h7 is about to drop off the board, leaving Black with a decisive advantage.

22 f4

22 Qf5 is met by 22...Qc6! followed by ...Qg6.

22...Kxh7 23 fxe5 Kg8 24 Re3 Rd5 25 Rf1 Re8 26 Rf5 Re7 27 Qe2 Qc8 28 g4 Qe8 0-1

The e5-pawn is about to be picked off, leaving White with nothing to show for being a bishop down. Black was rewarded here for a brave choice with 11...g5! and some ice-cool defending to follow.

Game 10
□ **G.Kaidanov** ■ **A.Zapata**
New York 1993

---

1 e4 c5 2 Nf3 e6 3 d3 d5 4 Nbd2 Nc6 5 g3 g6 6 Bg2 Bg7 7 0-0 Nge7 8 Re1 b6 9 c3 a5 10 a4 Ba6 (Diagram 47)

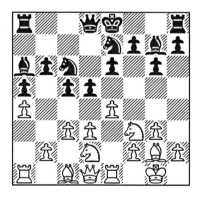
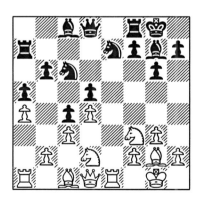

Diagram 47 (W)
Targeting d3

Diagram 48 (B)
Planning b2-b3

Hitting the d3-pawn like this is extremely tempting, especially with the insertion of the moves ...a7-a5 and a2-a4 – Black no longer has to worry about Qa4. However, there are a few reasonable alternatives for Black:

a) After 10...0-0 11 e5 Black can again unbalance things with 11...Qc7 12 Qe2 g5!?. White can opt to delay e4-e5 in favour of the preparatory 11 Qe2, when Black should probably continue with 11...Ba6. It looks tempting to gain time by playing 11...dxe4 12 dxe4 Ba6 but after the surprising self-pin 13 Nc4! Black doesn't have a good plan and White can unravel successfully: 13...Qc7 14 Bf1! Rfd8 15 Qc2 h6 16 Bf4! e5 17 Be3 Rab8 18 Rad1 Rxd1 19 Rxd1 (A.Strikovic-D.Rivera Kuzawka, La Coruna 1993) and White is enjoying the outposts on the queenside – Na3-b5 is one possibility.

b) After 10...d4!? Black intends to cement his space advantage with ...e6-e5, so White should cut across this idea with 11 cxd4 cxd4 12 e5!, opening up the possibility of Ne4. Black can create an outpost on d4 by recapturing with 11...Nxd4 but following 12 Nxd4 Bxd4 13 e5! Ra7 14 Nc4 Black misses the presence of his bishop on g7 – his dark squares (d6, f6 etc.) are looking very dodgy.

c) 10...Ra7!? is a refined move that some grandmasters have taken a liking to. One point is that the rook has vacated the long diagonal, thus Black eliminates many of the tactics White has here. Also, the rook has the option of going to d7, increasing the pressure on the d-file. Now 11 e5 is met by the typical 11...Qc7 12 Qe2 g5! so White should probably either play the noncommittal 11 Qe2 or 11 h4, or change plans altogether with 11 exd5. Now 11...Nxd5 12 Nc4 is similar to the main game, while after 11...exd5 White aims for d3-d4 with 12 Nb3. For example, 12...0-0 13 d4! c4 14 Nbd2 **(Diagram 48)** and now White prepares to break up Black's pawns with b2-b3. Black can prevent White's idea with 12...d4!? 13 cxd4 cxd4 when 14 Bf4 0-0 15 Ne5 looks roughly equal.

11 exd5 Nxd5

Presenting White with an outpost on c4, but after 11...exd5 White reverts to the plan mentioned in the previous note: 12 Nb3! 0-0 (12...d4 13 Nfxd4! makes good use of the pins) 13 d4, for example 13...c4 14 Nbd2 Nf5 15 b3! cxb3 16 Qxb3 Rb8 17 Ba3 and White was better in M.Müller-Glek, Berlin 1994.

12 Nc4 0-0 13 h4!?

With the idea of softening up Black's kingside with h4-h5.

TIP: Black should consider playing 13...h6!? here, meeting 14 h5?! with 14...g5!.

13...Qc7 14 h5! Rad8 15 Qe2 Rfe8 16 hxg6 hxg6 17 Ng5!

The opening of the h-file has given White some serious attacking possibilities, including Qe4-h4.

17...e5!? 18 Qe4 Bb7 19 Qh4 Nf6 20 Ne4! Nh7!

Cool. There was a temptation to exchange with 20...Nxe4? 21 dxe4, but then White could play Bg5 and Ne3-d5, making good use of d5.

21 g4! (Diagram 49)

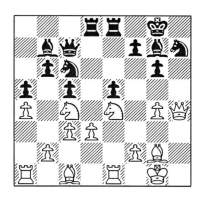

Diagram 49 (B)
Planning Re3-h3

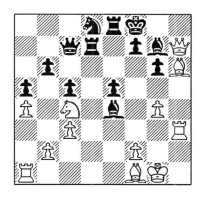

Diagram 50 (B)
Trading bishops

An inspired pawn sacrifice – White plans Re3-h3.

21...Rxd3 22 Bf1! Rd7 23 Re3 Nd8?

A decisive mistake in a difficult position. According to Dmitry Gurevich, Black should return the pawn with 23...g5!. Following 24 Nxg5 Nxg5 25 Qxg5 e4!?, intending ...Ne5, Black is still well in the game.

24 Rh3! Bxe4

Or 24...Nf8 25 Bh6! Bxe4 26 Bxg7 Kxg7 27 Qh8 mate.

25 Qxh7+ Kf8 26 Bh6! (Diagram 50)

Eliminating a crucial defender.

26...f6 27 Re1

Fritz likes 27 Qh8+ Kf7 28 Nxe5+! Rxe5 29 Qxg7+ Ke6 30 Qg8+ Nf7 31 f4 Red5 32 Re1 but the text is just as good.

27...Qb7 28 g5! fxg5 29 Qh8+! 1-0

It seems that White doesn't always need the spearhead of an e5-pawn to generate an attack on the kingside.

Black Plays 5...Bd6

1 e4 e6 2 d3 d5 3 Nd2 c5 4 Ngf3 Nc6 5 g3 Bd6 (Diagram 51)

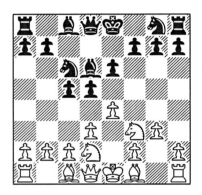
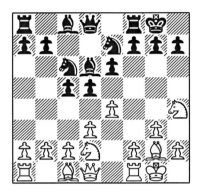

Diagram 51 (W)	Diagram 52 (B)
Black plays 5...Bd6	A change of scene

5...Bd6 introduces an incredibly solid set-up for Black, who intends to follow up with ...Nge7 and 0-0. In many ways this line can be compared to 5...g6, with Black's bishop controlling e5 from another diagonal. Crucially Black has not been forced to weaken his dark squares on the king-side with ...g7-g6, so he is much happier to commit his king to this side of the board at an early stage. On the other hand, the bishop is less active on this square, and Black finds it more difficult to create counterplay.

 WARNING: Black has trouble reaching this system if White 'accelerates' the fianchetto with 4 g3!? because following 4...Nc6 5 Bg2 Bd6? the pawn on d5 is en prise.

Black can attempt to get around this problem by playing 4...Bd6!? so that he is ready to meet 5 Bg2 with 5...Ne7, reaching the desirable set-up. However, White can throw a spanner in the works with 5 Qg4!?

when Black must either make some concession on the kingside with 5...Kf8 or 5...g6, or sacrifice the g-pawn with 5...Nf6 6 Qxg7 Rg8.

6 Bg2 Nge7

We've already seen via a different move order that 6...Nf6 7 0-0 0-0 8 Re1! is problematic for Black, who already faces the threat of e4-e5.

7 0-0 0-0 8 Nh4! (Diagram 52)

The normal 8 Re1 is covered in Game 11. This ambitious move, planning expansion with f2-f4, was introduced at the highest level by Bobby Fischer. Although less common than 8 Re1, 8 Nh4 has scored better and has been the choice of KIA experts such as Psakhis, Bologan and Dolmatov, so I've taken the liberty of promoting it to the 'main line'.

Black has quite a few choices here, although some of the moves are similar in motive and there one or two transpositions. 8...b6 is covered in Game 12, while 8...Bc7 and other options are covered in Game 13.

Strategies

White will rush forward on the kingside with f2-f4 after which Black often decides to employ one of the following defensive strategies:

1) Blocking the f-pawn in its tracks by meeting f2-f4 with ...f7-f5.

2) Restraining White's e- and f-pawns by meeting f2-f4 with ...f7-f6, thus preventing both e4-e5 and f4-f5-f6.

If Black chooses option (1) White generally ends up exchanging on f5 and trying to use the open e-file and the outpost on e5. In option (2) White slowly builds up on the kingside while Black seeks counterplay on the other side of the board.

Statistics

Black has scored a very good 51% in over 1600 games with 5...Bd6 although, as with 5...g6, on average those playing Black were rated higher than those with White. For White, 8 Nh4 has scored 52%, which compares favourably to the 46% of 8 Re1.

Game 11
☐ M.Omelka ■ V.Bashkov
Zlin 1996

---

1 e4 c5 2 Nf3 e6 3 d3 Nc6 4 g3 d5 5 Nbd2 Bd6 6 Bg2 Nge7 7 0-0 0-0

8 Re1

The automatic move for KIA players, but I don't think that this is as threatening as 8 Nh4 (see Games 12-13).

8...Qc7!

Simply preventing e4-e5.

9 c3 Bd7 10 Qe2 f6! (Diagram 53)

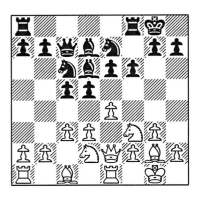

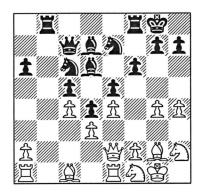

Diagram 53 (W)
What now?

Diagram 54 (B)
g3-g4 – not a bright idea

Faced with the threat of e4-e5 again, Black rules it out entirely. Black's position is extremely solid, he has more space than usual and his kingside is lacking dark-squared weaknesses. White should probably start action on the queenside with 11 a3! followed by b2-b4, but let's see what happens if he stubbornly continues to try something on the kingside.

11 Nf1?! d4!

Black will follow up with ...e6-e5, gaining even more space. This idea is particularly appropriate now that White's knight has moved away from d2 – there's no longer an immediate Nc4 to worry about.

12 c4

Or 12 h4 e5 13 h5 Bg4! 14 h6 g5! 15 N1h2 Be6 16 Rf1 Ng6! 17 Ne1 b5 with a clear advantage for Black, M.Klenburg-S.Grabuzov, Pardubice 1993. White's only pawn break on the kingside is f2-f4, but he is a million miles away from achieving this advance. Meanwhile, Black's 'counterplay' on the queenside is beginning to look menacing.

12...e5

As far as I can see, White has simply obtained a poor version of a King's Indian Defence with colour reversed. The normal plan would be to go for f2-f4 here, but with the rook on e1 and the knight on f1, White isn't in a very good position to do this. Instead he carries on in 'normal' mode.

13 h4 a6 14 N3h2 b5 15 b3 bxc4 16 bxc4 Rab8 17 g4? (Diagram 54)

Things go from bad to worse after this misconceived idea. Good or bad, White has to go for 17 h5 followed by Ng4, N1h2, Rf1 and finally f2-f4.

17...Ng6!

Taking full advantage of the newly-created outpost on f4.

18 h5 Nf4 19 Bxf4 exf4

White has three miserable minor pieces and Black is about to obtain domination with ...Ne5. In a desperate attempt for some air White gives up a pawn, but things have gone too far.

20 e5 Nxe5 21 Bd5+ Kh8 22 f3 Qa5 23 Red1 Qa3 24 Nd2 Rb2 25 Qf1 Ba4 26 Nb3 Rxa2 0-1

A good illustration of why plans must be altered to suit the needs of the position. Here the usual KIA attack against the French was simply not on.

Game 12
☐ **K.Lerner** ■ **S.Dolmatov**
Kharkov 1985

1 e4 e6 2 d3 d5 3 Nd2 c5 4 Ngf3 Nc6 5 g3 Bd6 6 Bg2 Nge7 7 0-0 0-0 8 Nh4 b6 (Diagram 55)

An outwardly attractive move – Black prepares to activate his bishop via either b7 or a6.

9 f4 dxe4!?

Instead of trying to restrain White's pawns, Black looks for counterplay by trading in the centre. Alternatively:

a) 9...f6 10 Ndf3 Bc7 transposes to Game 13.

b) 9...f5 10 exf5! exf5 11 Ndf3 is slightly better for White, who plans to utilise the open e-file. In the game M.Dvoretsky-V.Chekhov, USSR 1987 White's advantage increased after 11...Qc7?! 12 c3 Ba6 13 Re1

Rae8 14 Be3 h6 15 d4 Rd8 16 Bf2; White has e5 as an outpost, but it's very difficult for Black to use e4.

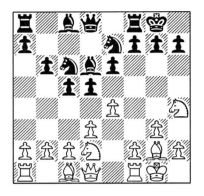

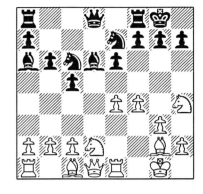

Diagram 55 (B)	**Diagram 56 (W)**
8...b7-b6	11 Rf1-e1

10 dxe4 Ba6 11 Re1 (Diagram 56) 11...Bc7

Or 11...c4 12 c3! (killing the bishop on a6 – 12 e5 Bc5+ 13 Kh1 c3! 14 bxc3 Rc8 was Black's idea) 12...Na5?! 13 e5! Bc5+ 14 Kh1 Nd5 15 Ne4 Bb7 16 Qh5! Ne7 17 g4! with a very strong attack, Fischer-Ivkov, Santa Monica 1966. The rest of game is quite instructive: 17...Bxe4 18 Bxe4 g6 19 Qh6 Nd5 20 f5 Re8 21 fxg6 fxg6 22 Nxg6! Qd7 23 Nf4 Rad8 24 Nh5 Kh8 25 Nf6 Nxf6 26 exf6 Rg8 27 Bf4 Rxg4 28 Rad1 Rdg8 29 f7! and Black resigned on account of 29...Qxf7 30 Be5+ R4g7 31 Qxh7 mate.

12 c3

Preventing ...Nd4 or ...Qd4+. The immediate 12 e5 is certainly also possible, when 12...Qd7?! 13 c3! transposes to the text but without allowing Black the possibility in the next note. However, 12...Qd4+ 13 Kh1 Rad8 gives Black some counterplay.

12...Qd7?!

12...Bd3! 13 e5 Qd7?! 14 Ne4! Rad8 15 Qg4 kicked off a menacing attack on the black king in S.Dolmatov-J.Lautier, Polanica Zdroj 1991. Black can improve on this by accelerating his queenside counterplay with 13...b5! 14 Ne4 c4 although I would still take White after 15 Qg4 Bb6+ 16 Kh1.

13 e5 Rad8 14 Qh5 (Diagram 57)

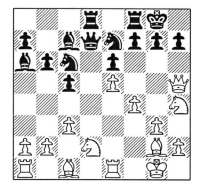

Diagram 57 (B)
Time for panic?

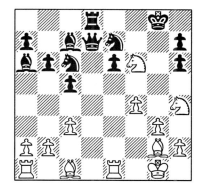

Diagram 58 (B)
A winning fork

14...f5?!

Black panics. Perhaps he was worried about 14...Bd3! 15 Ne4 c4 16 Nf6+!?, but after 16...gxf6 17 exf6 Kh8! 18 fxe7 Nxe7 Black's position is better than the one he gets in the game.

15 exf6 Rxf6?

This just loses material. Black must play 15...gxf6 although it's true his position after 16 Qg4+ Kf7 (otherwise e6 falls) 17 Ne4 looks very ropey.

16 Ne4 Rh6

Or 16...Rff8 17 Ng5!, hitting h7 and e6.

17 Qxh6!

Winning the exchange. Black could easily have resigned here.

17...gxh6 18 Nf6+ (Diagram 58) 18...Kf7 19 Nxd7 Rxd7 20 f5 exf5 21 Nxf5 Nxf5 22 Bxc6 Rd8 23 Be4 Kf6 24 Bxf5 Kxf5 25 Bxh6 Bd3 26 Rad1 c4 27 Rd2 b5 28 Rf2+ Kg4 29 Kg2 b4 30 Bf4 1-0

Game 13
□ P.Jaracz ■ P.Haba
Koszalin 1999

1 e4 e6 2 d3 d5 3 Nd2 c5 4 Ngf3 Nc6 5 g3 Bd6 6 Bg2 Nge7 7 0-0 0-0 8 Nh4 Bc7

A non-committal move: Black puts his bishop on a safer square and awaits White's push on the kingside before taking action. Here are a couple of alternatives:

a) I suspect that the outrageous 8...g5!? should be met simply with 9 Nhf3 when White hopes to prove that Black's advance on the kingside is more reckless than brave. Instead 9 Qg4?! f6 10 Nhf3 Qe8 11 Ne1 e5 saw White being driven back in B.Sadiku-N.Nikcevic, Pula 1990.

a) Ambitiously advancing on the queenside with 8...b5 makes sense. Play continues 9 f4 f5 (9...f6 is the other option) and now I don't really like the idea of advancing with 10 e5 because following 10...Bc7 Black's kingside is rock-solid and very difficult to breach. Instead 10 exd5 exd5 11 Ndf3 followed by Re1 and Be3-f2 seems a more attractive way for White to play the position.

9 f4 f6

Black opts to restrain White on the kingside. Again 9...f5 is playable, while 9...Ng6!? is another possibility.

10 Ndf3 b6

Black can simplify with 10...dxe4 11 dxe4 Qxd1 12 Rxd1, although White's extra space on the kingside should promise him a slight edge.

11 Qe1 Rb8 12 Be3 e5!? 13 f5! (Diagram 59)

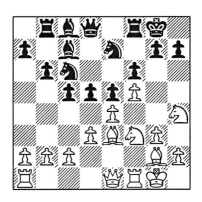
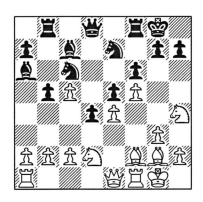

Diagram 59 (B)
The pawn wedge

Diagram 60 (B)
Offering an exchange sacrifice

 NOTE: After f4-f5 White has a typical King's Indian pawn wedge on the kingside.

13...Ba6 14 Nd2 c4!?

Mixing things up. After the slower 14...d4 15 Bf2 White will continue with g3-g4,Nhf3, h2-h4 and g4-g5 etc.

15 dxc4 d4!

15...dxc4 16 c3 makes the bishop on a6 look rather silly.

16 Bf2 b5 17 c5! (Diagram 60)

A promising sacrifice to keep the queenside relatively closed. White will have good light- squared control for the exchange.

17...b4 18 Qd1 Bxf1 19 Bxf1 Na5 20 Nb3 Nec6!

Unsurprisingly Black isn't keen to allow White's bishop to c4: 20...Nxb3?! 21 axb3 Nc6? 22 Bc4+! Kh8 23 Ng6+! hxg6 24 fxg6 and Qh5 mate is a graphic illustration of what could happen if Black's isn't careful.

21 Be1 Rf7 22 Nxa5 Nxa5 23 a3! bxa3 24 b4! Nc6 25 b5 d3!

Black's idea is 26 bxc6 dxc2! 27 Qxd8+ Bxd8 28 Bd3 Rb2 followed by ...a3-a2. Instead 25...Na5 26 Rxa3 leaves Black in some trouble, with 26...Kh8? 27 Qh5! not helping Black's cause, for example 27...Rf8 28 Bxa5 Bxa5 29 Ng6+ Kg8 30 Bc4+.

26 Bxd3 Nb4?? (Diagram 61)

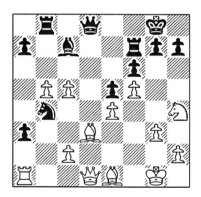

Diagram 61 (W)
Black blunders

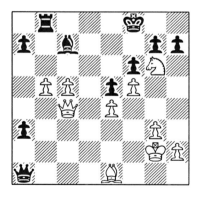

Diagram 62
Mate in 10!

Black had to try 26...Nd4!.

27 Bc4!

Not 27 Bxb4? Qd4+!.

27...Nxc2

Perhaps Black was relying on this tactic, but there's at least one massive flaw.

28 Qxc2! Qd4+ 29 Kg2 Qxa1 30 Bxf7+

30 Bc3, winning the queen, is more than adequate, but the text is rather nice.

30...Kxf7 31 Qc4+! Kf8 32 Ng6+!! (Diagram 62)

The knight re-enters the game with a vengeance. Now my *Fritz 8* announces mate in 10.

32...hxg6 33 fxg6 Ke8 34 Qe6+ Kd8 35 c6 1-0

Oh, why do these players resign so early? Here the spectators were denied the nice finish 35...Qd4 36 Qg8+ Ke7 37 Bb4+! Qxb4 38 Qf7+ Kd6 39 Qd5+ Ke7 40 Qd7+ Kf8 41 Qf7 mate.

3...Nf6 and Early Deviations

Now we'll look at lines where Black tries to exploit the fact that White is going for an early fianchetto with g2-g3. Because of this, very often White switches plans and develops classically. In fact, in the 'main line' the position is more a French Tarrasch than a KIA.

1 e4 e6 2 d3 d5

Most French players will play this move automatically, but it's certainly not forced. A couple of alternatives:

a) 2...c5 **(Diagram 63)** transposes into a Sicilian and following 3 Nf3 we reach a position that is discussed in Chapter 2. Instead 3 g3 will often reach the same positions, e.g. 3...Nc6 4 Bg2 g6 5 Nf3 Bg7 but White can also think about going into a Closed Sicilian with 5 Nc3 followed by f2-f4 or Be3 and Qd2.

b) 2...b6!? 3 g3 Bb7 4 Bg2 and now 4...d5 may well reach positions discussed previously, especially if Black continues with ...c7-c5. Another approach for Black is to strike at e4 with 4...f5!? 5 Nd2 Nf6. Now White can continue with 6 Ngf3! fxe4 7 dxe4, not worrying about the pawn grab with 7...Nxe4? on account of 8 Nh4! d5 9 Nxe4 dxe4 10 Qh5+ when Black is in some trouble.

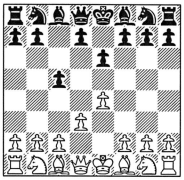

Diagram 63 (W)
Into a Sicilian

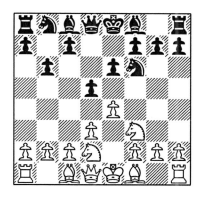

Diagram 64 (W)
Anticipating g2-g3

3 Nd2 Nf6 4 Ngf3

The most flexible move. Committing to the fianchetto with 4 g3 is possible, when a good way for Black to continue is 4...Nc6 5 Bg2 dxe4! 6 dxe4 e5 7 Ngf3 Bc5! – see the note to White's 5th move in Game 14.

4...b6!? (Diagram 64)

Anticipating White's kingside fianchetto, Black is ready to cause immediate problems down either the a6-f1 or a8-h1 diagonals. Because of this, 5 g3 loses much of its appeal.

4...Nc6 is a major alternative (see Game 14), while 4...c5 transposes to lines considered earlier.

5 c3!?

A tricky move, giving support to d3-d4 after e4-e5 and keeping all options open. Alternatively:

a) 5 e5 Nfd7 6 d4 c5 7 c3 transposes to the main line. White could also attempt to reach lines discussed earlier with 6 g3, but here the advanced e-pawn could come under heavy fire, for example 6...c5! 7 Bg2?! Nc6! 8 Qe2 Qc7!.

b) 5 g3 dxe4! is Black's idea. Following 6 dxe4 there's nothing wrong with 6...Bb7, while 6...Bc5!? is also promising. Now 7 Bg2 can be met by the very awkward 7...Ba6! 8 c4 Qd3!. White should probably forget about Bg2 in favour of 7 Bb5+, although even here 7...Bd7 8 Bd3 Nc6 followed by ...e6-e5 is fine for Black.

 NOTE: An advantage of avoiding ...c7-c5 is that this might become a useful post for a bishop.

5...c5

Now that White has virtually committed himself to the e4-e5 and d3-d4 plan, Black goes back to playing ...c7-c5. There are other options, though:

a) 5...Bb7 looks plausible, after which White should continue with 6 e5! Nfd7 7 d4. However, given that Black's plan normally involves exchanging the light-squared bishops with ...Ba6, it makes more sense to delay moving this bishop and play ...Bc8-a6 in one go.

b) 5...Be7 is a useful waiting move, after which 6 e5 Nfd7 7 d4 c5 transposes to the main line. White could also try the slightly disruptive 6 Qa4+!?, the point being to answer 6...Nbd7 with 7 e5! and 6...Qd7 with 7 Qc2! c5 8 e5! when on both occasions Black's f6-knight doesn't have d7 available as a natural retreat square. Because of this Black should probably play 6...c6.

c) 5...Ba6!? **(Diagram 65)** anticipates e4-e5 and d3-d4 so that Black can exchange light-squared bishops.

Diagram 65 (W)
Waiting for e4-e5

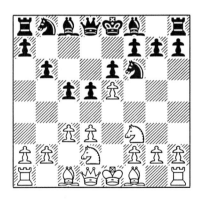

Diagram 66 (B)
Time for the push

Instead it may well be better for White to keep the tension in the centre for the moment: 6 Be2! Be7 7 0-0 0-0 (7...dxe4 8 dxe4 Bxe2 9 Qxe2 0-0

10 e5 Nd5 11 Ne4 grants White a pleasant space edge) 8 e5!? Nfd7 9 Re1 c5 10 Nf1 Nc6 11 Bf4 (L.Yudasin-C.Gelman, Chicago 1997) with a typical KIA position except for the fact that White's bishop is on e2 rather than g2. Even so, White can continue in normal fashion with g2-g3, h2-h4, N1h2 etc.

6 e5 (Diagram 66)

It's difficult to make any more constructive waiting moves, so White goes ahead with the central push. Again White can try the disruptive check with 6 Qa4+!? but this time following 6...Qd7! 7 Qc2 Black has time to get organised with 7...Qc7!, giving the f6-knight the d7-square after e4-e5. Instead 7 Qxd7+ is possible but a bit dull, and White can hardly hope for any advantage here. Finally, if White continues with 6 g3 it makes sense for Black to continue with 6...Ba6!, targeting d3.

6...Nfd7 7 d4

7 g3?! should be answered by 7...Ba6!.

7...Be7!

A clever waiting move. After 7...Ba6 8 Bxa6 Nxa6 we get to a position which can also be reached via a French Tarrasch after 1 e4 e6 2 d4 d5 3 Nd2 Nf6 4 e5 Nfd7 5 Bd3 c5 6 c3 b6 7 Ngf3 Ba6 8 Bxa6 Nxa6, where White's space advantage promises him a plus. Black's idea with 7...Be7 is to wait for 8 Bd3 when 8...Ba6! 9 Bxa6 Nxa6 leaves Black a tempo ahead of the line just mentioned.

8 Bb5!

White knows that an exchange of bishops is virtually unavoidable, so he looks to offer the trade on his terms (see his next move). 8 Qa4 prevents ...Ba6 for one move but Black can always play ...a7-a5 followed by ...Ba6.

8...Ba6

 NOTE: With the typical French pawn structure (d4 and e5 versus d5 and e6), it usually makes sense for Black to trade his 'bad' bishop for White's 'good' bishop (i.e. the light-squared bishops) if possible.

Black can gain time chasing the bishop with 8...a6 9 Ba4 b5 10 Bc2 but White isn't too unhappy about this – the bishop on c2 has found a good diagonal and Black can no longer force a trade.

9 a4! (Diagram 67)

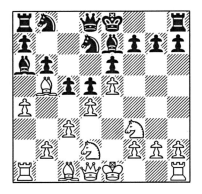

Diagram 67 (B)
9 a4!

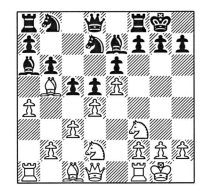

Diagram 68 (B)
A typical position

The point of White's previous move: following a recapture on b5 the pawn cramps Black and makes it difficult for him to develop his queenside.

9 Ba4?! keeps the light-squared bishops on the board but at too high a cost – with Black's bishop bearing down the a6-f1 diagonal White won't be able to castle for a while.

9...0-0

Despite the problems caused by 9 a4, it doesn't make sense for Black to opt out of exchanging bishops with 9...Bb7, for example 10 0-0 Nc6 11 Re1 cxd4 12 Nxd4!? Qc7 13 N2f3 0-0 14 Bxc6! Bxc6 15 Bg5! Bd8 16 Bxd8 Raxd8 17 b4 and White has a typical 'good knight versus bad bishop' situation, Anand-Dreev, London (rapid) 1995.

10 0-0 (Diagram 68)

White's space advantage on the kingside definitely gives him some attacking chances there, but Black can be happy that at least White's light-squared bishop, so often a major player in these attacks, will soon be traded off. Black will generally be on the defensive, but will hope to arrange some counterplay on the queenside (see Game 15).

Statistics

4...b6 has scored well for Black (50% in just over 1200 games), while 5 c3 has been White's most successful reply (55%). 4...Nc6 has scored 49% in around 1200 games.

Game 14
☐ **R.Schmaltz** ■ **M.Feygin**
Netherlands 2002

1 e4 e6 2 d3 d5 3 Nd2 Nf6 4 Ngf3 Nc6

A very direct move – Black plans ...e6-e5 and/or ...dxe4. It's also worth mentioning the relatively rare 4...Bc5!? which was given in the 3rd edition of John Watson's celebrated *Play the French* – the bible for many French Defence advocates. Probably the first thing to say is that playing in strict KIA fashion with 5 g3? falls to the tactic 5...dxe4 when 6 dxe4 Ng4! is highly embarrassing, and 6 Nxe4 also drops a pawn to 6...Nxe4 7 dxe4 Qxd1+ 8 Kxd1 Bxf2. Most White players have continued with 5 e5 Nfd7 and here 6 g3 is playable, while after the obvious tempo-gaining 6 d4 Black can play 6...Be7 or more ambitiously with 6...Bb6!?, planning ...c7-c5.

5 c3!?

A clever way to keep all the options open – White waits to see how Black proceeds before committing himself in the centre or with his f1-bishop.

If White plays in KIA style with 5 g3, Black exchanges with 5...dxe4! 6 dxe4 and then plays 6...Bc5!. This is the most active square for this bishop after an exchange on e4 and ...Bc5 is especially effective against an early g2-g3. Following 7 Bg2 e5 8 0-0 0-0 9 c3 Black prevents White from expanding on the queenside with b2-b4 by playing 9...a5! and will follow up with ...b7-b6 and ...Ba6!, creating problems down the a6-f1 diagonal.

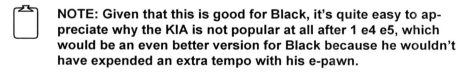

NOTE: Given that this is good for Black, it's quite easy to appreciate why the KIA is not popular at all after 1 e4 e5, which would be an even better version for Black because he wouldn't have expended an extra tempo with his e-pawn.

White's other option is to advance with 5 e5 Nd7 6 d4 (this position can be reached via 1 e4 e6 2 d4 d5 3 Nd2 Nc6 4 Ngf3 Nf6 5 e5 Nd7, but there it is White to move). Now Black should strike back in the centre with 6...f6!; after 7 exf6 Qxf6 Black wants to castle and then release the potential energy in his position with a swift ...e6-e5. White can try to keep a tighter rein on things with 7 Bb5 when a typical continuation is 7...fxe5 8 dxe5 Be7 9 0-0 0-0 (threatening e5) 10 Re1.

5...a5 (Diagram 69)

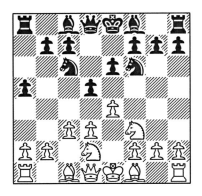

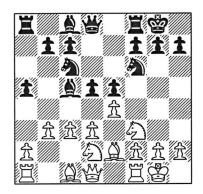

Diagram 69 (W)	Diagram 70 (W)
A waiting policy	How about 9 Re1 here?

Tit for tat – Black continues the shadow play with a high-class waiting move that prevents White from gaining space with b2-b4. Black is waiting for White to commit himself with g2-g3 before exchanging on e4 and playing ...Bc5.

5...dxe4 is possible but a bit premature, because following 6 dxe4 Bc5 White can develop his light-squared bishop more actively with 7 Bb5!.

5...e5 has been played quite a few times. After 6 b4!? Black usually either protects the e5-pawn with 5...Bd6 or prevents b4-b5 with 5...a6.

6 Be2

White is happy to continue quietly. The most ambitious way to play here is with 6 e5!? Nd7 7 d4 reaching a similar position to the one discussed in the note to White's 5th move. As you would expect, 6 g3 is answered by 6...dxe4 7 dxe4 Bc5!.

6...e5

Black can still play as against 6 g3 with 6...dxe4 7 dxe4 Bc5 but after, say, 8 0-0 0-0 9 Qc2 e5 the bishop is probably better placed on e2 than on g2. For one thing, there is no ...b7-b6 and ...Ba6 to worry about.

7 0-0 Bc5!?

The most active move, although the more restrained 7...Be7 has been played many times too.

8 b3!

White's plan is to slowly expand on the queenside with a2-a3, Rb1 and then b3-b4.

 WARNING: Trying to arrange b2-b4 more quickly with 8 Rb1 0-0 9 a3 runs into 9...a4! when any advance of the b-pawn is met by ...axb3, leaving White with an isolated a-pawn.

8...0-0 (Diagram 70) 9 a3

 WARNING: The plausible 9 Re1?? is actually a disastrous blunder punished by 9...Bxf2+! 10 Kxf2 Ng4+ 11 Kg1 Ne3, trapping the queen!

9...b6

Planning ...Bb7. A typical alternative here is the advance 9...d4 when White can decide between blocking the position up with 10 c4!? followed by Ne1-c2, Rb1 and b3-b4; or alternatively 10 Bb2, keeping the tension.

10 Rb1 Bb7 11 b4 axb4 12 axb4 Bd6 13 Qc2 Qe7 14 Re1 Rfe8!

Slowly both sides manoeuvre their forces. Black correctly keeps the tension in the centre; 14...d4?! would be premature after 15 b5! dxc3 16 Qxc3 Na5 17 Nf1 followed by Ng3.

15 Bf1 Qd7 16 exd5!?

Giving up the centre, but the positive side for White is that he forces off one of Black's bishops.

16...Nxd5 17 Nc4 f6 18 Nxd6 Qxd6 19 Nd2 Kh8 20 Ne4 Qd7 21 g3 Nd8

Planning to regroup with ...Ne6.

22 Bb2?!

22 Bg2 is safer.

22...Qc6!

Threatening ...Nxb4.

23 Qd2 (Diagram 71)

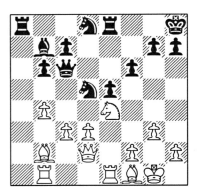

Diagram 71 (B)
A chance for Black

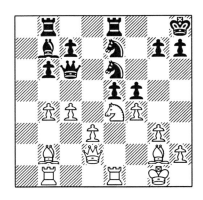

Diagram 72 (W)
A chance for White

23...Ne7

Missing an opportunity. After 23...f5 White cannot move the knight because 24 Ng5?? loses to 24...Nxc3!, threatening mate on h1. So White has to enter the complications of 24 b5, but Black can play 24...Qxb5! 25 c4 Qc6 26 cxd5 Qxd5.

24 c4! Ne6

Now it's too late for 24...f5 due to 25 b5 Qg6 26 Ng5, when 26...h6 can be answered by 27 Rxe5! hxg5 28 Rbe1 regaining the piece – 28...Qf7 29 Qxg5 is crushing.

25 Bg2 Rab8

Or 25...f5 26 b5! Qd7 27 Ng5! Bxg2 28 Nf7+ Kg8 29 Nxe5 and Kxg2.

26 f4! f5? (Diagram 72)

With the queen now protecting g2, suddenly the tactics on the long diagonal work in White's favour. 26...Nd4 had to be played.

27 Nf6! Qxg2+ 28 Qxg2 Bxg2 29 Nxe8 e4 30 Nxg7 Nxg7 31 Kxg2 1-0

Despite the final result, 4...Nc6 seems like a very reasonable line for Black.

Game 15
☐ M.Adams ■ E.Bareev
Sarajevo 1999

1 e4 e6 2 d3 d5 3 Nd2 Nf6 4 Ngf3 b6 5 c3 c5 6 e5 Nfd7 7 d4 Be7 8 Bb5 Ba6 9 a4 0-0 10 0-0 cxd4!

Black wants to play ...Qc8 in order to defend the a6-bishop and thus free the b8-knight. However, the timing of the exchange on d4 is important. The immediate 10...Qc8 is inaccurate as after 11 Re1 cxd4 White has the option of 12 Nxd4!. The game T.Sammalvuo-S.Brynell, Gothenburg 2003 continued 12...Bxb5 13 axb5 Qb7 14 Qg4! **(Diagram 73)**

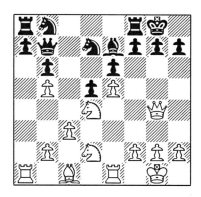

Diagram 73 (B)
Trouble ahead for Black

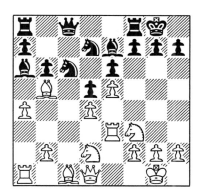

Diagram 74 (B)
Maybe a swinger?

with the makings of a strong attack, especially after 14...Re8 15 Nxe6! fxe6 16 Qxe6+ Kf8 (16...Kh8 17 Qf7!) 17 Re3.

11 cxd4

Now 11 Nxd4? merely leaves the e5-pawn en prise.

11...Qc8 12 Re1 Nc6 13 Re3! (Diagram 74)

With possible swinging ideas across the third rank.

13...Qb7

In a later game Bareev diverged with 13...Bxb5, and after 14 axb5 Nb4 15 Rc3 Qb7 16 Nf1 a6 17 bxa6 (17 Bg5!?) 17...Rxa6 18 Rxa6 Nxa6 an equal position was reached, Adams-Bareev, Frankfurt 2000.

14 Nf1 Rfc8 15 Bd2 Bxb5 16 axb5 Na5! 17 b3

Preventing ...Nc4. After 17 Bxa5 bxa5 18 Rxa5 Black wins his pawn back with 18...Bd8.

17...a6 18 bxa6 Rxa6 19 h4 Nc6 20 Rc1 Raa8 21 Rec3 b5 22 Ng3 b4

Preparing ...Na7-b5. Trading rooks with 22...Ba3 23 R1c2 Nb4 24 Rxc8+ Rxc8 25 Rxc8+ Qxc8 (Bareev) is another reasonable option for Black.

23 R3c2 h6?

Black was worried about something coming to g5, but ...h7-h6 presents Black with new problems. After the calm 23...Na7 24 Ng5 Rxc2 25 Rxc2 Nb5 26 Qg4 Nf8 (Bareev) White will find it more difficult to breach Black's defences.

24 Nh5 Bf8 25 g4!

Exploiting the negative side of ...h7-h6: g4-g5 is coming and the king-side will open up to White's advantage.

25...Ne7 26 Rxc8 Rxc8 27 Rxc8 Nxc8 28 g5! (Diagram 75)

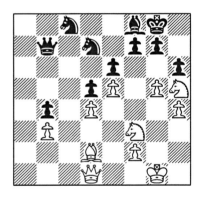
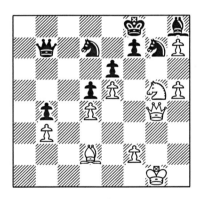

Diagram 75 (B)	Diagram 76 (B)
Charge!	No defence

28...Ne7

Trying to block things up with 28...g6 doesn't work due to 29 gxh6! gxh5 30 Ng5 Bxh6 31 Qxh5 Bxg5 32 Qxg5+ and now 32...Kf8 33 Qd8+ Kg7 34 h5! Kh7 35 h6 (threatening Qg5) 35...f5 36 exf6 Ndb6 37 Qf8! when there is no good defence to f6-f7 followed by mate on g8.

29 gxh6?

Missing a chance. White can crash thorough with 29 Nxg7! Bxg7 30 gxh6 Bh8 31 Ng5 (Bareev), for example 31...Nf5 32 h7+ Kf8 33 Qg4! (threatening Nxf7 or Nxe6+ followed by Qg8+) 33...Ng7 34 h5 **(Diagram 76)** when Black has no good defence to h5-h6. One possible finish is 34...f5 35 Nxe6+! Ke7! 36 Qg5+! Kxe6 37 Qg6+ Ke7 38 Bg5+ Kf8 39 Qd6+ Kf7 40 Qe7 mate.

29...gxh6 30 Qc1 Qc6!

Resilient play. By sacrificing the h-pawn Black reaches the sanctuary of the endgame where his queenside pressure will ensure a draw.

31 Bxh6 Qxc1+ 32 Bxc1 Nc6 33 Bg5 Na5 34 Nd2 Nc6! 35 Nf3

Or 35 Be3 Be7!, so White opts for a repetition.

35...Na5 ½-½

An Early Qe2

As we saw earlier in the chapter, White tends to plays Nd2 in order to avoid a queen swap should Black exchange pawns on e4. An alternative way to do this is to play Qe2, and this approach certainly has its advocates. One reason for preferring Qe2 over Nbd2 is that the c1-bishop isn't blocked and can thus be developed at an earlier stage than normal. Another point is that in some instances the b1-knight can be developed more actively on c3. The main coverage of Qe2 lines can be seen in the next chapter, as more often than not it arises from Sicilian move orders where Black plays a quick ...d7-d5. Here I'll just concentrate on lines that arise only from the French move order.

1 e4 e6 2 d3

White can even play the queen move as early as move two. The main attraction of 2 Qe2 is that it discourages Black from playing 2...d5 – after 3 exd5 Black must recapture with the queen. Even this is not that bad for Black, but if Black wishes to recapture on d5 with a pawn, then 2...Be7 blocks the e-file and prepares ...d7-d5. Following 3 Nf3 d5 4 d3 Nf6 we have reached note 'c' to Black's third move.

Another option worth considering for Black is 2...c5. After all, somehow to me the queen makes a funny impression standing on e2 in a Sicilian.

Play could continue 3 Nf3 Nc6 4 g3 g6 5 Bg2 Bg7 6 0-0 Nge7 7 c3 0-0 8 d3 d6 9 Nbd2 e5 with a position similar to ones discussed in the next chapter, except for the fact that White's queen is on e2 instead of d1.

2...d5 3 Qe2 (Diagram 77)

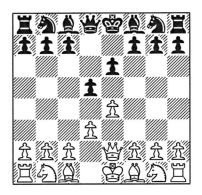
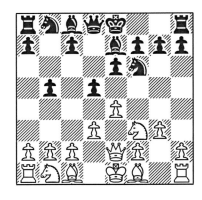

Diagram 77 (B)
No trade of ladies

Diagram 78 (W)
5...b5!?

Thus avoiding a queen swap.

3...dxe4!?

Opting for an open game where the placement of White's queen is more likely to come into question. Alternatively:

a) 3...c5 is likely to lead to lines discussed in the next chapter after 4 Nf3. Instead 4 exd5 Qxd5 5 Nc3 Qd8 isn't too worrying for Black, who will just develop normally with ...Nc6, ...Nf6, ...Be7 etc; White's unusual development doesn't leave him well placed to exploit Black's loss of time with his queen moves.

b) 3...Nc6!? 4 Nf3 e5!? is an ambitious idea along the same lines as 1 e4 e6 2 d3 d5 3 Nd2 Nf6 4 Ngf3 Nc6 5 c3 e5. White can either continue in solid fashion with 5 c3 Nf6 6 g3 etc. or change the character of the game with Morozevich's suggested 5 exd5!? Qxd5 6 Nc3 Bb4 7 Bd2.

c) 3...Nf6 4 Nf3 Be7 5 g3 is a popular continuation. Now Black can reach positions discussed in the next chapter with 5...c5 or else try the interesting 5...b5!? **(Diagram 78)**.

Black's play becomes more enticing after seeing 6 Bg2 dxe4 7 dxe4 b4!, which I believe was introduced by Korchnoi. Suddenly the idea of ...Ba6 looms large and Black has done well from this position so far. For example: 8 a3 Ba6 9 Qd2 Nc6! 10 e5 Nd5 11 Bf1 (what else?) 11...Bxf1 12 Kxf1 a5 and Black was more than comfortable in J.Timman-V.Korchnoi, Wijk aan Zee 2000; or 8 Nbd2 Ba6 9 Nc4 and now 9...Nc6 or 9...0-0 with good counterplay.

6 e5!? is an important alternative for White because it avoids all the ...Ba6 hassle. Following 6...Nfd7 7 Bg2 play may well transpose to the next chapter, but Black may also delay castling and try to punish White for playing e4-e5 rather earlier than normal – with the centre blocked the black king is reasonably safe on e8. For instance, 7...c5 8 h4 (to prevent ...g7-g5) 8...Nc6 9 0-0 h6!? 10 c3 g5! 11 hxg5 hxg5 12 d4 b4! with excellent counterplay for Black, S.Beshukov-J.Plaskett, Hastings 2000/01; or 10 Re1 g5! 11 h5 Bb7 12 c3 Qb6 13 a4 b4 with a very lively position, S.Belkhodja-V.Neverov, Dubai 2002.

 TIP: 5...b5!? looks like an attractive way for Black to liven up the proceedings.

4 dxe4 e5

4...b6!? is a significant alternative for Black – see Game 16.

5 Nf3 Nc6

Another option is 5...Nd7 6 Nbd2 c6 and now Morozevich likes the plan of 7 b3! and Bb2, adding pressure to e5.

6 c3 Nf6 7 Qc2! (Diagram 79)

A very good move – the queen was no longer well placed on e2 and now the bishop can develop on the f1-a6 diagonal. As we've already seen from similar positions, Black would be very happy after something like 7 g3 a5! 8 Bg2 Bc5! 9 0-0 0-0.

7...Bd6

Black can still develop the bishop more actively with 7...Bc5, but White can gain time by attacking it: 8 b4! Bb6 9 Be2 0-0 10 0-0 a6 11 Nbd2! Qe7 12 Nc4! (gaining more time) 12...Ba7 13 a4! Rd8 14 Bg5 and White has some initiative, A.Strikovic-Guerra Bastida, Orense 1996.

A more enticing option for Black is 7...a6!?, ruling out Bb5 and also giving the dark-squared bishop a haven on a7 so that Nbd2-c4 doesn't hit the bishop. In the game 0-1 D.Svetushkin-Y.Kruppa, Kiev 2000 White cut across Black's plan with 8 b4 but Black still reached a reasonable position after 8...Bd6 9 Nbd2 0-0 10 Nc4 h6 11 Be2 b5 12 Nxd6, and here Black played 12...cxd6! to strengthen the pawn centre.

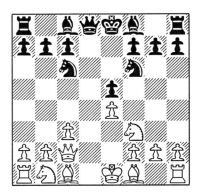

Diagram 79 (B)	Diagram 80 (W)
Freeing the f1-bishop	Ruling out Bg5

8 Nbd2 0-0 9 Nc4 h6! (Diagram 80)

Otherwise Bg5 would be annoying. With a symmetrical pawn structure there's not much to choose between White's and Black's chances. The game Zhang Zhong-J.Speelman, Bled Olympiad 2002 continued 10 Be2 Rb8!? (preparing ...b7-b5) 11 a4 b6 12 0-0 Bb7 13 Re1 Na5!? 14 Nxd6 cxd6! 15 Bf1 Qc7 16 b4 Nc6 with a roughly level position.

Statistics

Both 3 Qe2 and 2 Qe2 have scored well in practice (60% and 58% respectively), although these results are tempered by the fact that on average White's rating has been quite a bit higher than Black's. When facing 3 Qe2, Black's most popular response has actually been 3...Nf6 4 Nf3 Be7 5 g3 c5 6 Bg2 Nc6 7 0-0 0-0, reaching a position discussed in the next chapter, but I believe Black has better options than this.

Game 16
□ A.Morozevich ■ S.Lputian
Wijk aan Zee 2000

1 e4 e6 2 d3 d5 3 Qe2 dxe4 4 dxe4 b6!?

A logical move, trying to exploit the positioning of White's queen with an early ...Ba6.

5 Nd2!?

Certainly a brave move, but maybe a very good one too. White has two ways to meet ...Ba6: move the queen or block the diagonal. Moving the queen hasn't led to much for White: 5 c3 Ba6 6 Qc2 Bxf1 7 Kxf1 and now either 7...Nd7 or 7...Qc8 with the idea of ...Qb7 has done okay for Black. White can obviously block with c2-c4 (e.g. 5 Nf3 Ba6 6 c4 Nc6 7 Nc3 Nf6) but it's always possible that Black will at some point make good use of that outpost on d4.

Morozevich's idea of meeting ...Ba6 with Nc4 is the best solution positionally speaking; it's just a case of whether Black has anything tactical against White's deliberate self-pin. The early exchanges in this game suggest he doesn't.

5...Ba6 6 Nc4 Nf6 7 Nf3 Nc6 8 c3! (Diagram 81)

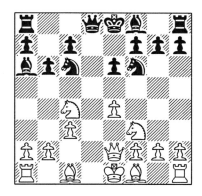

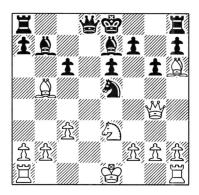

Diagram 81 (B)
...Na5 looks tempting

Diagram 82 (W)
A critical choice

Preventing ...Nd4 and preparing to answer ...Bc5 with b2-b4.

8...Be7!

8...Na5 looks tempting but Lputian was right to refrain from playing this because White has the resource 9 Qc2! Bxc4 10 Bxc4 Nxc4 11 Qa4+ Qd7 12 Qxc4, leaving him with a slight but persistent advantage.

9 e5!

Now White will be able to break the pin with Qe4.

9...Nd7 10 Qe4 Bb7 11 Qg4! g6

Of course not 11...0-0 on account of 12 Bh6. Now White can prevent Black from castling kingside, but the position becomes very complex as the tactics begin.

12 Bh6! b5! 13 Ne3 Ndxe5 14 Nxe5 Nxe5 15 Bxb5+ c6 (Diagram 82) 16 Qe4?

I suspect that Morozevich missed Lputian's deep idea here, otherwise he would have played 16 Qe2! (McDonald). Now after 16...cxb5 17 Qxb5+ Qd7 18 Qxe5 f6 19 Qa5 I don't think Black has enough for the pawn. 16...Qc7 followed by ...0-0-0 may objectively be stronger, but castling queenside isn't an ideal situation for Black.

16...Qc7 17 Be2 f5! 18 Qa4 Nf7!

The point of Lputian's play. This hardly obvious knight retreat leaves White's h6-bishop in a spot of trouble.

19 Bf4?

This loses a piece, and White only gets minor swindling chances in return. White must play 19 Bg7! Rg8 20 Bd4 when he is just about surviving the tactics after either 20...f4 21 Nc4 e5 22 Qa5! or 20...Kf8 (threatening ...c6-c5) 21 b4!.

19...e5 20 Bg3 f4 21 Nd5 Qd6 22 0-0-0 fxg3 23 Nf4 Qf6 24 Nd5 Qd6 25 Nf4 Qb8 26 Ne6 Ng5 27 Bc4 Nxe6 28 Bxe6 (Diagram 83) 28...gxh2?

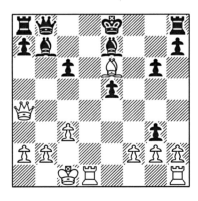

Diagram 83 (B)
Which pawn to capture?

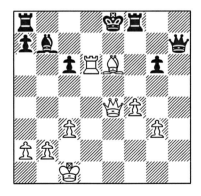

Diagram 84 (B)
No defence

I imagine here that Lputian and possibly even Morozevich were in some time trouble at this stage, and this influences their play. It doesn't look like a good idea to let White activate his rook so easily. It makes more sense to capture on f2 with 28...gxf2!; Black's king escapes after 29 Rhf1 Rf8! 30 Bd7+ Kf7 31 Rxf2+ Kg7.

29 Rxh2 Bd6? 30 f4?!

Fritz very much likes 30 Qb3! when suddenly Black has to deal with ideas such as Rxd6, Bf7+, and even Bg8.

30...e4?

This looks like a typical time-trouble move. Black must get his rooks into the game with 30...Qc7 and ...Rd8.

31 g3!

Ruling out the threat of ...Bxf4+ as well as lining up the possibility of Re2. Now Black is in real trouble.

31...Qc7 32 Qd4! Rf8 33 Qxe4 Qe7 34 Rxh7!

Morozevich is now in his element.

34...Qxh7 35 Rxd6 (Diagram 84)

Despite the extra rook, Black is in no position to defend himself. For example, 35...Rf6 36 Bf7+! Kxf7 37 Rd7+ Kg8 38 Rxh7 Kxh7 39 Qe7+, or 35...Qe7 36 Qxg6+ Rf7 37 Bxf7+ Qxf7 38 Re6+ Kf8 39 Rf6.

35...Qc7 36 Bf7+! Kxf7 37 Qxg6+ 1-0

It's mate after 37...Ke7 38 Qe6. An amazing game which White should never have won, but Morozevich's 5 Nd2 looks like a good try.

Arriving via a Flank Opening

Finally in this chapter a brief overview of how the lines we've looked at can be reached via Nf3, g3 etc. where Black commits himself to an early ...e7-e6. As you might imagine, both sides have quite a bit of scope with their move orders here – as well as 1 Nf3, White may begin with 1 g3 or even 1 d3. I'll just concentrate on the move orders most commonly seen in practice while pointing out transpositions to other main line openings.

1 Nf3

1 g3 d5 2 Bg2 c5 will come to the same thing after 4 Nf3. White can de-

lay the development of the king's knight with 3 d3 Nc6 4 Nd2 and e2-e4 but Ngf3 is likely to come at some stage in any case. Of course, Black also has to be ready for a transposition to the Bird's Opening with 3 f4.

1...d5 2 g3 (Diagram 85)

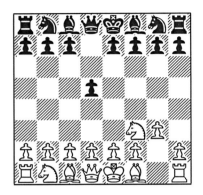

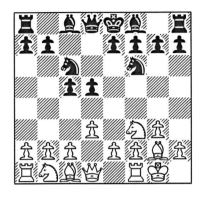

Diagram 85 (B)
1 Nf3 and 2 g3

Diagram 86 (B)
White prepares e2-e4

2...c5

Or 2...Nf6 3 Bg2 e6 4 0-0 Be7 when Black is ready for a Catalan after 5 c4 or 5 d4 0-0 6 c4. Instead a KIA can be reached after 5 d3 c5 6 Nbd2 Nc6 7 e4 etc.

3 Bg2 Nc6

With this move order Black has to be ready to meet the reversed Grünfeld with 4 d4.

4 0-0 Nf6

Alternatively:

a) 4...g6 5 d3 (5 d4!?) 5...Bg7 6 Nbd2 e6 (6...Nf6 reached a reversed King's Indian – see Chapter 4) 7 e4 Nge7.

b) 4...e6 5 d3 (again Black must be ready for 5 d4 or even 5 c4) 5...Bd6 6 e4 Nge7 7 Nbd2 although here White has the option of delaying developing the b1-knight in favour of 7 Qe2 or perhaps 7 Nh4.

5 d3 (Diagram 86) 5...e6

Here Black also has the option of playing 5...e5, 5...g6, 5...Bg4 and

5...Bf5, reaching a reversed King's Indian – see Chapter 4.

6 Nbd2 Be7 7 e4

Reaching one of the main lines in this chapter.

Points to Remember

1) After e4-e5 White's e5-pawn acts as a spearhead for a kingside attack. It gives White an enormous amount of space to manoeuvre and it deprives Black, in particular a black knight, the use of the f6-square.

2) White must get the timing right when playing e4-e5. This lunge is usually more effective once Black has committed himself to castling kingside, or when White can easily support the advanced pawn. Played too early, it may give Black the chance to surround it, or undermine it with ...f7-f6 or even ...g7-g5-g4.

3) In the traditional main line with 5...Nf6 it often ends up a battle between White's offensive on the kingside and Black's counterplay on the other wing. If Black doesn't fancy this he can consider lines with ...b7-b6, ...Bb7, ...Qc7 and 0-0-0.

4) In the 5...g6 line Black must be especially careful not to allow White an automatic attack against his castled king. It's usually worth trying to obtain counterplay with ...f7-f6 or ...g6-g5, even if this means weakening the kingside.

5) Against the 5...g6 line, White has an alternative way of handling the position involving exd5, which may be especially useful if Black is lagging behind in development.

6) For Black, 5...Bd6 is the most effective line to play if White insists on playing in typical KIA fashion with Re1, preparing e4-e5. Instead White should look closely at the Nh4 and f2-f4 plan.

7) Bear in mind ideas of h2-h4 for White. In the 5...g6 line Black often meets this with ...h7-h6, preparing to meet h4-h5 with ...g6-g5. Similarly, White often meets an unprovoked ...h7-h6 with ...h2-h4, making Black think twice about playing ...g6-g5.

8) In the 3...Nf6 line Black tries to exploit the fact that White is going for an early fianchetto with g2-g3. Because of this, very often White switches plans and develops more classically.

Chapter Two

KIA Versus the Sicilian

Introduction

From looking at my database, I've noticed that the positions discussed in this chapter arise from 1 e4 c5 the vast majority of the time. Therefore I've concentrated on this move order, but I do provide a summary of how to reach the positions via 1 Nf3 at the end of the chapter.

Black has quite a few different ways of playing the Sicilian against the KIA. After 1 e4 c5 White can play d2-d3 immediately, but instead it's worth flicking in 2 Nf3, as if going for an Open Sicilian. White doesn't lose anything with this feint (2...d5? 3 exd5 Qxd5 4 Nc3 doesn't make sense), and Black is forced to commit himself to some extent.

I've divided Black's options into two categories:

1) Black plays 2...e6

2) Black plays 2...Nc6 or 2...d6

You may have already guessed that the KIA is far more popular against the first set-up because, as we already know, ...e7-e6 is not a particularly useful move. Fischer sometimes played 2...e6 3 d3 when he didn't fancy playing an Open Sicilian, while more recently top-ten players Peter Leko and Alexander Morozevich have been seen taking the white side of this line.

Playing the KIA against 2...Nc6 and 2...d6 is less popular because Black has more flexibility over pawn structure – depending on circumstances he can leave his e-pawn on e7 or play ...e7-e5 in one go. Nevertheless, the fact that world champions Botvinnik and Smyslov, plus more recently grandmasters such as Emil Sutovsky and the 2005 European Champion Liviu Dieter Nisipeanu, have used the KIA here shows that it must also be taken seriously.

Black Plays 2...e6

1 e4 c5 2 Nf3 e6 3 d3 (Diagram 1)

There's nothing objectively wrong with 3 g3!? – it's a system in its own right. However, after 3...d5 White cannot reach the KIA set-up unless he's happy to allow Black the option of exchanging queens after 4 d3 dxe4 5 dxe4 Qxd1+ 6 Kxd1.

3...Nc6

The most flexible and by far the most common choice – in virtually all black set-ups the knight belongs on c6.

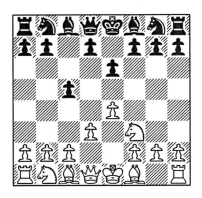

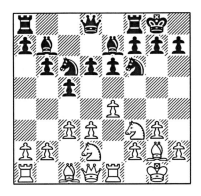

Diagram 1 (B)	**Diagram 2 (W)**
Building the foundations	Holding back with the d-pawn

 TIP: Just as against the French, it's vital for KIA advocates to play this move early.

3...d5 is also an important option, after which 4 Nbd2 transposes to Chapter 1 while 4 Qe2 is discussed later in this chapter. If Black is looking for something a bit different then 3...b6!? fits the bill nicely: 4 g3 Bb7 5 Bg2 d6! 6 0-0 Be7! (the most accurate; 6...Nf6 allows White the extra plan of 7 Nh4! followed by f2-f4 – here Black must be careful to avoid the trick 7...Be7?! 8 e5! Bxg2 9 exf6 Bxf1 10 fxe7 Qxe7 11 Qxf1 when White's bishop and knight should outweigh the rook and pawn) 7 Re1 (if White insists on the f2-f4 idea then he can play 7 Ne1 Nc6 8 f4) 7...Nf6 8 Nbd2 0-0 9 c3 Nc6 **(Diagram 2)** with a position that has been reached quite a few times.

By holding back on ...d5 Black doesn't allow White to obtain an e5-pawn wedge and thus a typical KIA plan of attack on the kingside is less effective. For example, 10 Nf1 b5 11 h4 a5 12 N1h2 a4 and it's clear that White's attack isn't as 'automatic' as usual. As an alternative, 10 d4 certainly comes to mind, while A.Morozevich-V.Ivanchuk, Moscow (rapid) 2002 continued 10 a3 (to prevent ...Nb4 after d3-d4, ...cxd4, cxd4) 10...Ne5!? 11 Nxe5 dxe5 12 Nc4 Qc7 (12...Nd7 is also possible) 13 f4 exf4 14 Bxf4 Qc6 15 Qe2 Rad8 with a roughly level position.

4 g3

This is the obvious continuation, but I should also mention 4 c3!?. As we'll see throughout this chapter, c2-c3 with the idea of d3-d4 crops up on numerous occasions, but playing it so early seems to be a rather new wrinkle. I guess one of the points is that if Black fianchettoes with 4...g6, White can forget about g2-g3 and simply continue with 5 d4 d5 6 e5 with an Advanced French where it's not clear whether Black's extra ...g7-g6 is a help or a hindrance.

If Black plays 4...d5 White should seriously consider playing 5 Qe2 (see the next section). Obviously 5 Nbd2 is also playable, when we're back into the territory of Chapter 1, but it's true that White doesn't normally commit his c-pawn so early in those lines. Let's take the line 5...Nf6 6 g3 Be7 7 Bg2 0-0 8 0-0 b5 9 Re1 a5 10 e5 Nd7 11 Nf1 Ba6 12 h4 b4 – here Black seems to be obtaining more queenside counterplay on account of White's advanced c-pawn.

4...g6 (Diagram 3)

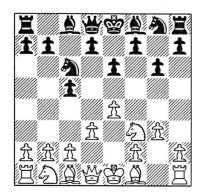

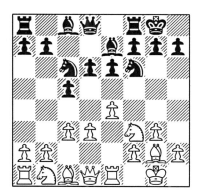

Diagram 3 (W)
The lure of the diagonal

Diagram 4 (B)
The 'classical' Sicilian set-up

Perhaps not the first move that an improving player would think of, but at club level 4...g6 has established itself as Black's favourite.

> **NOTE: In 'Closed Sicilians', with White playing e2-e4 and d2-d3, the most desirable place for Black's dark-squared bishop is the long a1-h8 diagonal. On here it has great influence both on the centre and the queenside.**

Even so, there are some important alternatives for Black:

a) For 4...Nge7 see Game 19.

b) 4...d5 5 Nbd2 transposes to Chapter 1, while 5 Qe2 is covered in the next section.

c) Black can also develop in 'classical' Sicilian style, for example 4...Nf6 5 Bg2 Be7 6 0-0 0-0 7 Re1 d6. Again, with Black's d-pawn held back on d6 and thus no white pawn wedge on e5, it makes sense for White to opt for the c2-c3 and d3-d4 plan with 8 c3 **(Diagram 4)**.

Now Black has two main ways of playing the position. Firstly, he can opt for a Ruy Lopez formation with 8...e5!? when White normally plays h2-h3 (to prevent ...Bg4) followed by d3-d4. Secondly, Black can aim for a French set-up with 8...Bd7 9 d4 cxd4 10 cxd4 d5, when White chooses between 11 e5 Ne4 and an isolated d-pawn with 11 exd5 Nxd5 12 Nc3.

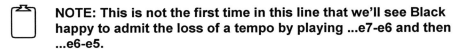

> **NOTE: This is not the first time in this line that we'll see Black happy to admit the loss of a tempo by playing ...e7-e6 and then ...e6-e5.**

d) Just so I don't get accused of ignoring the super-trendy, a quick mention should be made of the initially shocking 4...Bd6!?. In fact, positionally speaking this is quite a justifiable move because, as we've already seen, on the b8-h2 diagonal the bishop keeps an eye on the important e5-square, and the bishop can always drop back to c7 to allow the d-pawn to move. Play could continue 5 Bg2 Nge7 6 0-0 Bc7 and now against 7 c3 Black can either reach similar positions to those seen in Chapter 1 with 7...d5 or opt for a super-solid set-up with ...d7-d6 and ...e6-e5. A logical alternative for White is to play 7 Nh4 intending to gain space on the kingside with f2-f4.

5 Bg2

Again there are a number of alternatives for White: 5 d4!? and 5 Bg5 are covered in Games 17-18, while going for an immediate advance in the centre with c2-c3 and d3-d4 is once more an option, although perhaps it's not so effective here as on the previous move: 5 c3 Bg7 6 d4 cxd4 7 cxd4 d5 (7...Qb6!? also looks worrying for White) 8 e5 f6! 9 exf6 Nxf6! (illustrating an advantage of delaying ...Nge7) 10 Bg2 0-0 11 0-0 Ne4! and Black has good counterplay, O.Castro Rojas-S.Webb, Hamburg 1977.

5...Bg7 6 0-0

Virtually everyone plays this, but once more White can try to mix things up with 6 c3!? Nge7 and now:

a) 7 d4 cxd4 8 cxd4 d5 (as in note 'b', 8...Qb6!? must also be taken into account) 9 e5 0-0 10 0-0 transposes to Game 20.

b) 7 h4!? **(Diagram 5)** is an attractive possibility.

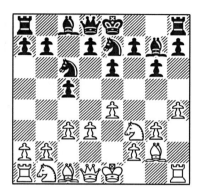

Diagram 5 (B)
A softening up procedure

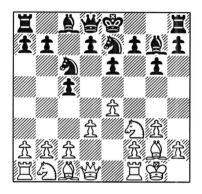

Diagram 6 (W)
Fluid development from Black

 NOTE: We saw the idea of h2-h4 in Chapter 1. White intends to 'soften up' Black's kingside with h4-h5. Black must decide whether he can live with this or whether to take action with 7...h6, when h4-h5 can be met by ...g6-g5!.

The game E.Sutovsky-B.Lindberg, Malmö 2003 continued 8 d4!? cxd4 9 cxd4 Qb6!? 10 d5!? Qb4+!? (10...Bxb2 11 Bxb2 Qxb2 12 Nbd2 exd5 13 exd5 Nxd5 14 0-0 0-0 –Gofshtein – is also critical, with Black's dark-squared weaknesses on the kingside giving White some hope) 11 Nfd2. Here Black should probably grab the pawn with 11...Bxb2, when 12 Bxb2 Qxb2 13 Nb3 would lead to a typically unclear mess that Emil Sutovsky seems to strive for in every game he plays, and in fairness to him this has led to some wonderfully creative victories.

6...Nge7 (Diagram 6)

Again this is the favoured square for the g8-knight because it doesn't block the g7-bishop and thus Black keeps greater control over the key squares e5 and d4.

After 6...Nf6 play could continue in a similar fashion to the main line after 7 c3 0-0 8 Re1 e5, but note here that Black is effectively a tempo down on the line considered in the third section of this chapter.

7 c3

7 Re1 will come to the same thing after 7...d6 8 c3 e5 or 7...0-0 8 c3 e5, but in this second line White has the option of 8 e5!?, temporarily shutting out the g7-bishop. Theoretically I don't think this is anything for Black to worry about, but it does give me a chance to include an early KIA miniature with a wonderful finish: 8...d6 (the simplest way) 9 exd6 Qxd6 10 Nbd2 Qc7?! (10...b6! 11 Nc4 Qd8 is known to be okay for Black) 11 Nb3! Nd4? 12 Bf4 Qb6 13 Ne5 Nxb3 14 Nc4! Qb5 15 axb3 a5 16 Bd6 Bf6 17 Qf3 Kg7 18 Re4 (18 Qxf6+!! is even quicker) 18...Rd8 (T.Petrosian-L.Pachman, Bled 1961) and here 'iron Tigran' produced the beautiful 19 Qxf6+!! Kxf6 20 Be5+ Kg5 21 Bg7! **(Diagram 7)**

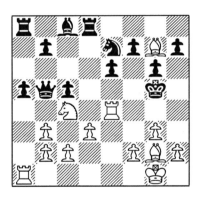

Diagram 7 (B)
A mating net

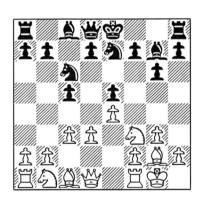

Diagram 8 (W)
Ruling out d3-d4

and Pachman resigned as there was no good way to prevent mate after 22 h4+ Kh5 23 Bf3 or 22 f4+ Kg4 23 Ne5+ Kh5 24 Bf3.

7 Nc3 is more of a Closed Sicilian move than a KIA move. Typically Black replies with 7...d6 8 Be3 e5 or 7...0-0 8 Be3 Nd4!.

7...0-0

As with all of the previous moves, Black once again has the option of playing 7...d5 when White decides between 8 Qe2 and 8 Nbd2. Black can also rule out d3-d4 with the immediate 7...e5!? **(Diagram 8)** although usually Black waits for White to commit himself with Re1 before playing this.

 NOTE: Playing ...e6-e5 is an integral part of Black's strategy in this line. Black reckons it's worth 'losing a tempo' to keep control of d4 and prevent d3-d4 for the foreseeable future.

It's worth noting that 8 Be3 d6 9 d4 exd4! 10 cxd4 Bg4! is fine for Black, while White can attempt to utilise the position of his king's rook by playing 9 Nh4 and f2-f4.

8 Re1

The more direct 8 d4!? is a critical alternative – see Game 20. White can also prepare d3-d4 with 8 Be3, hitting the c5-pawn. Following 8...d6 9 d4 cxd4 10 cxd4 (10 Nxd4!? is also possible) 10...d5 11 e5 White has gained the extra move Be3, but it's not clear whether this is good news or bad news as it's liable to be attacked by ...Nf5. Another option for Black after 8 Be3 is 8...b6!?. After 9 d4 cxd4 10 Nxd4 Bb7 Black can have no complaints, so White should probably prefer 10 cxd4.

8...e5!

Putting an end to White's ambitions of playing d3-d4, at least for now.

Black has a risky alternative in 8...d6!? when 9 d4!? cxd4 10 cxd4 d5?! 11 e5 leaves us in Game 20 except White has got the move Re1 for free – an obvious plus for him. However, 10...Qb6! **(Diagram 9)**, hitting d4, is more to the point.

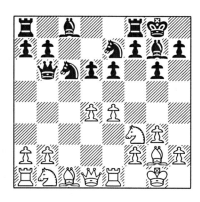

Diagram 9 (W)
Pressuring d4

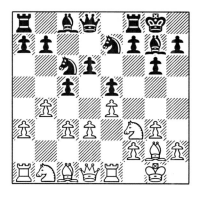

Diagram 10 (B)
Queenside expansion

Now a few games have continued along the tactical line 11 d5 Bxb2 (11...Nd4 is also possible) 12 Bxb2 Qxb2 13 dxc6 Qxa1 14 Qb3! Nxc6 15 Nc3 Nd4! 16 Rxa1 Nxb3 17 axb3, leading to an unclear ending. In the middle of this White also has the option of 13 Nbd2!?, intending to meet 13...exd5 14 exd5 Nxd5 with 15 Nc4.

9 a3

Changing plans – White is going for queenside expansion with b2-b4.

 NOTE: The plan of b2-b4 makes much more sense now that the a1-h8 diagonal has been blocked with ...e6-e5 – Black's g7-bishop is no longer so influential on the long diagonal.

Again playing for an early d3-d4 with 9 Be3 is well met by 9...d6 10 d4?! exd4 11 cxd4 Bg4!. Another possible plan for White is 9 Nbd2 planning a2-a4 and Nc4, but while looking a pretty set-up, this isn't particularly threatening for Black. For example, 9...d6 (9...d5 10 exd5 Nxd5 11 Nc4 gives us a type of position studied in Chapter 4, but with Black having lost a tempo with ...e7-e6-e5) 10 a4 (10 a3 followed by b2-b4 is still possible) 10...h6 11 Nc4 Be6 12 Rb1 a6 (12...f5!? also certainly comes into consideration) 13 b4 cxb4 14 cxb4 b5 and if anything I prefer Black.

9...d6

Alternatively:

a) 9...a5?! is covered in Game 21.

b) 9...d5!? has been played very little but doesn't look bad. If 10 exd5 Nxd5 11 Nbd2 we again reach a reversed King's Indian (see Chapter 4). Here, though, White's extra move (a2-a3) is not that valuable.

10 b4 (Diagram 10)

Strategies

Given the fluid pawn formation, there is more than one reasonable plan for both White and Black. White can couple expansion on the queenside with the preparation of an eventual d3-d4. The groundwork for this advance may include Nbd2-b3 and Be3 or Bb2. Another option for White is b4-b5, when the black knight usually goes to a5 – Black must be careful that this piece doesn't becomes sidelined from the action.

Black's most obvious pawn break is ...f7-f5, but depending on circumstances this is sometimes delayed or even omitted. Black sometimes builds up slowly, for example with ...Be6, ...Qd7 and a possible ...Bh3, while play on the queenside with ...b7-b5 and ...a7-a5 also cannot be ruled out. See Game 22 for further details.

Statistics

Overall White has scored 53% in nearly 9000 games with 3 d3. After 4...g6 White's most successful move has been 5 Bg5, which has scored a very impressive 67% over a relatively small number of games (just over 150).

Game 17
□ **E.Polovnikova** ■ **A.Iljushin**
Nizhnij No 1999

---

1 e4 c5 2 Nf3 e6 3 d3 Nc6 4 g3 g6 5 d4!?

What's this? Does White want to play an Open Sicilian after all? But hasn't he simply lost a tempo?

In fact 5 d4!? is a rather clever idea. Black's extra move is ...g7-g6, but there's an argument that this doesn't help him at all. Certainly ...e7-e6 together with ...g7-g6 creates a strange mix in an Open Sicilian – Black neglects his dark squares (especially d6 when the bishop is fianchet-toed).

5...cxd4 6 Nxd4 Bg7!?

With this move Black must be prepared to play an ambitious pawn sacrifice. From Black's point of view, I see no reason to avoid this, but if he wishes he can play 6...a6 (to prevent Nb5) followed by ...Bg7.

7 Nb5!? (Diagram 11)

The consistent choice and the only way to try and punish Black for his opening moves. Now if Black does nothing, Nd6+ will cause great disruption, so his next move is virtually forced.

7...d5! 8 exd5 exd5 9 Bf4?

Really upping the stakes, although objectively speaking this looks like a mistake.

Absolutely critical for the assessment of this variation is the continuation 9 Qxd5 (relying on the c7-fork) 9...Qe7+! 10 Be2 Bg4 11 f3 Rd8 12 Qg5 Bf5 13 Qxe7+ Ngxe7 (J.Halbritter-M.Diekers, Germany 1999) when Black's development advantage promises him very reasonable compensation for the pawn.

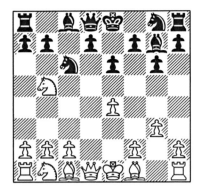

Diagram 11 (B)
Trying to punish Black

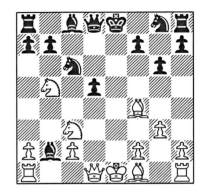

Diagram 12 (B)
What's going down?

9...Bxb2 10 N1c3!? (Diagram 12)

White's idea is that after 10...Bxa1? 11 Qxa1 he has domination over the dark squares and threats of Nc7+ and on the a1-h8 diagonal.

'Trading' rooks with 10 Nc7+ Kf8 11 Nxa8 Bxa1 is good for Black, e.g. 12 Bg2 Bf5 13 Nc7 g5! and the bishop cannot protect the knight.

10...Nf6!

An excellent move, maintaining the threats and preparing a very effective queen sacrifice. In I.Glek-T.Henrichs, Recklinghausen 1995 Black prevented Nc7+ with 10...Qe7+?! 11 Be2 Ne5?, the cheeky point being that White gets mated after 12 Nxd5?? Nf3+! 13 Kf1 Bh3. However, Glek simply played 12 0-0 and following 12...Nf6 13 Na4! Bxa1 14 Qxa1 Ned7 15 Bd6! Black was forced to resign.

11 Nc7+

In hindsight 11 Rb1 is a better try, even if 11...Bxc3+ 12 Nxc3 0-0 is favourable for Black.

11...Qxc7!! 12 Bxc7 Bxc3+ 13 Ke2 Bf5

This is stronger than the obvious 13...Bg4+ 14 f3 Nd4+ 15 Kd3 Bxf3 16 Kxc3 Bxd1 17 Kxd4, while *Fritz* approves of the aesthetically pleasing variation 13...Nd4+ 14 Kd3 Nb5! 15 Bf4 Bf5+ 16 Ke3 d4+ 17 Ke2 d3+

18 cxd3 Nd4+ 19 Ke3 Nd5 mate! **(Diagram 13)**.

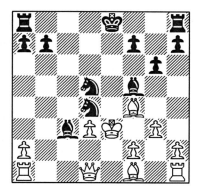

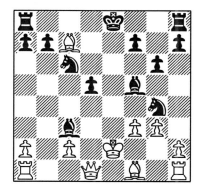

Diagram 13 (W)
A striking checkmate

Diagram 14 (W)
A 'minor piece' attack

14 f3 Ng4! (Diagram 14)

Threatening ...Nd4+ and regaining the queen with interest.

15 fxg4

White has nothing better, e.g. 15 Qxd5 Nd4+ 16 Kd1 Ne3+.

15...Bxg4+ 16 Kf2 Bxd1 17 Rxd1 d4

The fireworks have ceased and Black has a decisive two-pawn cushion. The rest of the game is largely uneventful, Black slowly but surely realising his material advantage.

18 Rb1 b6 19 Bh3 0-0 20 Bg2 Rac8 21 Bxc6 Rxc7 22 Ba4 f5 23 Rhd1 Kg7 24 Rd3 Re7 25 Rf3 Rf6 26 Bb3 Rc6 27 Rf1 Rc5 28 Kg2 h5 29 h3 a5 30 g4 hxg4 31 hxg4 fxg4 32 Rf8 Kh6 33 Rg8 Re2+ 34 Rf2 Rxf2+ 35 Kxf2 b5 36 Kg3 0-1

Black's enterprising play in this game seems to be a comprehensive solution to 5 d4!?.

Game 18
☐ **A.Shchekachev** ■ **D.Kuzuev**
St Petersburg 1998

---

1 e4 c5 2 Nf3 e6 3 d3 Nc6 4 g3 g6 5 Bg5!? (Diagram 15)

Developing the c1-bishop and causing a slight disruption in Black's camp. Naturally 5...Nge7? 6 Bf6! is not what Black was envisaging after 4...g6. The other blocks are playable, but I can see why many players are put off by 5...f6 and 4...Be7 – they don't exactly look very pretty.

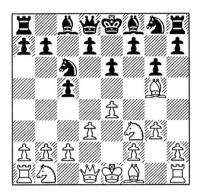

Diagram 15 (W)
Maximum annoyance value

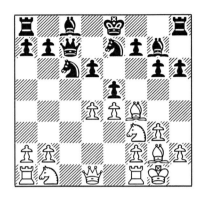

Diagram 16 (W)
11...e5!

5...Qc7

After 5...Qb6 White can defend with 6 Qc1, but much more in the spirit of things is 6 Nbd2!? Qxb2 7 Nc4, after which the queen fianchetto with 7...Qg7! has been played more than once.

6 Bg2 Bg7 7 c3 Nge7 8 0-0 d6

One of the points of 5 Bg5 is that following the logical continuation 8...0-0 9 d4 cxd4 10 cxd4 d5 11 e5, the pawn break ...f7-f6 looks less appetising because Black will be forced to part with his g7-bishop. Instead the game I.Glek-H.Kuijf, Holland 1996 continued 11...Qb6 12 Qd2 Nf5 13 Rd1 h6 14 Bf6! Bxf6 15 exf6 Qd8 16 g4 Nd6 17 Qxh6 Qxf6 18 Nc3 b6 19 h4 with good prospects on the kingside for White.

Glek is a real 5 Bg5 fan and his games are always worth checking out. For example, I.Glek-N.Short, Cap d'Agde (rapid) 1996 continued 8...d5 9 Na3 0-0 10 Re1 h6 11 exd5 Nxd5 12 Bd2 b6 and now White whipped up an attack out of nothing after 13 Qc1! Kh7 14 Re4!, intending 14...Nde7 15 Rh4 Nf5 16 Rh3 followed by g3-g4.

9 d4 cxd4 10 cxd4 h6 11 Bf4!

11 Be3 is met by 11...d5! as after 12 e5 Black can gain time on the

bishop with 12...Nf5.

11...e5! (Diagram 16) 12 dxe5

Black seems to be fine after this exchange, so perhaps White should onsider keeping the tension in the centre with 12 Be3!?.

12...dxe5 13 Be3 0-0 14 Qc1

This coupled with White's next two moves smacks of over-ambition in a position that doesn't justify such actions. White should probably make do with the equality on offer after 14 Nc3.

14...Kh7 15 b4 a6 16 Na3 Be6

The more ambitious 16...b5! (Smirin) looks logical – it's not clear what White's knight is doing on a3.

17 b5 axb5 18 Nxb5 Qb8 19 Qb2? Ra4! (Diagram 17)

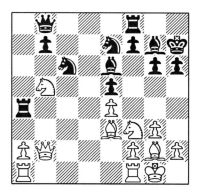

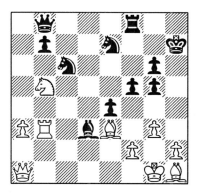

Diagram 17 (W)
A double threat?

Diagram 18 (B)
Draw?

This move is easy to overlook. The threat of ...Rb4 is obvious; the threat against e4 less so.

20 a3 Rxe4! 21 Ng5+ hxg5 22 Bxe4 f5!

Clearing the way for ...e5-e4, rejuvenating the bishop on g7.

23 Bh1 e4 24 Qc1

Deciding to give back the exchange. White can block the diagonal with 24 Nc3 but following 24...Nd5 25 Bd2 g4 followed by ...Nd4 or ...Ne5 Black's compensation is obvious.

24...Bxa1 25 Qxa1 Bc4 26 Rb1 Bd3 27 Rb3 (Diagram 18) 27...Bc4

Perhaps in time trouble, the lower-rated player heads for a repetition, even though following 27...f4! 28 Bc5 Rf5 Black has a clear plus. Perhaps Black missed that 29 Bxe7 Nxe7 30 Nd4 Rc5 31 Ne6 can be met by 31...Qe5!.

28 Rb1 Bd3 29 Rb3 Bc4 30 Rb1 ½-½

Game 19
□ **E.Mortensen** ■ **B.Lindberg**
Politiken Cup, Copenhagen 1998

---

1 e4 c5 2 Nf3 e6 3 d3 Nc6 4 g3 Nge7

Black often plays this move if he wishes to avoid having to face 4...g6 5 d4!? or 4...g6 5 Bg5!?. The point is that after 5 Bg2 g6 6 0-0 Bg7 we have reached the main line, but unfortunately for Black it's not quite as simple as that because White has one or two extra options.

5 h4!? (Diagram 19)

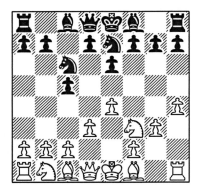
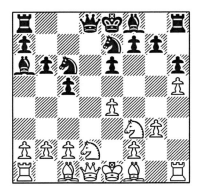

Diagram 19 (B)	Diagram 20 (B)
Shoving up the h-pawn	A surprising solution

Cutting across Black's plan – now 5...g6 is met by 6 h5!.

5...d5

Of course Black isn't forced to play this advance in the centre. Another option is 5...h6!?, preparing ...g7-g6 so that h4-h5 can be met by ...g6-g5. White can again prevent Black's idea, this time with 6 h5. This was played in the game I.Glek-O.Romanishin, Linz 1997, whereupon the

Ukrainian GM came up with a typically imaginative way of solving the problem of the e7-knight: 6...d6 7 Bh3!? Ng8!! (White has spent two tempi with his h-pawn, so why not?) 8 Nbd2 Nf6 9 Nh4 Be7 10 f4 Bd7 11 Ng2 Qc7 12 Ne3 0-0-0 with a very playable position for Black. It's noticeable that a few grandmasters have repeated this idea of ...Ng8-f6.

6 Nbd2

Naturally 6 Qe2 is also possible here.

6...h6

With the same idea as in the previous note. Another possibility is to gain more space in the centre with 6...e5!?, when the position is beginning to resemble a reversed King's Indian. Black has lost a tempo with ...e7-e6-e5, but he figures that White's extra move, h2-h4, is not that significant. For example, 7 c3 f6 8 a3!? Bg4! (exploiting the fact that there's no h2-h3 available) 9 Be2 Be6 10 b4 d4! with a reasonable position for Black, E.Lobron-J.Emms, Bundesliga 1997.

7 h5!?

7 Bg2 g6 takes us back to normal lines.

7...b6?!

The idea behind this move looks attractive, but it doesn't work out well for Black. There's an argument for continuing in the same vein as in the note to Black's 6th move with 7...e5!.

8 Bg2 dxe4 9 dxe4 Ba6

This was the idea behind 7...b6 – Black forgets his problems with the e7-knight for a moment to prevent White from castling. If now 10 c4 Black can continue with 10...Qc7 and ...0-0-0 before using the d4-square to re-rack his knights with ...Nd4 and ...Nec6. However...

10 Bf1! (Diagram 20)

 NOTE: This 'undevelopment' of the bishop is surprisingly effective – I haven't found a way for Black to exploit it.

Perhaps the best bet is 10...Bxf1 11 Kxf1. Then White's king will sit very comfortably on g2, but at least Black can play 11...Nd4 followed by ...Nec6.

10...Bb7 11 c3!

Preventing ...Nd4 once and for all.

11...g5

Extreme play – Black is willing to accept weaknesses so that he can develop his kingside. It's not easy to suggest an obvious improvement. Following 11...Qc7 12 Nc4 Rd8 13 Qc2 White threatens Bf4, and 13...e5 14 a4! secures the knight on c4 and still leaves Black pondering what to do about his kingside.

12 hxg6 Nxg6 13 Rh5! (Diagram 21)

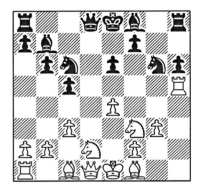

Diagram 21 (B)
5th rank action for the rook

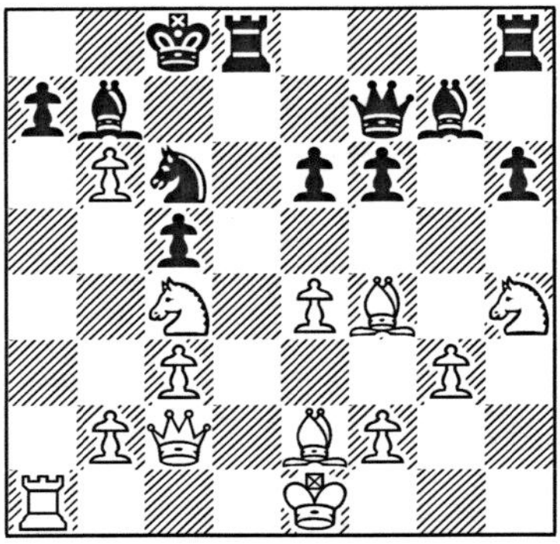

Diagram 22 (B)
Threatening Nd6+

A very deep move – this rook causes problems for Black on the 5th rank later on.

13...Qd7 14 Qc2 0-0-0 15 Be2 Bg7 16 Nc4 f6?!

Planning ...Qf7, but this is doomed to fail. If Black kicks the knight away with 16...b5 17 Ncd2 we see the rook coming to life on h5, with White threatening both Bxb5 and Rxc5.

Perhaps Black should simply move his king to a slightly safer square with 16...Kb8.

17 a4! Qf7 18 a5!

White is unconcerned with Black's threat of a discovered attack on the h5-rook because he is crashing through on the queenside.

18...Nf4

Or 18...b5 19 a6! Ba8 20 Na3, hitting b5 and c5.

19 Bxf4! Qxh5 20 Nh4 Qf7 21 axb6 (Diagram 22) 21...e5 22 Be3 Bf8 23 bxa7 Kc7 24 Qb3 Ba8 25 Bg4 1-0

There is no good defence to Qb6 mate. Aside from the Bg2-f1 idea, it was interesting how White imaginatively used both rooks on their 'home' files.

Game 20
□ **G.Vescovi** ■ **A.Volokitin**
Bermuda 2005

---

1 e4 c5 2 Nf3 e6 3 d3 Nc6 4 g3 g6 5 Bg2 Bg7 6 0-0 Nge7 7 c3 0-0 8 d4

 NOTE: 8 d4 is the most obvious continuation and in my opinion the critical try for an advantage in this line – White plays d4 before Black has a chance to prevent it with ...e6-e5.

8...cxd4

8...d5!? hasn't been played much but is interesting, the point being that after 9 e5 the omission of the exchange on d4 may help Black to some extent (for example, White doesn't have the c3-square for his knight). After 9 exd5 Nxd5 10 dxc5 Black can regain the pawn with 10...Qe7 Now the game Zhang Zhong-S.Rublevsky, Poikovsky 2004 continued 11 Nbd2 Qxc5 12 Ne4 Qa5 13 Bg5 h6 14 Bd2 Qc7 15 c4 Nde7 16 Nc3! a6 17 Re1 Rd8 18 Qc1 Kh7 with a roughly level position.

9 cxd4 d5 (Diagram 23)

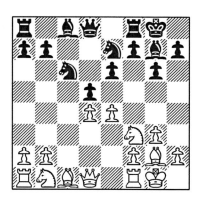

Diagram 23 (W)
Claiming some ground

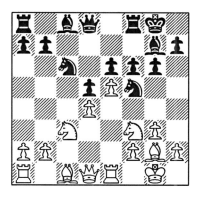

Diagram 24 (B)
Supporting e5

Striking back in the centre. Black can play more modestly with 9...d6 but after 10 Nc3 White's presence in the centre must promise him some kind of edge.

9...Qb6 is an attempt to refute White's early actions, but the tactics after 10 d5! look good for White: 10...Bxb2 11 Bxb2 Qxb2 12 dxc6 Qxa1 13 cxd7 Nc6 14 Qb3! Nd4 15 Nxd4 Qxd4 16 Rd1 Qf6 17 e5! Qe7 18 dxc8Q Raxc8 and White's two minor pieces are superior to Black's rook, M.Turov-V.Filippov, Moscow 1999.

10 e5

The only choice – 10 Nc3? dxe4! leaves White with a horribly vulnerable d-pawn.

10...Nf5

Adding pressure to the d4-pawn. The immediate 10...f6 is also possible, and a transposition is likely after 11 Re1 Nf5.

11 Nc3

The more passive option for this knight is 11 Na3, planning to defend the d4-pawn via c2. For example, 11...Qb6 12 Nc2 f6 13 g4 Nfe7 (13...fxe5!? 14 gxf5 e4 is an attractive piece sacrifice) 14 exf6 Rxf6 15 Re1 Bd7 16 Bg5 Rf7 17 Rb1 h6 18 Be3 Raf8 with good counterplay for Black, who plans ...g6-g5 and ...Ng6, L.McShane-J.Emms, Whitstable (rapid) 1998. Note that 19 Ne5 Nxe5 20 dxe5 Qc7 21 f4 can be answered by 21...Rxf4! 22 Bxf4 Rxf4 with excellent compensation.

The blunt 11 g4!? is worthy of consideration: 11...Nh4 12 Nxh4 Qxh4 13 f4 followed by Be3, Nc3 etc.

11...f6 12 Re1! (Diagram 24)

Giving up the e5-strongpoint makes no sense here, as after 12 exf6 Bxf6 White has immediate problems with his d4-pawn.

12...Kh8!

As Black wants to answer Bf4 with ...g6-g5 followed by ...g5-g4, it's a useful idea to tuck the king away in the corner.

Capturing on e5 hasn't fared well in practice: 12...fxe5 13 dxe5 h6 14 h4! (preventing ...g6-g5) 14...Bd7 15 Bf4 Be8 16 Qd2 Rc8 17 Rac1 Rc7 18 Nh2! Rcf7 19 Ng4 Kh7. Now in A.Morozevich-N.McDonald, British League 2002 the Russian GM surprisingly blundered with 20 b3?, allowing the tactic 20...Nxh4!. However, after McDonald's suggestion of 20 Ne2! Black is really gasping for air.

13 g4!?

13 h4 looks logical, but following 13...Bd7 14 Bf4 fxe5 15 dxe5 Black has the trick 15...Nxh4! 16 Nxh4 g5.

13...Nh4!

13...Nfe7 is obviously possible, but this sacrifice seems very promising.

14 Nxh4 fxe5 15 Nxg6+!? (Diagram 25)

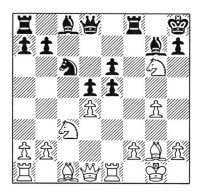

Diagram 25 (B)	Diagram 26 (B)
Sacrificing back	Threatening Rxe5 and Rf1

Deciding to offload the extra piece in order to weaken Black's king. 15 Nf3 exd4 followed by ...e6-e5 gives Black a huge centre.

15...hxg6 16 dxe5 Nxe5 17 Be3?!

In his notes to *Chess Informant*, Vescovi preferred shifting the rook via 17 Re3 Kg8 18 Rg3 with ideas of Be3-d4 and f2-f4.

17...Qf6! 18 Bc5 Rf7 19 Re3?

This pawn sacrifice shouldn't work.

19...Qxf2+! 20 Kh1 Kg8?

Allowing White right back into the game. After 20...Qf4!, threatening ...Nxg4, Black keeps a clear advantage.

21 Nxd5! exd5 22 Qxd5 (Diagram 26) 22...Bd7?

Black can limit White's advantage with 22...Bxg4 23 Rf1 Qxb2 24 Rxe5 Qxe5 25 Qxf7+ Kh7 26 Qxb7 Rd8 27 Qxa7.

23 Rxe5 Qxb2 24 Rf1 Qxg2+

This temporary queen sacrifice only manages to reach a losing endgame. The long line 24...Qxe5 25 Rxf7 Qxd5 26 Bxd5 Bc6! 27 Rf8+! Kh7 28 Rxa8 Bxd5+ 29 Kg1 b6 30 Rd8! Bxa2 31 Be3 (Vescovi) offers Black some practical chances, even though White should win with best play.

25 Kxg2 Bc6 26 Qxc6 bxc6 27 Rxf7 Bxe5 28 Re7 Bf4 29 Rxa7 Rxa7 30 Bxa7 Kf7 31 Bb6 Ke6 32 a4 Kd7 33 a5 Kc8 34 a6 Bd6 35 h3 Kb8 36 Kf3 Kc8 37 Be3 Kb8 38 Bf4! Bxf4 39 Kxf4 Ka7 40 h4 c5 41 h5 gxh5 42 gxh5 c4 43 h6 c3 44 Ke3 1-0

Game 21
□ **V.Bologan** ■ **N.Firman**
Moscow 2002

---

1 e4 e6 2 d3 c5 3 Nf3 Nc6 4 c3 Nge7 5 g3 g6 6 Bg2 Bg7 7 0-0 0-0 8 Re1 e5 9 a3 a5?!

Preventing b2-b4, but perhaps the antidote is worse than the illness.

10 a4! (Diagram 27)

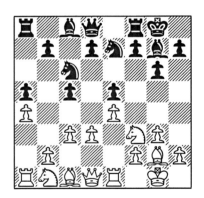

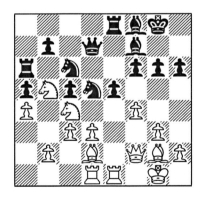

Diagram 27 (B)	Diagram 28 (B)
Enticing outposts on b5 and c4	Slow torture

Fixing b5 and c4 as outposts.

 NOTE: The idea of playing a2-a3, inducing ...a7-a5, and then continuing with a3-a4 is a common positional trick in the KIA.

10...d6

Given that Black plays ...d6-d5 very soon, there must be an argument for playing the immediate 10...d5.

11 Na3 h6

Eliminating the possibility of Ng5 in preparation of ...Be6.

12 Nd2!

White's knights are on excellent circuits – one is aiming for b5, the other for c4. These knights remain a problem for Black throughout the entire game.

12...Be6 13 Nb5 d5

13...f5 would be the consistent continuation, but 14 Nc4! (McDonald) leaves Black struggling to defend d6, with 14...fxe4 15 Ncxd6 exd3 16 Qxd3 offering White a major positional advantage – 16...Nf5 is met by 17 Bd5!.

14 exd5 Nxd5 15 Nc4 Ra6?

Understandably Black is keen to remove his rook from the long diagonal, but it is unfortunately placed on this square. 15...Rb8!, keeping the rooks connected, minimises White's advantage.

16 Qe2 Re8 17 Be3 Bf8 18 Bd2! f6 19 f4!

Black's centre is under great pressure. 19...exf4? 20 Bxd5! Qxd5 21 Nc7 illustrates one problem of 15...Ra6.

19...Bf7 20 Qf2 Qd7 21 Rad1 (Diagram 28)

Slowly building up the pressure. Due to White's positional advantages (the outposts on b5 and c4), there is no need to hurry.

21...Nb6?

Finally getting rid of one of White's knights, but in fact this only speeds up Black's demise.

22 Nxb6 Rxb6 23 Be3!

There is no way for Black to defend c5 and his positions falls apart.

23...Bb3 24 Bxc5 Bxd1 25 Bxb6 Bxa4 26 Nc7! Re7 27 Nd5! 1-0

White wins material after 27...Rf7 28 fxe5 fxe5 29 Nf6+. Positional wizardry from Bologan, but I believe White's position is generally easier to play after 10 a4!.

Game 22
☐ M.Piskur ■ O.Romanishin
Pula 1998

1 e4 c5 2 Nf3 e6 3 d3 Nc6 4 g3 Nge7 5 Bg2 g6 6 0-0 Bg7 7 Re1 d6 8 c3 e5 9 a3 0-0 10 b4 Kh8!? (Diagram 29)

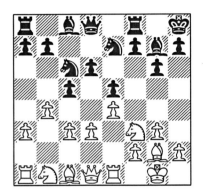
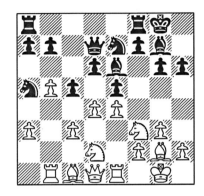

Diagram 29 (W)	**Diagram 30 (B)**
Preparing ...f7-f5	The desired advance

> NOTE: 10...Kh8 is a prophylactic measure against Ng5 and Qb3+ in preparation for the natural ...f7-f5 advance.

Black has tried several other moves here:

a) After 10...cxb4 White should reply with 11 axb4! opening the a-file for the rook and keeping a c-pawn to use in preparation for d3-d4.

b) 10...h6 (preparing ...Be6) 11 Nbd2 (11 b5!? Na5 12 c4!? followed by Nc3 is an attractive alternative) 11...Be6 12 Rb1 Qd7 13 b5! Na5 and now in V.Hort-E.Lobron, Biel 1986 White was able to push with 14 d4! **(Diagram 30)**, planning to meet 14...cxd4?! 15 cxd4 exd4 with 16 Qa4 b6 17 Nxd4.

c) 10...a6, preventing b4-b5, is a very sensible move. Now White has various ways to act, with one possible line being 11 Nbd2 h6 12 Rb1 Rb8 13 Bb2 (13 Nb3 b6 14 d4?! c4! 15 d5 cxb3 16 dxc6 Be6 favoured Black in S.Ansell-J.Nunn, British League 2000) 13...Be6 14 Ba1 Qd7 15 d4! cxd4 16 cxd4 exd4 17 Nb3 and White regains the pawn in the centre. The move 14...f5!? is a critical way to cut across White's plan, the position opening up with unclear consequences after 15 bxc5 dxc5 16 exf5 gxf5.

11 Nbd2

Given that Black seems to obtain a very comfortable position after this, there's something to be said for the continuation 11 b5!? Na5 12 c4, when the knight can be more actively developed via c3.

11...f5!

There's no need to delay this advance here – Black is well enough prepared.

12 Nb3

Or 12 b5!? Na5 13 Bb2?! (I prefer 13 c4!) 13...fxe4! 14 dxe4 (14 Nxe4 is met by 14...c4!, blocking out the b2-bishop) 14...Be6 15 Qe2 Nc8! (heading for b6 to eye the c4- and a4-squares) 16 c4 Nb6 17 Rac1 a6! with very good counterplay for Black, R.Soffer-I.Smirin, Israel 1998.

12...a5! (Diagram 31)

Black's idea is to answer 13 bxc5 with 13...a4 14 cxd6 Qxd6 15 Nbd2 Qxd3.

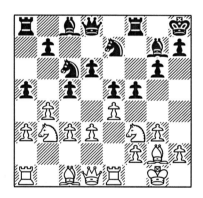

Diagram 31 (W)
12...a5!

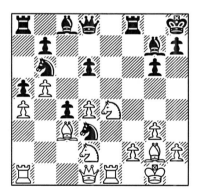

Diagram 32 (W)
An 'octopus' knight

13 b5 Nb8 14 a4

Perhaps 14 Nbd2, planning Nc4, is stronger.

14...Nd7 15 d4

Now Black is well placed to meet this advance, although 15 Nbd2 (planning Nc4) 15...Nb6! 16 c4 f4! isn't that appetising for White either.

15...exd4 16 cxd4 c4! 17 Nbd2 Nb6 18 Bb2 fxe4! 19 Nxe4 Ned5

Black's knights occupy good posts and the passed c-pawn is a threat. Black already has a good position, but now White self-destructs.

20 Nfd2?! Nb4! 21 Bc3? Nd3! (Diagram 32) 22 Nxc4

22 Re3 d5! wins material after 23 Nc5 Nxc5 24 dxc5 d4!.

22...Nxe1 23 Nxb6 Nxg2 24 Nxa8 Bf5 25 Qf3 Bh3! 26 Qe2 d5 27 Nc5 Qxa8 0-1

A good advert for 10...Kh8.

Black Plays 2...e6: Lines with Qe2

In Chapter One we discussed the idea of Qe2 against the French; here I'd like to take a look at Qe2 lines that normally arise via the Sicilian move order in which Black plays an early ...d7-d5 (naturally these positions can also arise from the French). As previously mentioned in Chapter One, White's two main reasons for preferring Qe2 over Nbd2 are:

1) White has the opportunity of developing the dark-squared bishop earlier.

2) The queen's knight may be developed more actively on c3 (this is usually after the advance c2-c4).

Let's take a look at some possible move orders to reach Qe2 positions before studying its effects in practical games:

1 e4 c5 2 Nf3 e6 3 d3 Nc6

Of course Black can play ...d7-d5 as early as move three: 3...d5 4 Qe2 Nc6 5 g3 reaches the main text.

4 g3

After 4 c3!? the possibility of White playing d3-d4 has very often induced Black into playing 4...d5 in practice. After 5 Qe2 **(Diagram 33)**

White has reached his desired set-up but at a slight cost: he has committed himself to the c2-c3 advance. It's true that White very often plays this move of his own free will, but there are a couple of points to bear in mind:

1) Given that White has already spent a tempo on c2-c3, the plan of c4

followed by Nc3 (see Games 25-26) becomes less desirable.

2) In certain lines Black's queenside counterplay is accelerated as the c3-pawn can be used as a point of attack.

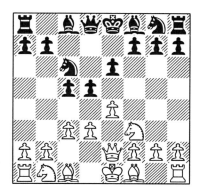

Diagram 33 (B)
Playing an early c2-c3

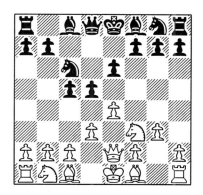

Diagram 34 (B)
The Qe2 set-up

Let's look at some variations:

a) 5...Nge7 6 g3 g6 7 Bg2 Bg7 8 0-0 transposes to the note to Black's 4th move.

b) 5...Nf6 (Black chooses the 'traditional main line') 6 g3 Be7 7 Bg2 and now:

b1) 7...0-0 8 0-0 b5 transposes to the note to Black's 7th move.

b2) 7...c4!? is a little-played but interesting attempt to exploit White's early c2-c3, with Black attacking the base of White's d3/e4 pawn chain. Now 8 dxc4 dxe4! has proved to be okay for Black in a few games, e.g. 9 Ng5 Ne5! 10 0-0 Qd3! 11 Re1 Qxe2 12 Rxe2 Nxc4 13 Nxe4 Nxe4 14 Bxe4 0-0 15 Nd2 Nd6. Instead, in D.Svetushkin-L.Gofshtein, Panormo 2001 White achieved an edge after 8 exd5!? cxd3 9 Qxd3 exd5 (perhaps Black should consider 9...Qxd5) 10 0-0 0-0 11 Nbd2 Bg4 12 Nb3 Qd7 13 Nbd4 Bd6 14 Be3 – the bishop on g2 is well placed to combat Black's isolated d-pawn.

4...d5

After 4...g6 5 Bg2 Bg7 6 0-0 Nge7 7 c3 we covered 7...0-0 and 7...e5 in the previous section. However, in practice Black often plays 7...d5!?

here. After 8 Qe2 Black's main two options are 8...0-0 (Game 24) and 8...b6 (Game 23).

Going back to 7...0-0, after 8 Qe2 Black still has the option of erecting a ...c5, ...d6, ...e5 structure, for example 8...d6 9 Nbd2 e5!. It's not clear here whether the queen is any better on e2 than on d1.

 NOTE: In general I believe the Qe2 set-up is less effective if Black hasn't committed himself to ...d7-d5.

5 Qe2 (Diagram 34)

5 Nbd2 leads us back into Chapter 1.

5...Nf6

Or 5...Nge7 6 Bg2 (as we saw in the previous section, 6 h4!?, intending to meet 6...g6 with 7 h5, is also possible; Black can play 6...e5!? here because 7 exd5 Nxd5 8 Nxe5?? Nd4! leaves White in big trouble) 6...g6 7 0-0 Bg7. Now 8 c3 transposes to the note to Black's 4th move, but given that White already has the Qe2 set-up in place, there's no need to play c2-c3 so early – White can wait for Black to commit himself and in some lines it may even be omitted. For example, 8 e5 h6 9 h4! (preventing ...g6-g5) 9...b6 and now White can continue with 10 Re1 Bb7 11 c3, e.g. 11...Qc7 12 Na3 a6 13 Nc2 (preparing d2-d4) which has been seen in a few games, or try something independent with 10 c4!? followed by Nc3 – we'll see more of this type of plan later on.

6 Bg2 Be7 7 0-0 0-0

Clearly the most popular move. However, as with Nbd2 lines, Black can also delay castling. The move 7...b6 is covered in Game 25, while the little-played 7...b5!? is certainly worthy of attention. The point is that after the natural 8 e5 Nd7 9 h4 we have transposed to a position covered in the Qe2 section of the previous chapter where Black is not forced to commit his king to the kingside – he can continue counterplay on the queenside or surround the e5-pawn with ...Qc7 and ...h7-h6, ...g7-g5 etc.

Another useful point of 7...b5 is that it makes the c2-c4 advance less desirable. A few games have continued 8 c3 0-0 (Black can still delay castling with 8...Bb7/8...a5 etc) 9 e5 Nd7 10 h4 a5 11 Bf4 (making use of the open diagonal to develop the bishop before playing Nbd2) 11...b4 and here the game I.Glek-V.Potkin, playchess.com (blitz) 2004 is noteworthy: 12 c4! (trying to keep the queenside as blocked as possible)

12...Nb6 13 Nbd2 Ra7! and Black obtained some counterplay with ...Rd7 followed by ...Bb7.

8 e5 (Diagram 35)

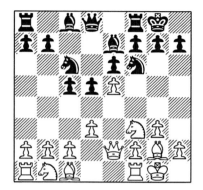

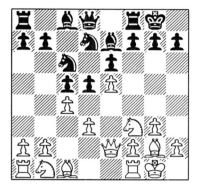

Diagram 35 (B)	Diagram 36 (B)
Here comes the lunge	A different approach

Now that Black has castled kingside, there's no longer any reason to delay the e4-e5 advance.

8...Nd7

 NOTE: There's a serious argument for Black to avoid the 'main line' by playing the rather unpopular 8...Ne8!?.

Regarding the above note, if White plays as against 8...Nd7 with 9 c4, Black continues with 9...Nc7! when the knight is quite well placed: it supports both the d5-pawn and queenside counterplay with ...b7-b5.

9 c4! (Diagram 36)

Strategies

It's the move c2-c4 that that really sets the Qe2 variation apart from Nbd2 lines. At first sight it seems slightly strange to strike out on the queenside, the place where Black is meant to hold all the aces, but there is good reason for this move. A few points to note about 9 c4:

1) White adds pressure to the d5-pawn, and this can be increased by Nc3.

2) If Black play ...dxc4 or ...d5-d4 White will gain access to the e4-square – a very good outpost for a knight, bishop, queen or even a rook that can be utilised in a kingside attack.

3) If Black exchanges on c4 White can transfer a rook to d1, using the open d-file.

4) On the negative side from White's point of view, Black may be able to make use of the newly created outpost on d4.

Black has more than one way to react to 9 c4, and his options will be covered in Game 26.

Statistics

White has scored an incredibly high 74% from the position after 9 c4. Even taking into consideration the fact that on average White was rated quite a bit higher, this is still an impressive score. Taking the position after 7 0-0, White score is still high at 67%, while Qe2 has also performed well against the ...g6, ...Bg7, ...Nge7 set-up.

Game 23
□ **A.Morozevich** ■ **A.Lastin**
Moscow (blitz) 2001

1 e4 c5 2 Nf3 e6 3 d3 Nc6 4 g3 g6 5 Bg2 Bg7 6 0-0 Nge7 7 c3 d5 8 Qe2 b6 9 Na3! (Diagram 37)

Diagram 37 (B)
A new knight circuit

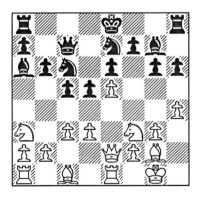

Diagram 38 (B)
Kingside or queenside?

Illustrating another feature of Qe2 over Nbd2. From a3 the knight is ready to jump into b5 in some circumstances, especially if Black plays the typical ...Qc7. If White plays e4-e5 the knight can use b5 as a stepping-stone to the d6-outpost. Alternatively, the knight can hop back to c2 where it supports both the d3-d4 and b2-b4 advances.

9...Ba6

A good move, preventing Nb5 and pressuring the tender d3-pawn.

10 e5 h6 11 h4 Qc7 12 Re1 (Diagram 38) 12...0-0-0

Not surprisingly Black doesn't fancy castling short and facing the usual pressure on the kingside. The game A.Stolte-A.Von Gleich, Germany 1989 is interesting: 12...0-0 13 Bf4 b5 (the only way to get queenside counterplay going, but...) 14 Nc2 b4 15 cxb4! Nxb4 16 Nxb4 cxb4 17 Qd2! Kh7 18 Rec1! Qb7 19 Nd4 Rfc8 20 Nb3 Qb6 21 Be3 Qb5 22 Bc5 (...White has taken over operations on the queenside!) 22...Nc6 23 d4 h5 24 Bd6 Bh6 25 f4 Qd3 26 Qf2 Qe2 27 Rc5 Qxf2+ 28 Kxf2 Bb7 29 Rac1 a6 30 R5c2 Ra7 31 Bf1 Ba8? 32 Na5! and Black resigned as material loss was inevitable.

13 Rb1!

Demonstrating how flexible White's position is – he can attack on either side of the board. The obvious idea is b2-b4, threatening a fork with b4-b5.

13...g5!?

Black desperately needs to find some counterplay somewhere, even at the price of a pawn. Passive defence with 13...Kb8 14 b4! cxb4 15 cxb4 Bb7 16 Nb5 leaves him with an unenviable position.

14 hxg5 Ng6

The point of 13...g5 – Black manages to get rid of White's e5-pawn.

15 gxh6 Bxe5 16 b4!

Typically direct from Morozevich. Now Black must do something about the threat of b4-b5.

16...Bxc3

In a later game Black tried 16...cxb4 17 cxb4 Nd4 but White kept an edge after 18 Nxd4 Bxd4 19 Nc2 Bc3 20 Bd2 Kb8 21 Rec1 Bxd2 22 Qxd2 Qe5 23 b5, D.Lobzhanidze-V.Gansvind, Dresden 2002.

17 b5 Bxe1 18 Qxe1 Bb7

18...Nb4 looks a better bet, but I still prefer White after 19 bxa6 Nxd3 20 Qe3 Nxc1 21 Rxc1. White will follow up with Nb5 and a2-a4, and it's difficult for Black to advance his central pawns without exposing his king further.

19 bxc6 Bxc6 (Diagram 39)

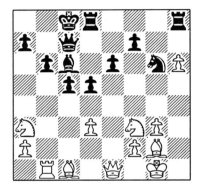

Diagram 39 (W)
White's in control

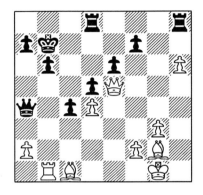

Diagram 40 (W)
Two good options

White has done well out of the tactical exchanges. As usual in a middlegame, a bishop and knight outweigh rook and pawn, and Black also has a very annoying passed pawn on h6 to deal with. If Black were able to get motoring with his central pawns he could create some counterplay, but White's next move puts a stop to this.

20 d4! c4 21 Nb5 Bxb5

21...Qd7 22 a4 a6 23 Nc3 doesn't help Black's situation.

22 Rxb5 Qc6 23 Rb1 Kb7 24 Ne5! Nxe5 25 Qxe5 Qa4 (Diagram 40) 26 Bg5

26 Bf4 also looks very strong. One line runs 26...Qxa2 27 Qc7+ Ka6 28 Rb4 (threatening Qc6) 28...Qa3 29 Rxc4!! dxc4 30 Qxc4+ b5 31 Bb7+! Kxb7 32 Qxb5+ Ka8 33 Qc6 mate.

26...Qxa2 27 Re1 Rc8 28 Qg7! Rhf8 29 Rxe6! c3 30 Re7+ Ka8 31 Rxf7 Rfe8 32 Bxd5+! 1-0

A nice finish – White wins after 32 Bxd5+ Qxd5 33 Rxa7+ Kb8 34 Bf4+.

Game 24
□ **G.Vescovi** ■ **B.Gulko**
Buenos Aires 2003

1 e4 c5 2 Nf3 e6 3 d3 Nc6 4 g3 g6 5 Bg2 Bg7 6 0-0 Nge7 7 c3 d5 8 Qe2 0-0 9 e5

As we've seen many times before, White is happy to carry out this lunge once Black is committed to kingside castling.

9...h6 10 h4 f6

Given that White has advanced with c2-c3, Black has a hook on the queenside to help with his counterplay, so an immediate advance in that sector looks logical: 10...b5 11 Bf4 a5 12 Nbd2 a4 13 Rac1 Bb7 14 Rfe1 Qb6 15 Nh2 a3! 16 b3 b4! 17 c4 Nd4 18 Qd1 Kh7 19 Nhf3 Nxf3+ 20 Nxf3 Rad8 21 Qe2 dxc4 22 dxc4 Nf5 23 Rcd1 with a roughly level position, J.Gallagher-J.Mestel, British League 1999.

Another enticing idea for Black is 10...Nf5!? 11 Bf4 f6! and now 12 exf6 Qxf6 13 Re1 allows the trick 13...Nxh4! 14 Nxh4 g5 15 Bd6 Rd8 16 Bxc5 gxh4, when Black has good counterplay. Instead, G.Vescovi-A.Gershon, Bermuda 2003 continued 12 Nbd2 g5! 13 exf6 gxf4! 14 fxg7 Rf7 15 Ne5 Rxg7 16 Nxc6 bxc6 17 Qe5! fxg3 18 fxg3 Nxg3 19 Rf4 Bd7 20 Kh2 when Black was a pawn ahead but White enjoyed some dark-squared control.

11 exf6 Rxf6 (Diagram 41)

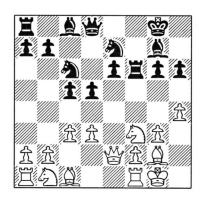

Diagram 41 (W)
The e5-pawn has gone

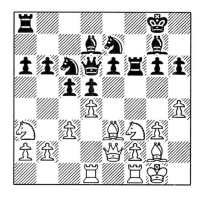

Diagram 42 (W)
A costly error

12 Be3

Controlling the crucial e5-square with 12 Bf4 is logical, but this gives Black the option of the speculative exchange sacrifice 12...Rxf4!? 13 gxf4, shattering White's pawns on the kingside.

12...Qd6

It's tempting to gain a tempo on the bishop with 12...d4, but the downside is that this move gives away the e4-square: 13 cxd4 cxd4 14 Bc1! (keeping the d2-square free) 14...e5 15 Nfd2! (Vescovi) and White will follow up with Ne4 and Na3-c4.

13 d4 b6?

Trying to maintain a pawn on c5, but Black gets into trouble after this move. 13...cxd4 14 cxd4 Nf5 was the way to go.

14 Na3! a6

Now 14...cxd4 can be met by 15 Nxd4! e5 (15...Nxd4 16 Bxd4!) 16 Nxc6 Qxc6 (16...Nxc6 17 Qd2 – Vescovi – hits d5 and h6) and now I like the move 17 c4!, when Black's centre is starting to creak.

15 Rad1 Bd7? (Diagram 42)

One mistake is quickly followed by another. Perhaps Black should release the tension with 15...c4, but following 16 Qd2 Kh7 17 Ne5! (Vescovi) White is winning the positional battle. Note here that 17...Nxe5? 18 dxe5 Qxe5 can be met by 19 Nxc4!.

16 dxc5! bxc5 17 Nd2

Threatening Ne4 – Black must lose at least a pawn.

17...Qb8 18 Ne4! Rf7 19 Nxc5 Bc8 20 Rfe1 Qd6 21 Na4 Rb8 22 Nc4! Qc7 23 Bb6 Qb7 24 Nd6!

Black's position collapses.

24...Qd7 25 Nxc8 Nxc8 26 Qxe6 Nxb6 27 Nxb6 Qa7 28 Bxd5 Nd8 29 Qxg6 1-0

Game 25
□ **V.Chekhov** ■ **M.Krasenkow**
Polish Team Ch., Lubniewice 1994

1 Nf3 c5 2 e4 e6 3 g3

As we saw earlier, this move order is inaccurate if White wants to play a KIA under any circumstances because Black can play 3...d5, not allowing White time for d3 and Qe2 (or Nbd2).

3...Nc6 4 Bg2 Nf6 5 d3 d5 6 Qe2 Be7 7 0-0 b6 8 e5 Nd7 9 c4! (Diagram 43)

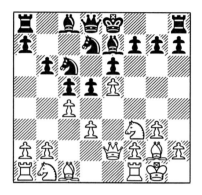

Diagram 43 (B)
9 c2-c4!

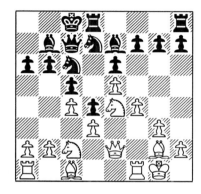

Diagram 44 (B)
Planning b2-b4

 NOTE: The idea of c2-c4 seems to be particularly effective against an early ...b7-b6 because Black no longer has the possibility of supporting the d5-pawn with ...Nb6.

9...dxc4?

This move has been played quite a few times, but with little success. The problem is that Black loses considerable influence in the centre, while White will be able to utilise the open d-file with his f1-rook. Some alternatives:

a) After 9...0-0 White can claim the e4-square with 10 Nc3! d4 11 Ne4. Black cannot capture on e5 because of 11...Ndxe5 12 Nxe5 Nxe5 13 Nd2!, attacking e5 and a8.

b) Following 9...Bb7!? 10 Nc3 d4! 11 Ne4 Black can get away with capturing on e5, so perhaps White should opt for 10 cxd5 exd5 11 e6!? fxe6 12 Qxe6 when Black has some issues to work out over king safety.

c) 9...d4 (Black's main move) 10 Nfd2!? (White wishes to support the e5-pawn with f2-f4 and make the most of the e4-outpost with his knight; a more standard KIA sequence would be 10 h4 Bb7 11 Bf4 h6! 12 h5! Qc7 13 Nbd2 0-0-0) 10...Bb7 (10...Ndxe5?? loses material to 11 f4!) 11 f4 Qc7

12 Ne4 0-0-0 13 Na3! a6 14 Nc2! **(Diagram 44)** and White's plan is to play for b2-b4. Black will seek counterplay on the kingside with ...h7-h5-h4 and/or ...f7-f6.

10 dxc4 Bb7 11 Nc3 a6

Already the knight on c3 shows its worth, with Black having to expend a tempo preparing ...Qc7.

12 Rd1! Qc7 13 Bf4 0-0-0

Now Black gets hit by a big tactical blow. However, White can also do the same if Black castles short: 13...0-0 14 Nd5! exd5 (14...Qd8 drops a pawn to 15 Nxb6!, while 14...Qc8 15 Nxe7+ Nxe7 16 Qd3 is unpleasant for Black) 15 e6! Bd6 (15...Qd8 is met by 16 cxd5! [Morozevich], while 15...Qc8 16 exd7 Qxd7 17 cxd5 Nd4 18 Nxd4 cxd4 19 Be5 is also very strong) 16 Bxd6 Qxd6 17 Rxd5! Nd4 (17...Qxe6 18 Qxe6 fxe6 19 Rxd7 Na5 20 Ne5 leaves Black in a grim ending) 18 Nxd4! Bxd5 19 Bxd5 cxd4 20 exf7+ Kh8 21 Bxa8 (A.Morozevich-D.Sermek, Moscow Olympiad 1994) and now 21...Rxa8 loses to 22 Qe8+ Qf8 23 Qxd7.

The idea of 13...g5 failed in spectacular fashion in the game S.Belkhodja-B.San Marco, Paris 1994 after 14 Bxg5 Bxg5 15 Nxg5 Qxe5 (or 15...Ndxe5 16 f4 Nd7 17 Nxe6! fxe6 18 Qxe6+ Kd8 19 Nd5 Qb8 20 Nxb6 and White wins) 16 Rxd7! (16 Nxf7! is more ruthless, but not quite as much fun) 16...Qxe2 17 Rxb7! Qxb2 18 Bxc6+ Kf8 19 Rd1 h6 20 Rxf7+ Kg8 21 Bxa8 hxg5 22 Re7 Kf8 23 Rc7 and, facing mate, Black resigned.

14 Nd5! (Diagram 45)

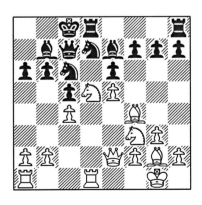

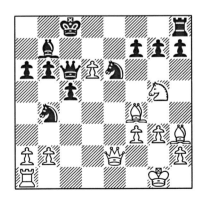

Diagram 45 (B)
Don't touch!

Diagram 46 (B)
Stay calm!

All the elements are perfect for this knight sacrifice to work. Perhaps Black should allow the knight to remain on d5 with 14...Qb8.

14...exd5 15 cxd5 Nb4

Or 15...Ncxe5 16 Nxe5 Nxe5 17 Bxe5 Bd6 18 Bxg7 with a clear extra pawn for White, A.Strikovic-V.Moskalenko, Mesa 1992.

16 d6! Bxd6 17 Rxd6 Nf8

After 17...Nd5 I like the simple 18 Rxd5! Bxd5 19 e6!.

18 Bh3+ Ne6 19 Ng5! Rxd6 20 exd6 Qc6 21 f3 (Diagram 46)

Calmly preventing the mate on h1. Meanwhile, the threats against e6 and f7 are becoming unbearable for Black.

21...Kb8 22 Bxe6 fxe6 23 Nf7!

Winning a rook because d6-d7-d8 is also a threat. Black could have resigned here.

23...Nc2 24 d7+ Ka7 25 d8Q Rxd8 26 Nxd8 Qd5 27 Qxc2 1-0

I suspect 9...dxc4 should be avoided.

Game 26
□ **D.Bronstein** ■ **B.Kelly**
Hastings 1995

---

1 e4 c5 2 Nf3 e6 3 d3 Nc6 4 g3 d5 5 Qe2 Nf6 6 Bg2 Be7 7 0-0 0-0 8 e5 Nd7 9 c4! d4 (Diagram 47)

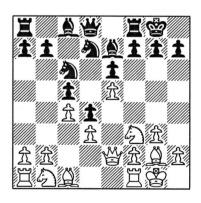

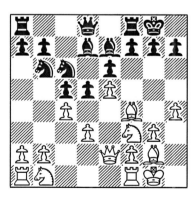

Diagram 47 (W)
The easy option

Diagram 48 (B)
How to get counterplay?

In some ways this is the easiest move for Black to play because he no longer has to worry about the tension in the centre, and this probably explains why 9...d4 has been played many times. However, most experts would agree that White has an advantage here based on the e4-outpost, even if in practice it's not so easy to utilise it because the e5-pawn requires constant attention.

Black's alternatives include:

a) Just as in the previous game, 9...dxc4?! doesn't inspire much confidence, for example 10 dxc4 Qc7 11 Bf4 b6 12 Nc3 a6 13 Rad1 Bb7 and now White can play 14 Nd5!.

b) 9...f6 10 exf6 Nxf6 11 Nc3 (11 Bf4 also looks reasonable) 11...Nd4 12 Qd1! has been played more than once. White has been temporarily forced backwards, but Black has long-term problems with his shaky pawn structure.

c) To me 9...Nb6! looks the most logical way forward. Black maintains considerable presence in the centre and puts some pressure on c4. If White captures on d5 Black can recapture with the e-pawn, freeing the c8-bishop and maintaining control of e4. The only real negative behind 9...Nb6 is that it blocks the b-pawn, leaving it more difficult for Black to arrange queenside counterplay (this is why 8...Ne8 9 c4 Nc7! should be considered). Now 10 Nc3 Nd4! is slightly awkward for White, so play continues with 10 Bf4 Bd7 11 h4 (**Diagram 48**) and now a couple of examples:

c1) 11...Nd4 12 Nxd4 cxd4 13 Nd2 Bc6 14 Rad1 Na4 15 Nb3! dxc4 16 dxc4 Bc5 17 Bxc6 bxc6 18 Nxc5 Nxc5 19 Be3! d3 20 Qg4! Qe7 21 Bg5 1-0 D.Bronstein-R.Dzindzichashvili, Soviet Ch. 1972 – White wins after 21...Qc7 22 Bf6 g6 23 Qg5 and Qh6.

c2) 11...a5! 12 Nbd2 a4! 13 a3 Na5 14 Rac1 Bc6 15 Rfe1 Qd7 with reasonable counterplay for Black, J.Gallagher-D.Knoedler, Zürich 1999. Instead of 12 Nbd2, White can opt for 12 a4!?. This blocks Black's counterplay at a cost of giving away the b4-square – a good trade in my opinion.

10 h4 a6

Alternatively:

a) 10...Kh8!? (planning ...f7-f6) 11 Bf4 f6 (Black's idea is to build a strong centre after 12 exf6 gxf6, the point being that 13 Qxe6? can be met by 13...Nde5 and ...Nxd3) 12 Nbd2 Qe8! (12...Ndxe5 13 Nxe5 fxe5 14 Bxe5 Nxe5 15 Qxe5 leaves White clearly better) 13 Bh3!? f5 14 Ng5! Bd8 15 Bg2 h6 16 Nh3! (L.Psakhis-I.Smirin, Haifa 1995) and White will follow up with h4-h5, Bf3, Kg2, Rh1 and perhaps g3-g4.

b) 10...Qc7 11 Bf4 b6 12 Nbd2 Bb7 13 Rae1 (13 Rfe1 and Nd2-f1-h2 is more typical) 13...Rae8 14 Ne4! (this doesn't seem possible, but...) 14...Ncxe5 15 Nxe5 Nxe5 16 Qh5 f6 17 Ng5! fxg5 18 Bxe5 Qd7 19 hxg5 Bxg2 20 Kxg2 with a very nice position for White, Z.Hracek-V.Rasik, Karvina 1989. Here Angus Dunnington points out the very pretty variation 20...g6? 21 Qxh7+!! **(Diagram 49)**

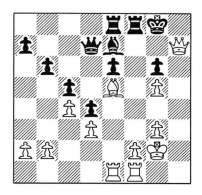

Diagram 49 (B)
21 Qxh7+!!

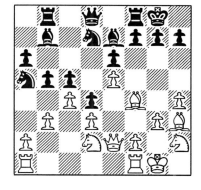

Diagram 50 (B)
A bold decision

21...Kxh7 22 Rh1+ Kg8 23 Rh8+ Kf7 24 Rh7+ Kg8 25 Rg7+ Kh8 26 Rh1 mate.

 TIP: In this type of position there are instances where White can use the e4-outpost even if it means giving up the e5-pawn.

11 Bf4 Rb8 12 Nh2!

This knight is heading for g4 while the other one covets e4. Also, Black's queenside counterplay is slowed down due to the attack on c6.

12...Na5 13 Nd2 b5 14 b3 Bb7 15 Bh3!? (Diagram 50)

An interesting decision: White avoids an exchange of bishops and temporarily gives up control of the long diagonal because he feels that the bishop will become a very useful addition to the kingside attack.

15...bxc4 16 bxc4 Nc6

16...Ba8, answering 17 Ng4 with 17...Rb2, looks more active, but perhaps Black was worried about 17 Ne4.

17 Ng4 Ba8 18 Nf3 Rb4 19 Ng5 Qb6 20 Bg2!

Now the bishop heads to e4.

20...Rb2 21 Qd1!

White wants to play Be4 before bringing the queen to f3.

21...Qa5 22 Be4

The sheer weight of White's minor pieces around Black's king must surely signal a successful attack. For example, 22...h6 can be met by 23 Nxe6! fxe6 24 Nxh6+! gxh6 25 Qg4+ Kh8 26 Qg6 when Black's survival chances are minimal.

22...g6 23 Qf3 Qc7? (Diagram 51)

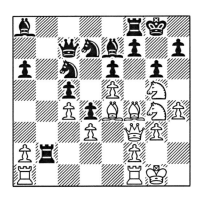

Diagram 51 (W)
White to play and win

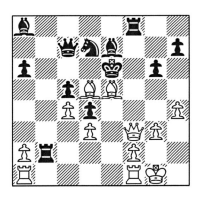

Diagram 52 (B)
Mate is coming

Allowing a combination, although in fairness Black was already under the cosh.

24 Nh6+! Kg7 25 Nhxf7! Ncxe5

25...Rxf7 26 Nxe6+ is White's idea.

26 Nxe6+ Kxf7 27 Bxe5+ Kxe6 28 Bd5+ (Diagram 52) 28...Bxd5 1-0

Black resigned instead of waiting for 29 Qxd5+ Kf5 30 Bxc7+ (*Fritz* prefers mate with 29 cxd5+ Kxe5 30 Rfe1+ Kd6 31 Re6).

Black Plays 2...Nc6 or 2...d6

1 e4 c5 2 Nf3 Nc6 (Diagram 53)

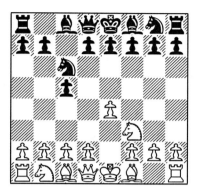

Diagram 53 (W)
Black plays 2...Nc6

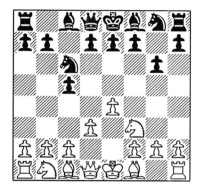

Diagram 54 (W)
Again the fianchetto

2...d6 is likely to reach the same positions, but is slightly more committal as far as Black is concerned. For example, Black no longer has the opportunity of reaching a Reversed King's Indian (see the note to Black's 3rd move) unless he's willing to lose a tempo with ...d6-d5.

Given that ...d6-d5 is unlikely, White may also delay d2-d3, hoping to play d2-d4 in one go. For example, 3 g3 g6 4 Bg2 Bg7 5 0-0 Nc6 6 c3!? Nf6 (6...e5 7 d3 transposes to the note to Black's 6th move). Now 7 d3 transposes to the main line, but White can also defend the e-pawn with 7 Re1!? when the idea of playing d2-d4 in one go is still feasible (see the final section for more on this). If Black wishes to play a ...Nf6 system then it's probably more accurate to play 3...Nf6!, encouraging White to play d2-d3.

3 d3

Now if White plays 3 g3 he has to take into consideration the reply 3...d5!? 4 exd5 Qxd5 5 Nc3 and now the slightly disruptive 5...Qe6+ (this position is more often reached via the move order 1 e4 c5 2 g3 d5 3 exd5 Qxd5 4 Nf3 Nc6 5 Nc3 Qe6+).

3...g6 (Diagram 54)

Once again the king's fianchetto beats everything else in the popularity stakes. However, another good approach by Black is to reach a Reversed King's Indian with 3...Nf6 4 g3 d5 5 Nbd2 (5 Qe2? Bg4! is very annoying) and now 5...e5, 5...g6 or 5...Bg4 (see Chapter 4 for more details).

4 g3 Bg7 5 Bg2 d6

5...Nf6 6 0-0 d5 7 Nbd2 0-0 again reaches a reversed King's Indian, while; 5...e6 will transpose to one of the first two sections of this Chapter.

6 0-0 Nf6

Opting for 'classical' development. Another popular choice is to clamp down on d4 with 6...e5 7 c3 Nge7 **(Diagram 55)**

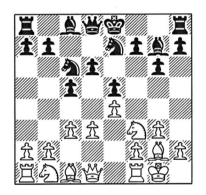

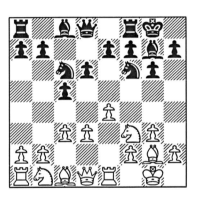

Diagram 55 (W)
A familiar position?

Diagram 56 (B)
Defending e4

when we reach a position very similar to the main line in the first section of this chapter, the differences being that Black hasn't lost a tempo with ...e7-e6-e5 and White's rook is on f1 instead of e1. Now White can proceed in typical fashion with 8 a3 followed by b2-b4, while another approach is to utilise the fact that the rook is on f1 with 8 Nh4, planning f2-f4.

 WARNING: Following 8...0-0 9 f4 exf4 10 gxf4 Black must strike back with 10...f5! because allowing White to play f4-f5, threatening f5-f6, would really force Black onto the defensive.

7 c3

7 Re1 will transpose to the main line after 7...0-0 8 c3. Instead, 7 Nbd2 0-0 8 a4, intending Nc4, was fashionable for a while after Botvinnik and Smyslov played it with some success. I think Black's most solid choice here is 8...e5 9 Nc4 h6!, intending ...Be6, ...Qc7, rooks to the centre and an eventual ...d6-d5.

7...0-0 8 Re1 (Diagram 56)

Defending the e4-pawn and thus making d3-d4 a real possibility. 8 Nbd2 is very similar to 8 Re1 and indeed there are many transpositions.

After 8 Re1 Black has more than one way to proceed. The two main moves both add pressure to the d4-square: 8...Bg4 (Game 27) and 8...e5 (Game 28). Both sides have numerous plans and these will be discussed in the following games.

There's also an argument that, despite appearances, White isn't actually threatening d3-d4 here, so Black isn't obliged to take action just yet. For example, 8...Rb8!? (planning typical queenside counterplay with ...b7-b5-b4) 9 d4 cxd4 10 cxd4 and now Black can quickly attack the centre by playing 10...Bg4 with ideas of ...Qb6 and ...Nd7. Of course White can take prophylactic measures; for instance 9 h3 and, after 9...b5, only now 10 d4!.

Game 27
☐ **L.Ljubojevic** ■ **V.Anand**
Monaco (rapid) 1994

---

1 e4 c5 2 Nf3 d6 3 g3 Nf6 4 d3 g6 5 Bg2 Bg7 6 0-0 0-0 7 Re1 Nc6 8 c3 Bg4 (Diagram 57)

With this pin Black shows that he is happy to give up the bishop pair if it means preventing White from advancing in the centre.

9 h3

9 d4?! looks all wrong now, and after 9...cxd4 10 cxd4 Qb6! White's centre is under tremendous pressure. To avoid losing material White has to play 11 d5 but 11...Ne5 12 Nc3 Rac8 promises Black excellent counterplay.

There's an argument here for playing 9 Nbd2!?. The idea is to recapture on f3 with the knight, after which White will be better placed to engineer the d3-d4 advance. A typical continuation is 9...b5 10 h3 Bxf3 11 Nxf3 Nd7 12 d4 b4.

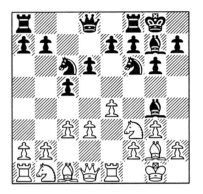

Diagram 57 (W)
The battle for d4

Diagram 58 (B)
Which queen move?

9...Bxf3 10 Bxf3

10 Qxf3 has also been played, for example 10...Rb8 11 Be3 Nd7 (preventing d3-d4) and now 12 Qd1, once more preparing d3-d4, actually transposes to the text.

10...Nd7

Preventing d3-d4. Next on the agenda for Black is ...Rb8 followed by the advance ...b7-b5-b4, making inroads into White's queenside.

11 Bg2

A sensible move, safeguarding the bishop against any ...Ne5 ideas and protecting the h3-pawn. 11 Be3, preparing d3-d4, could be met by 11...Qb6 (compare with the next note).

11...Rb8 12 Be3 (Diagram 58) 12...Qc7

In a later game, Y.Visser-S.Atalik, Groningen 1999, the Turkish GM tried to improve with 12...Qb6!?, and following 13 Qd2 Qa6 14 Bf1 b5 White should have continued 15 d4 (Atalik) with a complex position.

 WARNING: Black must avoid 12...b5?! 13 e5! when either knight capture on e5 loses material to 14 f4!.

13 Na3 b5 14 Nc2 b4 15 d4 a5 16 Qd2?

It turns out that the queen is poorly placed on this square – White admits as much with his 19th move. Yasser Seirawan claims a clear advantage for White following 16 Qd3!, although to me it still looks like Black has reasonable counterplay on the queenside after 16...a4 or 16...b3!?.

16...a4 17 Bf1 bxc3 18 bxc3 Qa5! 19 Qd3 Rb2! 20 Na3 cxd4 21 cxd4

21 Nc4 loses to 21...dxe3! 22 Nxa5 exf2+ 23 Kh1 fxe1Q 24 Rxe1 Nxa5, when Black's assorted pieces outweigh the queen.

21...Nde5! (Diagram 59)

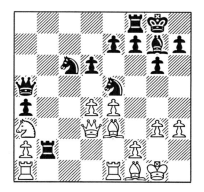

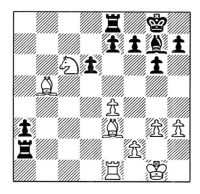

Diagram 59 (W)	Diagram 60 (W)
21...Nde5!	Touchdown is imminent

A nice little combination. Black will gain a rook and two pawns for two knights. Crucially, one of the pawns is a2, leaving Black with a runner on a4.

22 dxe5 Nxe5 23 Nc4

23 Qd1 can be met by 23...Qxe1! 24 Qxe1 Nf3+ 25 Kg2 Nxe1+ 26 Rxe1 Rxa2 (Seirawan) when the a-pawn should decide matters, e.g. 27 Nb5 Rb8 28 Rb1 Rb2!.

23...Nxd3 24 Nxa5 Nxe1 25 Rxe1 Rxa2 26 Nc6 Re8 27 Bb5 a3! (Diagram 60)

An exchange sacrifice to ensure a safe passage home for the a-pawn.

28 Nb4 Rb2 29 Bxe8 Rxb4 30 Bg5 a2 0-1

Game 28
□ **L.Yudasin** ■ **R.Mascarinas**
Manila 1990

1 e4 c5 2 Nf3 Nc6 3 d3 g6 4 g3 Bg7 5 Bg2 d6 6 0-0 Nf6 7 c3 0-0 8 Re1 e5 **(Diagram 61)**

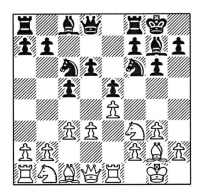

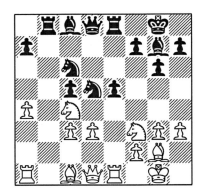

Diagram 61 (W)	**Diagram 62 (W)**
A familiar pawn structure	Problems with c3

We've seen this pawn structure before, but that was with Black's knight on e7. With the knight on f6 it makes less sense for Black to play for ...f7-f5 (for obvious reasons – the knight has to move again), but more sense to play in the centre (the knight controls both d5 and e4). Notice also that Black has not lost a tempo with ...e7-e6-e5, and this proves to be important in a2-a3/b2-b4 lines.

9 Nbd2

Alternatively:

a) Black's previous move was designed to discourage 9 d4?!, and Black certainly has nothing to worry about after 9...exd4! 10 cxd4 Bg4 11 dxc5 (or 11 d5 Nd4) 11...dxc5.

b) 9 a3 is the beginning of the typical offensive on the queenside with b2-b4. However, as in the main game, it is less effective here than normal after 9...b5! (you should know by now that 9...a5?! can be met by 10 a4!, netting b5 and c4 as outposts) 10 b4. If it were White to move here, he could seize the initiative with 11 a4!. However, with Black to play, 10...a5! takes over the operation on the queenside.

c) 9 Na3!? is worth studying. It has similar motives to 9 Nbd2, but here the c1-bishop is free to move: 9...Re8 (9...h6!?) 10 Bg5!? (White aims to dominate the d5-square) 10...h6 11 Bxf6 Bxf6 12 Nc4 b5 13 Ne3 Be6 14 Nd5 Bg7 15 a4 b4 16 Nd2 Na5 with a roughly level position, V.Malakhov-Z.Efimenko, Moscow 2005.

9...Re8!

A good, Ruy Lopez-style move, adding extra support to e5 in case of an eventual ...d6-d5, while making it more difficult for White to achieve d3-d4 due to the X-ray effect on the e4-pawn.

Another plan is to go for ...f7-f5, but Black must be careful with preparation. For example, 9...Nh5 10 Nc4! f5?! 11 exf5! Bxf5 (11...gxf5 is met by 12 Nfxe5! with a discovered attack on h5) 12 Qb3! Kh8 13 Qxb7 Bxd3 14 Bg5! and the complications seem to favour White.

10 a3?!

As mentioned previously, Black is well prepared for the plan of b2-b4, so White should look elsewhere. One option is 10 a4, allowing White to play Nc4 without having to worry about it being kicked away by ...b7-b5. A typical continuation is 10...h6 (preventing Ng5 and thus preparing ...Be6) 11 Nc4 Be6, and now 12 Rb1? with the idea of b2-b4 fails to the tactic 12...Nxe4! 13 Rxe4 d5. Instead White can play 12 Nfd2 with a queenside expansion plan including a4-a5, Qa4 and perhaps b2-b4.

10...b5!

Following Black's play in note 'b' to White's 9th move. Now 11 b4 a5! grabs the initiative, so White wisely lowers his ambitions.

11 a4! b4 12 Nc4 Rb8 13 h3?!

White doesn't have the time for this. Instead 13 Bd2!, adding support to c3, takes the sting out of Black's forthcoming idea.

13...bxc3 14 bxc3 d5! 15 exd5 Nxd5 (Diagram 62)

Suddenly White has major problems defending his c3-pawn. For example, 16 Bd2 is met by 16...e4! (Horn), while 16 Ra3? Nxc3! 17 Rxc3 e4 is also unpleasant for White. Perhaps the best chance is 16 Bg5, intending to retreat to d2 only after 16...f6 when the long diagonal is blocked.

16 Qc2 Nxc3! 17 Bb2!

17 Qxc3? e4 is disastrous for White.

17...e4! 18 dxe4

Or 18 Bxc3 Bxc3 19 Qxc3 exf3 20 Rxe8+ Qxe8 21 Re1 Be6 22 Bxf3 Nd4! and White is struggling.

18...Nd4

18...Nb4! 19 Qb3 Qd3! also secures a clear plus. After 20 Bxc3 Qxc3 21 Ra3 Qxb3 22 Rxb3 Be6 Black's raking bishops enjoy the open position.

19 Nxd4 cxd4 20 Bxc3 dxc3 21 Rad1 Qe7 22 e5 Qb4 23 Bd5 Bf5 24 Qa2 c2 25 Bxf7+? (Diagram 63)

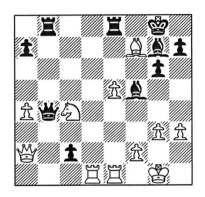

Diagram 63 (B)
Desperation?

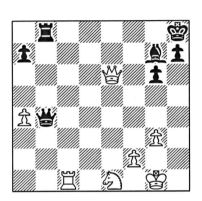

Diagram 64 (B)
Careful!

A bluff?

25...Kh8

...which works! 25...Kxf7?? walks into checkmate after 26 Nd6+! Ke7 27 Qf7+ Kd8 28 Nb5+ Kc8 29 Qc7. However, *Fritz* soon spots 25...Kf8! 26 Rc1 Re7! 27 Bd5 Qxe1+! 28 Rxe1 Rb1 with a winning position for Black after 29 Qa1 Rxa1 30 Rxa1 Rd7 31 Bf3 Rc7 32 Be2 Rxc4! 33 Bxc4 Bxe5 34 Re1 Bb2.

26 Rc1 Re7 27 Ne3 Rxe5 28 Nxc2 Rxe1+ 29 Nxe1 Bxh3 30 Be6 Bxe6 31 Qxe6 (Diagram 64) 31...Qxa4??

A terrible blunder, which allows a basic mating idea. Following 31...Rf8! it would still be Black pushing for the advantage.

32 Rc8+ Rxc8 33 Qxc8+ 1-0

Arriving via a Flank Opening

Just as with the French, there are many different move orders via flank openings to reach the typical KIA versus Sicilian positions. Below I've noted some of the more popular ones while also pointing out some transpositions to other openings. Of some interest here are the lines where White tries to gain an advantage by holding back on d2-d3.

1 Nf3

Or 1 g3 c5 2 Bg2 Nc6 3 e4 g6 4 d3 Bg7 and now 5 Nf3 is a KIA, while 5 f4 and 5 Nc3 are Closed Sicilian territory.

1...c5 (Diagram 65)

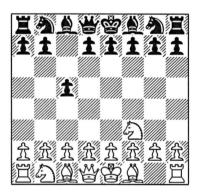

Diagram 65 (W)
Inviting a Sicilian

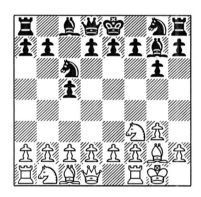

Diagram 66 (W)
Time to commit

This is a popular reply to 1 Nf3 amongst Sicilian advocates (they are obviously happy with a transposition via 2 e4). Alternatively:

a) 1...g6 2 g3 Bg7 3 Bg2 c5 4 0-0 Nc6 reaches the main line here.

b) 1...Nf6 (remaining flexible over the placement of the central pawns) 2 g3 g6 3 Bg2 Bg7 4 0-0 0-0 5 d3 (the KIA move; 5 c4 is an English, 5 d4 d6 is a regular King's Indian, and 5 d4 d5 is a kind of Grünfeld) 5...c5 (5...d5 6 Nbd2 c5 7 e4 Nc6 is a Reversed King's Indian – see Chapter 4) 6 e4 Nc6 7 Re1 d6 8 c3 reaches the third section of this chapter.

2 g3 Nc6 3 Bg2 g6

This has been the most common choice in practice. Both 3...e5 and

3...d5 are likely to reach the Reversed King's Indian.

4 0-0 Bg7 (Diagram 66)

If Black wishes to play a system with ...Nf6 then it is more accurate to play it here. After 4...Nf6 White is more or less obliged to play d2-d3 in order to play e2-e4, thus giving up the option of d2-d4 in one go.

5 e4!?

The most ambitious move. The safest way to ensure a KIA is with 5 d3 followed by e2-e4. Note that 5 c4 leads to the Symmetrical English.

5...d6

Black has a few alternatives here:

a) 5...Nf6 6 Re1 0-0 7 c3 d6 reaches the main text.

b) 5...d5!? is a direct way of trying to punish White's 5 e4. Now White can play 6 d3 although he must then be willing to enter the endgame if Black decides to swap on e4. The other option is 6 exd5 Qxd5 7 Nc3, gaining time on the queen. Black's most principled move here is 7...Qd7 **(Diagram 67)** supporting the c6-knight and preparing ...b7-b6 and ...Bb7.

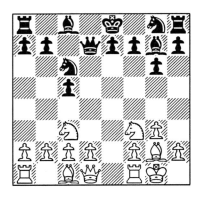

Diagram 67 (W)
Preparing ...b7-b6

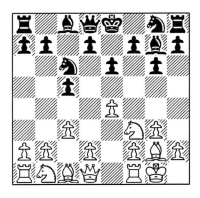

Diagram 68 (B)
Trying to gain a move

If Black is allowed to complete his set-up then White has no chance of an advantage, so White must play dynamically, e.g. 8 d3 b6 9 Bf4 Bb7 10 Nb5!? 0-0-0 (10...e5? loses to 11 Nxe5! Nxe5 12 Bxb7 Qxb7 13 Nd6+) 11 Re1 e5 12 Rxe5!? a6 13 Na3 Nxe5 14 Nxe5 Bxe5 15 Bxe5 Bxg2 16 Nc4! with complications, E.Dignum-R.Cifuentes Parada, Hoogeveen 2000.

c) 5...e5 6 c3 Nge7 7 d3 0-0 leads us to a type of position we're familiar with. An attempt to spice things up with 7 d4?! backfired after 7...cxd4 8 cxd4 exd4 9 Bf4 d5 10 e5 Bg4 11 Re1 Qb6 (F.Nijboer-T.Ernst, Groningen 1991), when White had insufficient compensation for the pawn.

d) After 5...e6!? White can reach the first section of this chapter with 6 d3, but 6 c3!? **(Diagram 68)** planning d2-d4 is more ambitious.

Now 6...Nge7?! 7 d4! cxd4 8 cxd4 d5 9 e5 0-0 10 Nc3 leaves White a tempo ahead in a position we've discussed before. The way to cut across White's plan is with 6...d5!? when White has two choices:

d1) 7 exd5 exd5 8 d4 cxd4 9 Nxd4! and now White probably has a slight nibble after either 9...Nge7 10 Be3 0-0 or 9...Nxd4 10 cxd4 Ne7 11 Nc3 0-0 12 Bg5 – in both cases Black's d-pawn is a bit vulnerable.

d2) 7 d3!? is an attempt to reach a KIA set-up with Qe2 or Nbd2. Black has the option of trading queens here but in practice Black normally chooses 7...Nge7. In fact after 7...dxe4 8 dxe4 Qxd1 9 Rxd1 the ending is probably a bit better for White; Black has some weak spots (the c5-pawn and the d6-square), and White can play Be3 and Na3-b5/c4.

> **NOTE: An exchange of queens on d1 doesn't always solve Black's problems.**

6 c3 Nf6 7 Re1 0-0 (Diagram 69)

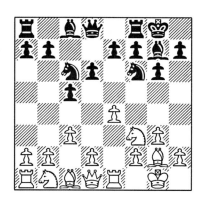

Diagram 69 (W)
Decision time

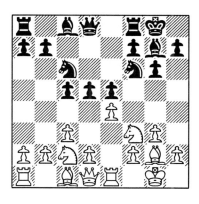

Diagram 70 (W)
9...d6-d5!

Now 8 d3 transposes directly to the third section of this chapter (2 Nf3 Nc6). However, White can also prepare to play d2-d4 in one go:

a) The immediate 8 d4 gives Black counterplay after 8...cxd4 9 cxd4 Bg4!, preparing to gang up on d4 with ...Qb6 and ...Nd7.

b) 8 h3 e5 9 d4!? cxd4 10 cxd4 exd4 11 Nxd4 and now 11...Nxd4 12 Qxd4 Re8 or 11...d5!? seems to give Black sufficient counterplay.

c) 8 Na3!? e5! and now White probably doesn't have anything better than 9 d3, transposing to the previous section, as 9 Nc2 d5! **(Diagram 70)** looks fine for Black.

So in the final analysis it doesn't look like Black has too much to worry about with White delaying d2-d3.

Points to Remember

Black Plays 2...e6

1) The KIA holds more promise against 2...e6 than it does in other lines – Black's e-pawn is poorly placed on e6.

2) The ...d7-d5 advance, moving back into French territory, remains an option for Black. White needs to play d2-d3 very early in order to meet ...d7-d5 with Nbd2 or Qe2. White has some extra positional options after Qe2, and this move has scored very well.

3) If Black wants something offbeat, then 3...b6 is an attractive option.

4) 5 Bg5 is a tricky sideline that has done well in practice.

5) White often uses the h2-h4 thrust against Black's kingside fianchetto. Again Black usually replies with ...h7-h6, ready to meet h4-h5 with ...g6-g5. Sometimes White will even play h2-h4 before Black plays ...g7-g6, thus discouraging Black from fianchettoing (see Game 20).

6) In the main line Black isn't afraid of losing a tempo by playing ...e6-e5 if it prevents White from carrying out the d3-d4 advance.

Black Plays 2...Nc6 or 2...d6

1) While the KIA is certainly playable here, theoretically speaking Black is not under the same pressure as he is in the 2...e6 lines.

2) If Black plays 2...Nc6 he has the option of transposing into a Reversed King's Indian with an early ...d7-d5.

3) In the ...Nf6, ...e7-e5 line, White's queenside expansion plan of a2-a3 and b2-b4 isn't as effective as usual.

Chapter Three

The KIA versus the Caro-Kann

Introduction

The King's Indian Attack is not quite as popular against the Caro-Kann as it is against the ...e6 Sicilian and the French, probably because of a couple of reasons. Firstly, Black hasn't committed his e-pawn to e6, so it can either be left on e7 or can go to e5 in one go. Secondly, perhaps in general White players are happier to meet the Caro-Kann head on in the main lines than they are in certain lines of the Sicilian and the French.

Even so, this restrained way of playing against the Caro still demands some respect. It was brought into prominence in the 1960s by the four-time Soviet Champion Leonid Stein. Later on it was taken up by the popular Yugoslav grandmaster Ljubomir Ljubojevic, and more recently it's been used by Sergei Tiviakov.

Black Plays 3...e5

1 e4 c6 2 d3 d5 3 Nd2 e5 (Diagram 1)

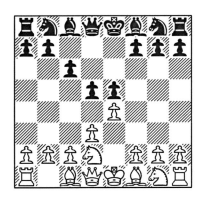
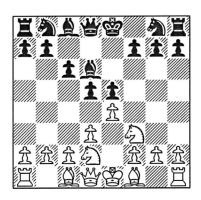

Diagram 1 (W)
Black plays 3...e5

Diagram 2 (W)
Defending the e-pawn

Not surprisingly 3...e5 is both the most popular and most ambitious choice here, with Black immediately occupying the centre.

4 Ngf3

I believe that this is the most accurate move; White is always going to play Ngf3 so there's no point delaying it, and it forces Black to do something about the defence of the e5-pawn.

4 g3 may reach the main line after 4...Nf6 5 Bg2 Bd6 6 Ngf3, but Black also has the option of developing his dark-squared bishop more actively with 5...Bc5. Following 6 Ngf3 0-0 the pawn grab with 7 Nxe5 is risky after 7...dxe4 8 dxe4 Bxf2+! 9 Kxf2 Qd4+ and ...Qxe5.

4...Bd6 (Diagram 2)

The most common choice, Black developing a piece, defending the e5-pawn and preparing to castling kingside.

If Black harbours any ambitions to develop the dark-squared bishop more actively on c5, then 4...Nd7 is the logical try. However, there are a couple of possible drawbacks to this move. Firstly, the knight blocks the c8-bishop, although this is only a problem if Black intends playing an early ...Bg4. Secondly, the paradoxical 5 d4!?, which is also playable against 5...Bd6 (see the next note), may be even stronger here. For example, 5...dxe4 6 Nxe4 exd4 and now both 7 Qxd4, as played by Tal, or the gambit with 7 Bc4, intending Ng5, look promising for White. Instead 5...exd4 is safer, but following 6 exd5 cxd5 7 Nxd4 Black's knight would prefer to be on the more active c6-square (compare this with note 'b' to White's 5th move).

5 g3

The typical KIA move, but there are a couple of alternatives that are worthy of a mention:

a) 5 Qe2 has been played quite a few times, but to me its value is unclear because Black isn't even forced to defend the e5-pawn. Following 5...Nf6!, the continuation 6 exd5 6...cxd5 7 Nxe5 0-0 looks quite treacherous for White, while 6 d4!? exd4! 7 e5 0-0! 8 exd6 Re8 9 Ne5 Ng4 (*ECO*) is also not much fun. It's true that White can simply continue developing as in the main line with 6 g3 0-0 7 Bg2 Re8 8 0-0 but, as we see later, there are more useful moves to play than Qe2 here.

b) It seems bizarre that White could even contemplate trying for an advantage with the tempo-losing 5 d4!? (Diagram 3) but it's actually quite a tricky move.

After 5...dxe4? 6 Nxe4 Black's position suddenly looks quite dodgy, and I also prefer White after 5...Nd7 6 exd5 cxd5 7 dxe5 Nxe5 8 Nxe5 Bxe5

9 Nf3. The solution for Black lies with 5...exd4! 6 exd5 cxd5 7 Nxd4, although he must be willing to play with the isolated d-pawn. One possible continuation is 7...Nc6 8 N2f3 Nf6 9 Be2 0-0 10 0-0 with a roughly equal position.

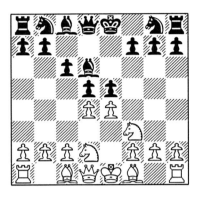

Diagram 3 (B)
Two steps to d4

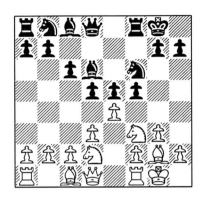

Diagram 4 (W)
An aggressive set-up

5...Nf6

More adventurous players with Black may prefer the uncompromising 5...f5!? 6 Bg2 Nf6 7 0-0 0-0 **(Diagram 4)** when Black certainly has considerable presence in the centre. I can't resist quoting the game J.Rudd-T.Dickinson, British League 2003, if only because of its pleasing finish (for one side at least): 8 c3 fxe4 9 dxe4 Bg4 10 Qc2 Nxe4? 11 Nxe4 dxe4 12 Ng5! Qc7? 13 Bxe4 h6? 14 Bd5+!! and Black is getting mated by Qh7.

An earlier game, R.Hübner-A.Miles, Tilburg 1986, is more critical for the evaluation of this line: 8...Kh8 9 Re1 fxe4!? (perhaps 9...Qc7!?) 10 dxe4 Bg4 11 h3 Bh5 12 g4 (or 12 exd5 cxd5 13 g4 Nxg4! – Miles) 12...Bg6 13 exd5 Nxd5. Here 14 Nxe5? Bxe5 15 Rxe5 Nd7 followed by ...Nf4 promises Black good compensation for the pawn, so instead White headed for the unclear complications after 14 Nc4 e4 15 Nfe5.

6 Bg2 0-0

Amusingly, Black has the option here of reaching lines discussed in Chapter 6 with 6...Bg4!? 7 0-0 Nbd7. As a rule, I'll leave these lines alone until we reach that chapter. Here I'll discuss lines where White prevents ...Bg4 with h2-h3 or Black forgoes playing the move.

7 0-0 Re8 (Diagram 5)

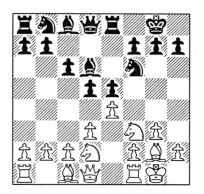

Diagram 5 (W)
More support for the centre

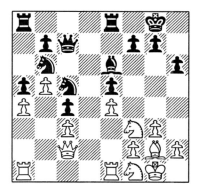

Diagram 6 (W)
A hole on d3

A shrewd move, giving added support to the centre. 7...Nbd7 is also possible, but slightly less flexible – it gives up on ...Bg4 ideas, and the knight doesn't always go to d7 (see the notes to Game 29). White normally continues with 8 Re1 or 8 b3, and a transposition to 7...Re8 certainly cannot be discounted.

After 7...Re8 we are going to look at two options for White: 8 b3 (Game 29) and 8 h3 (Game 30). The main ideas in this line will be discussed in these two games.

In practice White often chooses 8 Re1, although there are many transpositions because White usually plays b2-b3 at some stage. Another approach after 8...Nbd7 is 9 c3 but this looks less logical – for a start the d3-square looks a bit weak. For example, 9...dxe4 10 dxe4 Qc7 11 b4 Bf8 12 Bb2 Nb6 13 Qc2 h6 14 a3 c5! 15 b5 c4! 16 a4 Be6 17 Ba3 Bxa3 18 Rxa3 a5 19 Raa1 Nfd7 20 Nf1 Nc5 **(Diagram 6)** with a very pleasant position for Black, M.Tempone-J.Gomez Baillo, Corrientes 1984 – Black has certainly exploited the d3-weakness!

Game 29
☐ **S.Buchal** ■ **P.Treffert**
Germany 1988

---

1 g3

NOTE: As the beginning of this game demonstrates, the KIA versus the Caro-Kann can also be reached via a flank opening move order.

1...d5 2 Bg2 e5 3 d3 c6 4 Nf3 Bd6 5 0-0 Nf6 6 Nbd2 0-0 7 e4 Re8 8 b3 a5 (Diagram 7)

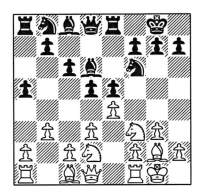

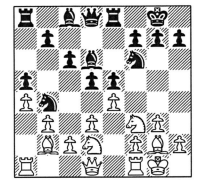

Diagram 7 (W)	Diagram 8 (W)
An a-pawn leap	An annoying beast on b4

Typically gaining space on the queenside and seeking some a-file action via ...a5-a4.

Blocking the centre with ...d5-d4 must always be considered. Following 8...d4 Black plans to follow up with an eventual attack on the queenside, while White's plans will revolve around arranging a kingside assault with f2-f4. In short, typical Reversed King's Indian play.

9 Bb2!?

This is hardly ever played, as many are nervous about Black's a-pawn lunge and seek to do something about it. For example:

a) 9 a4 Na6! 10 Bb2 Nb4! **(Diagram 8)**.

 TIP: After a2-a4, the plan of ...Na6-b4 is an attractive option for Black.

On b4 the knight adds pressure to c2 and d3. White can only eject the knight with c2-c3, but this weakens the d3-square. The game M.Adams-A.Dreev, FIDE World Championship (rapid), Las Vegas 1999 continued 11 Re1 Qc7 12 h3?! dxe4 13 dxe4 b5! 14 Nf1 Bc5 15 Qe2 Ba6

with good counterplay for Black on the queenside.

b) 9 a3 (planning to answer ...a5-a4 with b3-b4!) 9...Nbd7 10 Bb2 Nf8
11 Re1 Ng6 and now one possibility for White is to play 12 exd5!? cxd5
13 c4!? d4 reaching a reversed Modern Benoni pawn structure. J.Hickl-
J.Maiwald, Bern 1996 continued 14 Qc2 h6 (to prevent Ng5) 15 c5! Bc7
16 Nc4 Bd7 17 Re2 Bc6 18 Rae1 Qb8 19 b4 with White combining pressure on the e5-pawn with queenside play.

9...Nbd7

I think Black should grab the opportunity to play 9...a4! here. This tension on the queenside is uncomfortable for White, who always has to
reckon with the possibility of ...a4-a3. White can force Black's hand
with 10 a3, intending b3-b3, but the pawn structure after 10...axb3 11
cxb3 must be seen as a slight improvement on Black's part.

10 a4!

Not giving Black another chance. 10 a3 is also possible, but it's nice to
play a2-a4 without having to worry about the possibility of ...Na6-b4.

10...Qc7

 **NOTE: A typical manoeuvre for Black in this type of position is
...Nd7-f8-g6.**

On g6 the knight supports e5 and is no longer in the way of the c8-
bishop. After 10...Nf8 11 Re1 Ng6, White's position is all set up for a
strike in the centre with 12 d4!.

11 Re1 d4?!

Hoping to solve the problems in the centre by blocking things up, but
this doesn't help Black. 11...Nf8 followed by ...Ng6 still looks the best
bet.

12 c3! dxc3

Black can keep the centre blocked with 12...c5, but following 13 Rc1!
Qb8 14 Nc4 Bf8 Black will find it very difficult to arrange queenside
counterplay while White eventually lines up the f2-f4 break.

13 Bxc3 b6 14 Nc4 (Diagram 9) 14...Bb4?

Even though it completely cripples Black's queenside ambitions, 14...c5,
preventing d3-d4, had to be played.

15 Bxb4 axb4 16 d4!

Now White takes over the centre and his pieces begin to dominate the action.

16...exd4 17 Nxd4 Bb7 18 Nf5!

Eyeing the juicy d6-square.

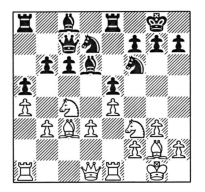

Diagram 9 (B)
Problems for Black

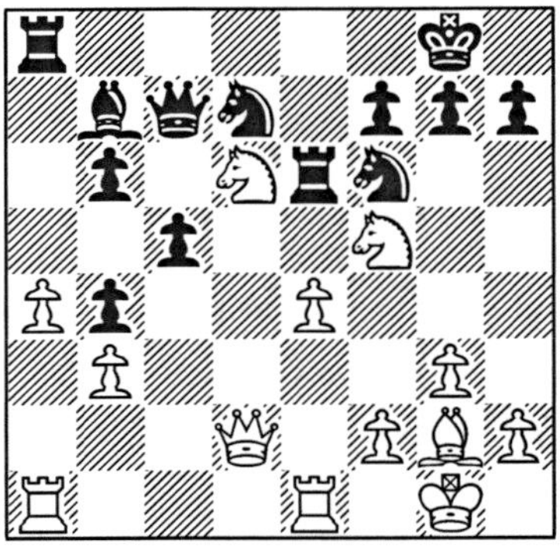

Diagram 10 (B)
The knights dominate

18...Re6 19 Qd2 c5 20 Ncd6! (Diagram 10) 20...Ne8

This loses straightaway, but it's difficult to suggest a better defence. For example,

20...Bc6 21 Qg5! g6 22 Nh6+ Kg7 23 e5! Nxe5 24 Nhf5+ Kg8 25 Bxc6 Qxc6 26 Rxe5! Rxe5 27 Nh6+ Kg7 28 Qxe5 and White wins.

21 Nxb7 1-0

Recapturing on b7 allows the devastating 22 e5, so Black chooses not to continue. An example of the nuances that both sides must deal with in this line.

Game 30
☐ **P.Petran** ■ **Y.Yakovich**
Cappelle la Grande 1993

1 e4 c6 2 d3 d5 3 Nd2 e5 4 Ngf3 Bd6 5 g3 Nf6 6 Bg2 0-0 7 0-0 Re8 8 h3 (Diagram 11)

Preventing ...Bg4, although many players forego h2-h3 because it does give Black an extra tempo to develop play elsewhere.

8...Nbd7

Black can also begin queenside operations immediately with 8...a5!? 9 Re1 and now:

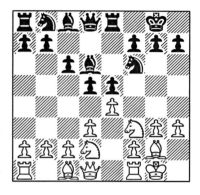

Diagram 11 (B)
Preventing ...Bg4

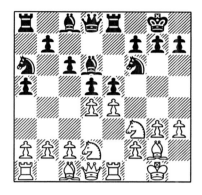

Diagram 12 (B)
Raising the stakes

a) 9...Na6?! (not a bad move in general, but Black's previous two moves have achieved nothing in the centre and now White is allowed to carry out a powerful idea) 10 d4! **(Diagram 12)** 10...dxe4 11 Nxe5 Bxe5 12 dxe5 Rxe5 13 Nxe4 Bf5 14 Nxf6+ Qxf6 15 Rxe5 Qxe5 16 c3 when White's bishop pair in an open position gave him a small but long-lasting advantage in G.Sax-A.Martin, Hastings 1983/84.

 NOTE: Both players must keep in mind the option of d3-d4, increasing the tension in the centre.

b) 9...dxe4! 10 dxe4 Bc5 and now White should prevent Black's a-pawn from moving any further with 11 a4!. In V.Anand-V.Malaniuk, Frunze 1987 the young Indian GM failed to do this, and following 11 c3? a4! 12 Qc2 Nbd7 13 Nf1 h6 14 Ne3 Bf8 15 Nf5 Nc5 16 Rd1 Qc7 17 Nh2 Be6 18 Be3 Red8 19 Rxd8 Rxd8 20 Ng4 Nxg4 21 hxg4 b5 Black had created an impressive bind on the queenside.

9 Re1 Qc7 10 b3 a5 11 a3?!

I think I would prefer 11 a4 here because after the text move Black soon takes over the initiative on the queenside.

11...dxe4 12 dxe4 b5!

Not just preventing Nc4, but also planning ...a5-a4.

13 Bb2 Nb6 14 Nh4

Nh4-f5 is a typical idea for White, against which Black normally drops his bishop back out of harm's way onto f8.

14...Bf8 15 Qe2 a4! 16 b4 Be6!

Coveting the desirable c4-outpost. The battle now centres around this square.

17 Nf5 Nc4 18 Nxc4 Bxc4 19 Qf3 Nd7! 20 Ne3 Nb6!

Keeping a firm hold over c4.

21 Red1 c5! (Diagram 13)

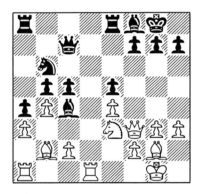
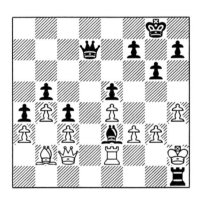

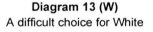

Diagram 13 (W)	Diagram 14 (W)
A difficult choice for White	Forcing checkmate

22 c3?

Securing the b4-pawn but making life truly miserable for the b2-bishop. I suspect that White's best move was 22 bxc5, even if after 22... Bxc5 it does leave him with weak queenside pawns.

22...Bb3!

Using the newly-created outpost on b3, Black takes over control of the d-file.

23 Rd2 Rad8 24 Rxd8 Rxd8 25 Bf1 Qc6 26 Qe2 Nc4 27 Nxc4 Bxc4 28 Qf3 Bxf1 29 Rxf1 c4!

The strangulation continues, with ...Rd3 next on the list. White cannot oppose rooks because 30 Rd1 simply loses a pawn after 30...Rxd1+ 31 Qxd1 Qxe4.

30 Qe2 Rd3 31 Kg2 g6 32 f3 Qd7 33 Rf2 Bh6! 34 Qc2 Rd1 35 h4 Be3! 36 Re2 Rg1+ 37 Kh2 Rh1+! (Diagram 14) 0-1

A nice tactical finish to a positional masterpiece from Yakovich. White is mated after 38 Kxh1 Qh3+ 39 Rh2 Qf1.

Black Plays 3...g6

1 e4 c6 2 d3 d5 3 Nd2 g6 (Diagram 15)

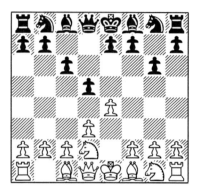

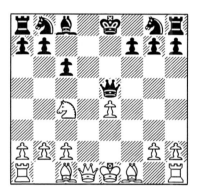

Diagram 15 (W)
Black plays 3...g6

Diagram 16 (B)
The d6-square beckons

3...g6 is second only to 3...e5 in the popularity stakes – we've already seen many times the value of the fianchettoed bishop on g7 against the KIA. There are a couple of third-move alternatives worth mentioning:

a) 3...dxe4 4 dxe4 e5 5 Ngf3 Bc5? has been played more than once, Black's tactical point being that after 6 Nxe5! he can regain his pawn with 6...Bxf2+ 7 Kxf2 Qd4+. However, following 8 Ke1 Qxe5 9 Nc4! **(Diagram 16)** Black is suddenly in some trouble, despite the fact that it's White's king who has been forced to move twice (Black's miserable score of 19% from this position tells its own story). After 9...Qxe4+ the knight is invading on d6; for example, 10 Be2 (10 Kf2 is also strong) 10...Qxg2 11 Nd6+ Kf8 12 Rf1 Be6 13 Nxf7! threatening Qxd8, or 10...Qe6 11 Nd6+ Ke7 12 Rf1! and White has a massive attack. Instead of 5...Bc5, Black should protect his e5-pawn with something like 5...Qc7. However, as mentioned before, it doesn't make a whole lot of sense to trade on e4 early – White can develop his bishop actively on the f1-a6 diagonal with 6 Bc4.

b) 3...Nf6!? invites the move 4 e5!?, and following 4...Nfd7 5 d4 c5 6 c3 we could quite easily reach a French Defence if Black plays ...e7-e6. Instead 4 Ngf3 is a more flexible approach by White, after which Black can take the opportunity to develop his light-squared bishop outside the pawn chain with 4...Bg4, attempting to reach a set-up covered in more detail in Chapter 6.

 WARNING: The automatic KIA move 5 g3? loses a pawn to the tactic 5...dxe4 6 dxe4 Nxe4!.

White can break the pin with 5 Be2 or play more ambitiously with h2-h3 followed by g2-g4, for example 5 h3 Bh5 6 Qe2 Qc7 7 g4!? Bg6 8 Bg2 e6 9 0-0 Be7 10 Nh4, G.Sax-L.Vadasz, Budapest 1977.

4 Ngf3 Bg7 5 g3 e5 (Diagram 17)

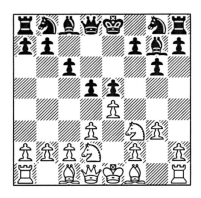

Diagram 17 (W)
Occupying the centre

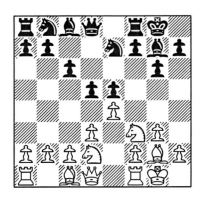

Diagram 18 (W)
A typical position

Taking a greater share of the centre. 5...Nf6 is the main alternative – see Game 32.

6 Bg2 Ne7

So that the g7-bishop isn't blocked and the e5-pawn remains protected.

7 0-0 0-0 (Diagram 18)

Strategies

White has more than one way of playing this position, but the one constant is Black's e5-pawn, which can expect a severe examination from White's pieces. In Game 31 White takes advantage of Black blocking the long diagonal with ...e7-e5 by playing the enterprising 8 b4!?, gaining space on the queenside and preparing to pressure e5 with Bb2.

White's other main option here is the more traditional 8 Re1 and now:

a) 8...d4 and here White can prepare Nc4 by playing 9 a4, while another option is 9 c3!?, when 9...dxc3?! 10 bxc3 Qxd3 11 Ba3 Re8 12 Bf1 Qd8 13 Nc4 (Spiridonov) gives White very active piece play for the sacrificed pawn.

b) After 8...Nd7 White can move back into the realms of Game 31 with 9 b4. However, in the game A.Gelman-A.Lastin, Ekaterinburg 1996 White played imaginatively with 9 exd5!? cxd5 10 c4!, allowing Black to reach a Modern Benoni structure with 10...d4. The game exploded into life after 11 b4 h6 12 a4 g5 13 Ba3 Ng6 14 Ne4 f5 15 Nd6, when it was pretty obvious which sides of the board White and Black were attacking.

Statistics

Black has scored rather well in the main line after 7...0-0: 51% in just under 500 games. His score is less impressive after 5...Nf6 6 Bg2 0-0 7 0-0: down to 38% from a similar number of games.

Game 31
□ **L.Aronian** ■ **I.Khenkin**
Bundesliga 2002

---

1 e4 c6 2 d3 d5 3 Nd2 g6 4 Ngf3 Bg7 5 g3 e5 6 Bg2 Ne7 7 0-0 0-0 8 b4!?

Gaining space on the queenside and preparing to pepper the e5-pawn with Bb2.

8...Na6!?

The more logical way to attack the b4-prong is with 8...a5!. Now White can keep his pawn structure tidy with 9 Bb2 Nd7 10 a3, but most players have been happy to accept weaknesses for the sake of piece play with 9 bxa5!?. It's true that after, say, 9...Qxa5 10 Bb2 d4 11 a4! Qc7 12 c3! dxc3 13 Bxc3 White, with Nc4 and Qb1 looming, is looking very active.

9 a3 Nc7 10 Bb2 f6

There's certainly a temptation for Black to block things up in the centre with 10...d4?!, but White shouldn't be deterred. Indeed, 11 c3! demonstrates a huge positive of b2-b4: Black is unable to hold the centre with ...c7-c5. Instead the old game L.Stein-R.Hartoch, Amsterdam 1969 continued 11...Bg4 12 Qc2 Ne6 13 cxd4 Bxf3 14 Nxf3 Nxd4 15 Nxd4 exd4 and now White opened up his pawn umbrella on the kingside with 16 f4!.

11 Re1 b6

Logical play – Black wishes to play ...d5-d4 followed by ...c6-c5, certainly blunting White's fianchettoed bishop on b2. However, White gets to strike in the centre before Black can arrange this.

12 d4! (Diagram 19)

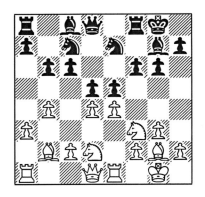
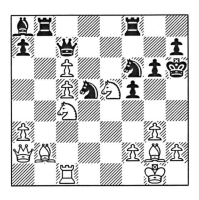

Diagram 19 (B)
Central action

Diagram 20 (W)
Going on a walkabout?

12...dxe4?

Perhaps Black underestimated the strength of White's following play, otherwise he might have chosen to create even further tension in the centre with 12...f5!? with the intention of meeting 13 exd5 with 13...e4!.

13 Rxe4 f5 14 Rxe5!

Not so difficult to see, but nice all the same. White is going to get massive positional compensation for a token material deficit.

14...Bxe5 15 Nxe5 Bb7 16 c4 Rb8 17 Qb3 Ne8

Black doesn't want to go backwards, but there is very little choice. Following 17...Ne6 White continues as in the main game with 18 c5! Nd5 19 b5!, totally undermining Black's defences on the a2-g8 diagonal.

18 c5+! Nd5 19 b5! Nef6 20 bxc6 Ba8 21 Qa2 Kg7 22 Ndc4 Qc7 23 Rc1 bxc5 24 dxc5 Kh6 (Diagram 20)

This absurd move simply highlights the hopelessness of Black's position – this is the safest place for the king!

25 Nd6 Ne7 26 Nef7+ 1-0

A nice example of how White can sometimes blow open the centre with a timely d3-d4.

Game 32
□ **R.Fischer** ■ **I.Ibrahimoglu**
Siegen Olympiad 1970

---

1 e4 c6 2 d3 d5 3 Nd2 g6 4 Ngf3 Bg7 5 g3 Nf6 6 Bg2 0-0 7 0-0 (Diagram 21)

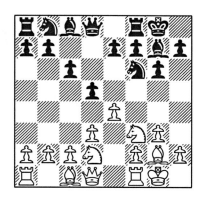

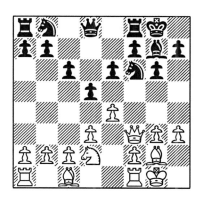

Diagram 21 (B)	Diagram 22 (B)
More than one route	Rock-solid!

NOTE: This line of the KIA versus the Caro-Kann is more often reached via a flank opening move order. For example, 1 Nf3 d5 2 g3 c6 3 Bg2 Nf6 4 0-0 g6 5 d3 Bg7 6 Nbd2 0-0 7 e4.

7...Bg4

Not the only move but a reasonable one. Black's idea is to give up the bishop pair and then erect a solid pawn centre (or at least it should be – in this game something goes awry).

8 h3 Bxf3 9 Qxf3 Nbd7

In the later game V.Ivanchuk-A.Chernin, Lvov 1987, the Russian GM demonstrated the way for Black to play this position: 9...e6! **(Diagram 22)** 10 Qe2 a5 11 a4 Na6! (leaving the d7-square free for the other knight in case of e4-e5) 12 c3 dxe4 (only now, as 13 dxe4 Nc5 14 Rd1 Qd3! looks okay for Black) 13 Nxe4 Qe7 14 Bg5 Nc5 15 Qe3 Ncd7 16 h4 Rfe8 17 Rfe1 Qf8 and White's advantage was minimal.

10 Qe2 dxe4?

Why give up the centre and open the position after giving away the bishop pair? I prefer 10...e6 or 10...e5.

11 dxe4 Qc7 12 a4 Rad8 13 Nb3 b6 14 Be3 c5

Preventing White from using d4, but at a cost of weakening the light squares. This wouldn't be so serious except Black got rid of the main protector on move eight.

15 a5 e5 16 Nd2!

Watch this knight go!

16...Ne8?! 17 axb6 axb6 18 Nb1! (Diagram 23)

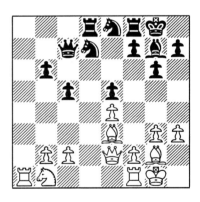

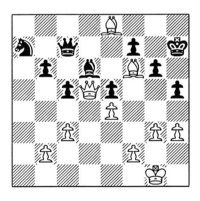

Diagram 23 (B)
Nd2-b1!

Diagram 24 (B)
The end

A fine retreat, highlighting Black's light-squared problems. The b5- and d5-squares beckon.

18...Qb7 19 Nc3 Nc7 20 Nb5 Qc6 21 Nxc7 Qxc7 22 Qb5 Ra8 23 c3

Rxa1 24 Rxa1 Rb8 25 Ra6 Bf8 26 Bf1!

White's domination of the light squares remain. This bishop may be redeployed actively on c4 or b5.

26...Kg7 27 Qa4 Rb7 28 Bb5 Nb8

A horrible place the knight – it's totally corralled by White's light-squared bishop. Mind you, Black's other minor piece isn't having much fun either!

29 Ra8 Bd6 30 Qd1!

Preventing the simplifying ...Ra7 as now this would hang the bishop on d7. Black is being stretched to the limit: White's rook and light-squared bishop are doing the business on the queenside, while White's queen and remaining bishop prepare to make inroads on the other flank.

30...Nc6 31 Qd2! h5 32 Bh6+ Kh7 33 Bg5 Rb8 34 Rxb8 Nxb8 35 Bf6 Nc6 36 Qd5 Na7 37 Be8! (Diagram 24)

Breaking Black's resistance and winning a pawn, the conclusion of a masterful display by Fischer.

37...Kg8 38 Bxf7+ Qxf7 39 Qxd6 1-0

Black Plays 2...e5

1 e4 c6 2 d3 e5 (Diagram 25)

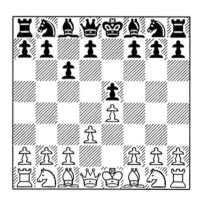

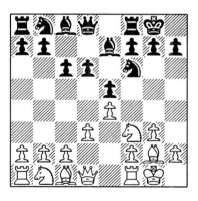

Diagram 25 (W)
No ...d7-d5?

Diagram 26 (W)
Restrained play

This ultra-solid approach from Black isn't particularly popular because most Caro-Kann players are unwilling to hold back with their d-pawn (...d7-d5 is, after all, the whole point of Black's first move). Nevertheless, 3...e5 has been used by some very strong grandmasters, including ex-world champion Anatoly Karpov.

3 Nf3

If White suddenly decides to go in to 'King's Gambit mode' then 3 f4!? is the move to play, with Black's most obvious responses being 3...exf4 4 Bxf4 d5 or the immediate 3...d5!?.

3...Nf6

3...d6 usually comes to the same thing, but the text sets a little trap...

4 g3

4 Nxe5?? drops a piece to 4...Qa5+!, although in two out of the three games on my database where this occurred, White fought back to win!

4 Be2 has also been played here – see Game 33.

4...d6

Solid – giving White nothing to aim at in the centre.

5 Bg2 Be7

Black can also play in copycat fashion with 5...g6 6 0-0 Bg7. For example, 7 a4 a5 (L.Ljubojevic-J.Hjartarson, Rotterdam 1989) and now Hjartarson's suggestion of 8 Nbd2 followed by Nc4 looks like a reasonable way to continue. I guess this is the rare case of the King's Indian Attack versus the King's Indian Defence!

6 0-0 0-0 (Diagram 26)

Strategies

Black is happy to sit behind his 'Philidor' pawn structure and let White dictate play in the centre. White can aim for a very quick d3-d4 after protecting the e-pawn with 7 Re1, but it might be more effective to hold back on this advance until he is fully mobilised with moves such as Nbd2 and c2-c3, or b2-b3 and Bb2.

Statistics

White has scored 54% against 2...e5 in over 250 games.

Game 33
□ **L.Ljubojevic** ■ **V.Ivanchuk**
Linares 1990

1 e4 c6 2 d3 e5 3 Nf3 Nf6 4 Be2

Ljubojevic experimented with this move a couple of times, without great success. We've seen the idea of keeping the bishop on the f1-a6 diagonal before (for example, where Black plays an early ...e6-e5 in the French).

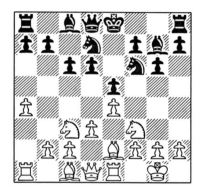

Diagram 27 (B)
The wrong plan

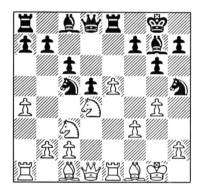

Diagram 28 (B)
Black has a tactic

4...d6 5 0-0 Nbd7 6 Re1 g6 7 a4!? Bg7 8 Nc3?! (Diagram 27)

After this and White's following move we reach a kind of harmless variation of the Pirc Defence where White has lost a tempo by playing d2-d4 in two steps.

In his notes to this game Ivanchuk suggests continuing queenside expansion with a4-a5 followed by c2-c3 and perhaps Nd2-c4. Another option that White could consider is b2-b3, Bb2/Ba3, Nbd2 and an eventual d3-d4.

8...0-0 9 d4?! exd4!

Black doesn't have to give up the centre like this, but the counterplay he obtains against the e4-pawn is a good reason to do so.

10 Nxd4 Re8 11 Bf1?!

This automatic move is another inaccuracy according to Ivanchuk. 11

f3?! d5! 12 exd5 Nxd5 13 Nxd5 Nb6! is also very pleasant for Black, so White should probably make do with 11 Bf3!, offering Black the opportunity to repeat the position after 11...Ne5 12 Be2.

11...Nc5 12 f3

Weakening the king's position, but what else?

12...d5!

Wasting no time in striking back in the centre. Now 13 exd5 Rxe1 14 Qxe1 Nxd5 is quite uncomfortable for White.

13 e5 Nh5 14 g4? (Diagram 28)

Blundering a crucial pawn. White can stay in the game with 14 f4!, although Ivanchuk's continuation of 14...f6! 15 e6! (15 g4? loses to 15...Nxf4! 16 Bxf4 fxe5) 15...f5! 16 Nxf5! gxf5 17 Qxh5 Bxe6 still sees Black in control.

14...Rxe5! 15 Rxe5 Bxe5 16 gxh5 Qh4 17 f4 Qg4+!

Perhaps White had missed this little move, the point being that 18 Qxg4 is answered by the intermezzo 18...Bxd4+ followed by ...Bxg4.

18 Bg2 Qxd1+ 19 Nxd1 Bxd4+ 20 Be3 Bxe3+ 21 Nxe3 d4 22 b4 Ne6

Winning a second pawn – the game is as good as over as a contest.

23 Nc4 Nxf4 24 Nd6 Nxg2 25 Kxg2 Bf5 26 Rd1 Bxc2 27 Rxd4 Rd8 28 a5 Kf8 29 Nb5 Rxd4 30 Nxd4 Ba4 31 Kg3 Ke7 32 Kf4 f6 33 hxg6 hxg6 34 h4 Kd6 35 Ne2 Bc2 36 Nc3 Ke6 37 Kf3 Kf5 38 Ke3 Kg4 39 b5 cxb5 40 Nxb5 Ba4 41 Nxa7 Bd7 42 Kd4 f5 43 Kc5 f4 44 Kd6 Ba4 0-1

Points to Remember

1) The KIA is not quite as popular against the Caro-Kann as it is against the French and ...e6 Sicilians.

2) In the ...d5/...e5 lines White can sometimes arrange to attack the centre with a timely d3-d4.

3) In the ...d5/...e5 lines where Black fianchettoes with ...Bg7, White often puts pressure on the e5-pawn with Re1 and b2-b4 (or b2-b3) followed by Bb2.

4) Holding back with ...d7-d5 is quite rare, but this is a very solid system for Black.

Chapter Four

The Reversed King's Indian

Introduction

In this chapter we'll take a look at lines where Black plays ...c7-c5 and ...d7-d5, and chooses a line that sees White playing the King's Indian Defence with colours reversed and an extra tempo. In my opinion this is a very respectable way for Black to proceed because theoretically speaking it's unclear how useful the extra tempo is for White. On the other hand, of course the King's Indian Defence is an especially viable option when playing Black, and in a practical sense those who know the intricacies of the King's Indian as Black should be very happy playing it with the extra tempo as White. Also, from a practical point of view it should be mentioned that Black can only reach the Reversed King's Indian from certain move orders, and he must also be prepared for White entering into alternative systems, such as the Reversed Grünfeld.

Black Plays ...e7-e5

This is the most obvious way of playing the Reversed King's Indian, with Black setting out for mass pawn occupation in the centre.

1 Nf3 d5 2 g3 c5 3 Bg2 Nc6 (Diagram 1)

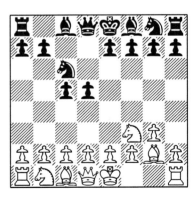
Diagram 1 (W)
Ready for 4 d4 here?

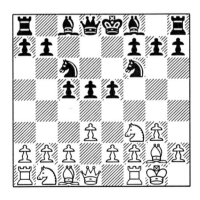
Diagram 2 (W)
Classical development

4 0-0

WARNING: Those playing Black must be prepared to meet more than just the KIA here. Indeed, 4 d4!, reaching a Reversed Grünfeld, is a serious option for White that puts many Black players off using this move order.

4...e5 5 d3 Nf6 (Diagram 2)

Sämisch fans might prefer 5...f6 when a typical continuation would be 6 e4 d4 7 Nh4 Be6 8 f4 Qd7 followed by ...0-0-0. However, given that ...c7-c5 is such a popular approach against the Sämisch these days, there's an argument for continuing with 6 c4, when 6...d4 7 e3 Be6 8 exd4 cxd4 reaches a reversed Modern Benoni pawn structure.

Black can also consider 5...Be7!? which will usually transpose to the main line, but Black's idea is to eliminate White's option of playing 6 Bg5 against 5...Nf6.

6 Nbd2

This move, preparing e2-e4, has traditionally been White's most popular here. Alternatively:

a) 6 Bg5!? is covered in Game 34.

b) Given that ...Na6 lines have recently become popular in the King's Indian, it's perhaps not surprising that 6 Na3!? has been tried here. Of course there are both similarities and transpositions to 6 Nbd2. For example, 6...Be7 7 e4 d4 leads to the note to Black's 7th move. An independent line continued 7...0-0 8 exd5 Nxd5 9 Re1 f6 10 c3 Nc7 11 Nh4!? g5 12 Be4!? gxh4 13 Bxh7+! Kxh7 14 Qh5+ Kg8 15 Qg6+ Kh8 16 Re4 f5! 17 Qh6+ with a draw by perpetual check, C.McNab-D.Gormally, York 2000.

c) The immediate 6 e4 is of course very possible, and this has the advantage of retaining the option of playing as in the Classical King's Indian with Nc3. However, there are a couple of points that perhaps discourage White from playing like this. The first is that the 'boring' exchange variation, only enough for equality with White, looks good enough for equality for Black too after 6...dxe4 7 dxe4 Qxd1 8 Rxd1 Bg4 (but not 8...Nxe4?! 9 Nxe5! Nxf2?? 10 Bxc6+!). A second point is that after 6...Be7 7 Nc3 d4 8 Ne2 Nd7 9 Nd2 Black can actually make use of the fact that he is a tempo behind a normal King's Indian. With colours reversed White would have castled by now, but why castle into an automatic attack? Instead in E.Van den Doel-G.Sosonko, Rotterdam

1997, Black took the initiative on the kingside after 9...h5! 10 f4 h4! 11 Nf3 h3 12 Bh1 Nf6 13 Nd2? Ng4! 14 Nb1 g5!.

6...Be7

Continuing in 'classical' mode. Given that White has temporarily lost the opportunity of pressuring d5 by playing Bg5, there's an case for Black playing 6...Bd6 here, and indeed this has occurred in a number of games. The point is that after 7 e4 d4 8 Nc4 the bishop can drop back to c7. Nevertheless, most prefer the e7-square for the bishop.

7 e4 0-0! (Diagram 3)

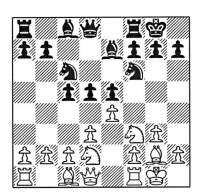

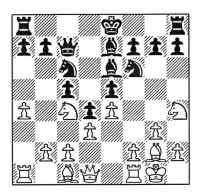

Diagram 3 (W)
Flexibility is the key

Diagram 4 (B)
Arranging f2-f4

The usual, most flexible, and I suspect the most accurate way forward. Black doesn't show his hand in the centre just yet – he waits for White to commit himself with one further move.

Exchanging on e4 here is in White's favour, especially if he can make use of the potential outpost on d5. For example, 7...dxe4 8 dxe4 0-0 9 c3 Qc7 10 Qe2 h6 11 Nc4 Be6 12 Nh4! Rfe8 13 Ne3! Rad8 14 Nhf5 Bf8 15 Qf3 Nh7 16 Nd5!, A.Gelman-A.Kopylov, Krasnodar 1998.

There's a temptation to seal up the centre with 7...d4, after which the plans for both sides become more obvious: White goes for a kingside attack by arranging f2-f4 while Black looks to the other wing for counterplay. J.Piket-J.Timman, Dutch Championship 1996 continued 8 Nc4 Qc7 9 a4! (preventing ...b7-b5 for a while) 9...Be6 and here Piket suggests the direct 10 Nh4!? **(Diagram 4)** with ideas of both Nf5 and f2-f4.

Going back to the position after 7...0-0, White must make a decision on his approach. He can try to induce Black into playing ...d5-d4, or he can utilise his extra tempo with an exchange on d5 followed by an attack in the centre. These possibilities are covered in Game 35.

Statistics

White has scored 50% in approximately 1000 games from the position after 5...Nf6, while 5...f6 has scored pretty well for Black at 55%.

Game 34
☐ **E.Vladimirov** ■ **G.Agzamov**
USSR 1977

1 Nf3 d5 2 g3 c5 3 Bg2 Nc6 4 0-0 e5 5 d3 Nf6 6 Bg5 (Diagram 5)

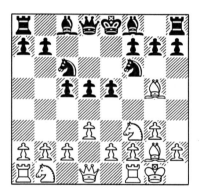

Diagram 5 (B)
6 Bg5

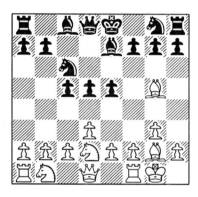

Diagram 6 (W)
A clever retreat

A more aggressive option than either 6 Nbd2 or 6 e4. White's plan is reasonably straightforward: exchange on f6 and then pressure the d5-pawn.

6...Be7 7 Nfd2!?

All part of the plan against d5. 7 Nc3 d4! 8 Bxf6 Bxf6 9 Ne4 Be7 has been played more than once and looks okay for Black.

7...Be6

A very sensible move, bolstering d5. However, Black has a couple of alternatives here:

a) 7...0-0 is similar to the text and can easily transpose. For example, 8 Nc3 Be6 (8...d4 9 Bxf6 Bxf6 10 Nd5 is White's idea) 9 e4 and now 9...d4 10 Bxf6 Bxf6 11 Nd5 transposes to the main game. In another Vladimirov game Black instead opted for 9...dxe4?!, but after 10 Bxf6 Bxf6 11 dxe4 White was in a great position to utilise the d5-outpost, and following 11...Qd7?! 12 Nd5! Bd8 13 Nc4! White enjoyed a substantial advantage in E.Vladimirov-Voskanian, USSR 1977.

b) The paradoxical 7...Ng8!? **(Diagram 6)** is worth knowing about, especially since it may even be Black's best move here!

White can hardly avoid an exchange of bishops, so a typical continuation is 8 Bxe7 Ngxe7 9 e4 d4 (there doesn't look anything wrong with 9...Be6 either), as in J.Nikolac-G.Sosonko, Wijk aan Zee 1979. It's worth giving the rest of this game in full as it demonstrates typical attacking and defensive ideas for both sides: 10 f4! 0-0 11 f5 f6 12 a4 (holding up Black's queenside play) 12...b6 13 Nf3 a6 14 Rf2 Bd7 15 Bf1 (vacating g2 for the rook and holding up ...c5-c4) 15...Nc8 16 Nbd2 Nd6 17 Be2 b5 18 g4 (finally g4-g5 is in the air) 18...Rb8 19 axb5 axb5 20 Rg2 Nf7 21 h4 h6 22 Kf2 Nb4 23 Nb3 c4 24 Nc5 Rc8 25 Nxd7 Qxd7 26 g5 fxg5 27 hxg5 hxg5 28 Nxg5 Nxg5 29 Rxg5 cxd3 30 Bxd3 Rf7 31 Kg1 Rf6 32 Rg2 Nxd3 33 cxd3 Qf7 34 Rc1 Rfc6 35 Rxc6 Rxc6 36 Qd2 Qh5 37 Rg3 Rh6 38 Kf2 Qh1 39 Rg2 Qh4+ 40 Rg3 Qh1 ½-½.

8 Bxf6

The immediate 8 Nc3 is obviously possible, but then White has to consider 8...Ng8!.

8...Bxf6 9 Nc3 0-0

9...d4!? is more ambitious. Then after 10 Na4 Be7 White can take the brave decision to play 11 Bxc6+!? bxc6, crippling Black's queenside pawns at a cost of giving up the fianchettoed bishop.

10 e4 d4

10...dxe4?! 11 dxe4 transposes to note 'a' to Black's 7th move.

11 Nd5

White's opening strategy has borne fruit, and he has occupied the d5-outpost. It's true that Black is immediately able to get rid of this knight, but White still keeps an edge because he is able to get moving with f2-f4.

11...Nb4!

11...Bxd5 12 exd5 Ne7 13 d6 is good for White. Following 13...Qxd6 14 Bxb7 Rab8 15 Nc4 White's bishop is much more active than its counterpart.

12 Nxf6+ Qxf6 13 f4! exf4?!

This only succeeds in accelerating White's attack on the kingside. Holding firm with 13...Nc6 is more resilient, even if White was a bit better after 14 f5 Bd7 15 Nf3 Qd6 16 f6!? (16 g4 f6 17 h4 is also possible) 16...Qxf6 17 Nxd4 Qd8 18 Nf5, N.Cummings-A.Dyakov, correspondence 2002.

14 gxf4 Qh6 15 f5! Bd7 16 Rf3 (Diagram 7)

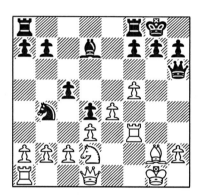

Diagram 7 (W)	Diagram 8 (B)
The rook's a swinger	27 Nf4-e6!

The rook plans to swing to h3, gaining time on Black's queen in the process.

16...Nc6 17 Rh3 Qf6 18 Qh5 h6 19 Kh1!

Planning Rg1.

19...Kh8 20 Rg1 Nb4?

Black is showing a nonchalant disregard for White's attack. After 20...Ne5! (Vladimirov) it would be much harder work for White to break through.

21 Qd1 Nxa2 22 Nf1! a5 23 Ng3 Qe5 24 Qd2 Ra6 25 Bf3 Kh7 26

Nh5 Rg8 27 Nf4! Rd6 28 Bh5! Be8 29 Ne6! (Diagram 8)

Winning. Black must sacrifice material because 29...fxe6 allows a mate in four after 30 Bg6+ Bxg6 31 fxg6+ Kh8 32 Rxh6+! gxh6 33 Qxh6.

29...Rxe6 30 fxe6 Qxe6 31 Bg4! Qd6 32 Bf5+ Kh8 33 Rg6! 1-0

A nice double rook sacrifice to finish Black off. White mates after 33...fxg6 34 Rxh6+! gxh6 35 Qxh6.

Game 35
☐ **A.Fedorov** ■ **A Suetin**
Moscow 1992

---

1 Nf3 d5 2 g3 c5 3 Bg2 Nc6 4 0-0 e5 5 d3 Nf6 6 Nbd2 Be7 7 e4 0-0 8 exd5!?

An early ...exd4 is playable but relatively unusual in the Classical Variation of the King's Indian Defence. Here White hopes to utilise the extra tempo in order to put pressure on Black's centre.

White can keep the tension for one more move with 8 Re1, forcing Black to do something in the centre. Unfortunately, if Black now blocks the centre with 8...d4! White's rook isn't ideally placed for the f2-f4 break. In fact, it would prefer to be back on f1!

8...Nxd5 9 Re1 (Diagram 9)

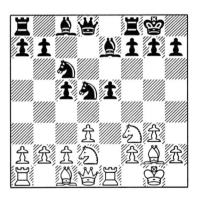

Diagram 9 (B)
Hitting the e5-pawn

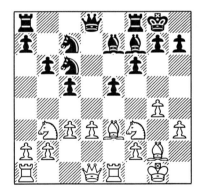

Diagram 10 (W)
What's the plan?

9...f6!

This weakens Black's kingside a bit – he has to watch out for tactics on the a2-g8 diagonal. On the other hand, Black's centre is now rock-solid. In contrast, 9...Qc7? loses a pawn to the discovered attack 10 Nxe5! Nxe5 11 Bxd5, while 9...Bf6 10 Ne4 gives Black problems to solve over the c5-pawn.

10 c3

Introducing ideas of d3-d4 and Qb3. The price White pays for this is a vulnerable d3-pawn. However, as we saw in Kaidanov-Zapata (Game 10), White is often happy to put up with this weakness.

10...Nc7

Sensible play; the knight was a sitting duck in the middle of the board, while now it's also more difficult for White to arrange d3-d4. Following 10...Be6 Black certainly has to reckon on 11 d4!.

11 Nb3 Bg4 12 h3 Bh5 13 g4 Bf7 14 Be3 b6 (Diagram 10) 15 Nfd2

White's play in the game G.Keller-K.Litz, correspondence 2000 is worth studying, as he gradually builds up pressure on the kingside by manoeuvring his pieces around: 15 Nh4!? Nd5 16 Be4! Re8 17 Qf3 Rc8 18 Bd2 Bf8 19 Nc1! Nce7 20 Ne2 Qd7 21 Kh2 a6 22 Rg1 Be6 23 Rad1 b5 24 Ng3 b4 25 Nh5 when White had the makings of a powerful kingside attack. This certainly looks more promising than what happens in the main game.

15...Qd7 16 f4?

Nibbling away at Black's centre but at a real cost of weakening his own king's position. This becomes more important as the game progresses.

16...exf4 17 Bxf4 Nd5 18 Bg3 Bd6! 19 Bxd6 Qxd6 20 Ne4 Qc7 21 Qf3 Rad8 22 Rf1 Nde7! (Diagram 11)

Planning ...Bd5 and possibly ...Ng6-h4.

23 Rad1 Bd5 24 Qf2 f5!

Eliminating another pawn in front of White's king.

25 gxf5 Nxf5 26 Nc1 h6!

But not 26...Bxe4? 27 Bxe4 Ng3?? 28 Bd5+!.

27 Qe1 Ne5 28 Rd2 Ng6! 29 Rdf2 Ngh4 (Diagram 12)

Due to a lack of pawn cover, Black's pieces are beginning to find welcome posts right in front of White's king.

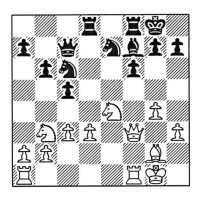

Diagram 11 (W)
Exploiting weaknesses

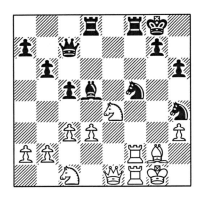

Diagram 12 (W)
Black's pieces invade

30 Ne2 Nxg2 31 Rxg2 Bxe4!

Winning a decisive amount of material.

32 dxe4 Ne3 33 Rxf8+ Rxf8 34 Rg3

Or 34 Rf2 Rd8!! (Suetin) followed by ...Rd1.

34...Rf1+! 35 Qxf1 Nxf1 36 Kxf1 Qf7+ 37 Ke1 Qxa2 38 e5 Qb1+ 39 Kf2 Qf5+ 40 Rf3 Qxe5 0-1

Black Fianchettoes

An early ...g6 and ...Bg7 in conjunction with ...d7-d5 and ...c7-c5 is another popular system for Black, who is effectively playing the Fianchetto Variation of the King's Indian a tempo down.

1 Nf3 d5

Of course there is more than one way to reach the main position after seven moves. Another common route is 1...Nf6 2 g3 g6 3 Bg2 Bg7 4 0-0 0-0 5 d3 d5 (5...c5 6 e4 d6 would be the KIA versus the Sicilian) 6 Nbd2 c5 7 e4 Nc6.

2 g3 c5 3 Bg2 Nc6 4 0-0 Nf6

Black can also develop his knight on e7, although if White captures with exd5 a transposition to the main line is likely: 4...g6 5 d3 Bg7 6 Nbd2 e5 7 e4 Nge7 8 exd5 Nxd5 9 Re1 0-0 10 c3 Re8 leads us to Game 36.

5 d3 g6 (Diagram 13)

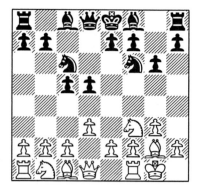

Diagram 13 (W)
Black fianchettoes

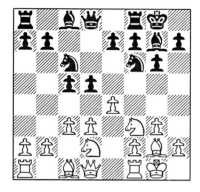

Diagram 14 (B)
White plays 8 c3

It's worth pointing out here that Black can also choose to develop his light-squared bishop with ...Bf5 or ...Bg4 before playing the move ...e7-e6, thus reaching similar positions to those discussed in the following two chapters. For example, 5...Bg4 6 Nbd2 e6 7 h3 Bh5 (7...Bxf3 is also possible, but most players prefer to keep the bishop) 8 e4 Be7 9 c3 0-0 10 g4! Bg6 11 Nh4 dxe4 12 Nxg6! hxg6 13 dxe4 when White will hope to expand on the kingside with his pawns.

 WARNING: 12 dxe4? loses a pawn to the trick 12...Bxe4! 13 Nxe4 Nxe4 14 Bxe4 Bxh4.

6 Nbd2 Bg7 7 e4 0-0 8 c3 (Diagram 14)

Giving Black something to think about, as now there is the very real possibility of playing e4-e5 followed by d3-d4. Black has two main ways of continuing here: occupying the centre with 8...e5 (Game 36), and exchanging on e4 with 8...dxe4 (Game 37).

8 Re1 is also popular and leads to very similar play. Indeed, there are many transpositional possibilities, especially if White captures on d5.

Statistics

White has scored 50% in just under 700 games from the position after 8 c3. The move 8 Re1 has fared less well: 45% in just over 700 games.

Game 36
☐ **K.Foerster** ■ **J.Ullrich**
Correspondence 1987

1 Nf3 d5 2 g3 c5 3 Bg2 Nc6 4 0-0 Nf6 5 d3 g6 6 Nbd2 Bg7 7 e4 0-0 8 c3 e5 9 exd5 (Diagram 15)

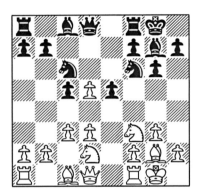

Diagram 15 (B)	**Diagram 16 (B)**
9 exd5 – the most aggressive plan	Increasing the pressure

Not the only way to play the position, but the most active. White gives up the centre but expects to obtain some action with his pieces and some target practice on c5 and e5.

9...Nxd5 10 Re1 Re8 11 Nc4 h6!

This little move is very important as it prevents a white piece (particularly a knight) coming to g5. It's quite easy for Black to underestimate his problems and drift into trouble by playing natural moves. For example, 11...Bf5?! 12 Qb3! Nb6 13 Ng5! (now f7 is vulnerable) 13...Qc7 (or 13...Nxc4 14 Qxc4 Qd7 15 Bd5! Re7 16 Nxf7! Rxf7 17 g4!, winning material) 14 Nd6! and White reached a winning position in M.Todorcevic-F.Sanz Alonso, Salamanca 1990 because 14...Qxd6 loses to 15 Qxf7+ Kh8 16 Qxe8+! Rxe8 17 Nf7+ and Nxd6.

12 Qb3!? (Diagram 16).

Keeping up the pressure in the centre. Another option here is to cement the knight's placing on c4 with 12 a4, after which one continuation is 12...Bf5! (ganging up on d3) 13 Nh4! Be6 14 a5, when White will follow up with Qa4 with the idea of a5-a6.

NOTE: Although c2-c3 leaves White with a weakness on d3, it's still considered worthwhile because the pawn on c3 keeps Black's knights out of b4 and d4.

12...Nc7

Sensibly removing a target from the centre. With White's queen on b3 and the bishop on g2, there were always discovered attacks on d5 to worry about.

Another retreat worth considering is 12...Nb6. Now 13 Nfd2 is a perfectly reasonable reply, while 13 Be3, hitting the c5-pawn, has occurred in a few games. Now 13...Qxd3 14 Nxb6 axb6 15 Qxb6 looks a bit better for White, so Black should probably prefer 13...Be6!, after which the continuation 14 Nfd2! Qxd3 15 Bf1 Qd8 16 Bxc5 Nxc4 17 Nxc4 Na5 18 Qa4 Nxc4 19 Bxc4, which looks roughly equal, has cropped up more than once.

13 Nfd2!?

Uncovering the bishop on the long diagonal while preparing Ne4, which will watch both the pawn on c5 and the square on d6.

13...Qxd3?

Black finds the temptation of the d3-pawn too great, but this soon leads him into real trouble.

In M.Bosboom-L.Van Wely, Vlissingen 1998 the Dutch grandmaster covered his weakness with 13...Ne6 14 Ne4 Bf8, although following 15 a4 I still prefer White. It's true that Black can push away one of those pesky knights with 15...f5, but after 16 Ned2 Black has been saddled with more weaknesses and the e5-pawn is very tender.

14 Ne4! (Diagram 17)

Threatening both to capture the c5-pawn and to plonk one of the knights into d6. Black has to be careful with his queen, for example 14...Na6 15 Ned6! Rd8 16 Be4! sees it being trapped in the middle of the board.

14...Be6 15 Qxb7! Bxc4 16 Qxc6

Material is still level, but Black's position is full of vulnerable spots (c5, c7, the long h1-a8 diagonal). It's unsurprising that Black soon ends up losing something.

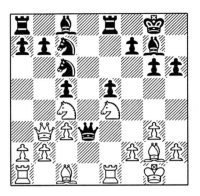

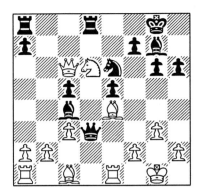

Diagram 17 (B)
The threats loom

Diagram 18 (B)
No choice for the queen

16...Ne6 17 Nd6! Red8 18 Be4! (Diagram 18) 18...Qxd6

The queen had no other move.

19 Qxd6 Rxd6 20 Bxa8 1-0

White is the exchange ahead. Perhaps it's a bit early for Black to resign, but playing on in losing positions in correspondence chess is usually just a waste of stamps (or it was before email arrived).

Game 37
□ **L.Vogt** ■ **M.Petursson**
San Bernardino 1990

---

1 e4 c5

As we saw in Chapter 2, the Reversed King's Indian occasionally arises from the Sicilian.

2 Nf3 Nc6 3 d3 Nf6 4 g3 d5 5 Nbd2 g6 6 Bg2 Bg7 7 0-0 0-0 8 c3 dxe4

A less ambitious and safer move than 8...e5; Black releases the tension and is happy not to have to defend some central pawns.

9 dxe4 Qc7 10 Re1 Rd8 11 Qe2

Preparing e4-e5; the immediate 11 e5? only succeeds in losing a pawn after 11...Ng4!.

11...Ng4! (Diagram 19)

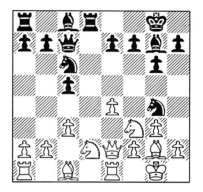

Diagram 19 (W)
The battle for e5

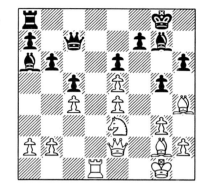

Diagram 20 (W)
Regaining the piece

Black takes White's idea seriously and decides to prevent it – a good decision I think. Instead, 11...b6 12 e5! Nd5 (12...Ne8 13 Ng5! h6 14 Nxf7! Kxf7 15 Qf3+ was even worse for Black in A.Strikovic-I.Penillas Mendez, Leon 1997) 13 Nc4 b5 14 Ne3 Rb8 15 Nxd5 Rxd5 16 Bf4! e6 17 h4! left White in control in K.Van der Weide-W.Van Rijn, Dieren 1997. The position resembles ones discussed in Chapter 1 – White has an automatic attack on the kingside.

12 Nc4 b6

I prefer the immediate 12...Nge5!.

13 Bf4 Nge5

It's tempting to force the bishop back with 13...e5 14 Bg5! f6 15 Bc1!, but then Black has permanently weakened his d5-square and also the knight on g4 is looking a bit silly.

14 Nfxe5 Nxe5 15 Ne3! e6 16 Bg5

In a later game, S.Safin-N.Vorontsov, Ashkhabad 1996, White achieved some advantage with 16 Ng4! h5 17 Nxe5 Bxe5 18 Bg5! Re8 19 f4 Bg7 20 e5! Bb7 21 Red1 – Black has some problems as he cannot oppose White's rook on the d-file.

16...Rd7!

An imaginative defence by the Icelandic GM. Following 16...Re8 17 f4! Nd7 18 e5 (Petursson) White has a very pleasant position.

17 f4 h6! 18 Bh4 Nd3 19 Red1 Ba6! 20 c4

It seems that 20...Nb4 is forced, after which White opens up his bishop with 21 e5!. However...

20...Ne5! 21 fxe5 Rxd1+ 22 Rxd1 g5 (Diagram 20)

The point: Black regains his piece by trapping the bishop.

23 Bxg5 hxg5 24 Ng4 Rd8 25 Nf6+

25 Rf1!? Qd7 26 b3 Qd3 27 Qf2 might still be a bit better for White (Black probably should force the exchange of queens with 27...Qd4). However, Petursson's prophylactic 25...Kf8!? may well be an improvement as now Nf6 can simply be answered by ...Qxe5.

25...Kf8 26 b3 Ke7 27 Ng4?

After this move White is firmly on the defensive. 27 Rxd8 Qxd8 28 Qb2! Qd1+ 29 Kf2 maintains an equal position.

27...Rxd1+ 28 Qxd1 Bxe5 29 Nxe5 Qxe5

Now the endgame will provide White with plenty of suffering. Every white piece is weaker than its counterpart, while White also has an inferior pawn structure (the pawn on e4 is particularly vulnerable).

30 Qd2 Bb7 31 Kf2 f6 32 h4? gxh4 33 gxh4 Bxe4 34 Bxe4 Qxe4 35 Qh6 Kf7 36 h5 e5 37 Qh8 Qf5+ 38 Ke1 Qb1+ 39 Kd2 Qxa2+ 40 Kc3 Qb1 41 h6 Qc1+

Black's winning plan is seen after 42 Kd3 Qd1+ 43 Kc3 Qf3+ 44 Kb2 Qg2+! 45 Kc3 Qg8!, checkmating the white queen!

Points to Remember

1) From a theoretical standpoint Black doesn't have too many problems in the Reversed King's Indian. The positions that arise aren't to everyone's tastes, but this line may appeal to Black players who are used to facing the King's Indian Defence as White.

2) Often the most aggressive way for White to use the extra tempo is to play an early exd5 followed by active piece play and an attack on Black's remaining central pawns (c5 and e5).

3) In the 'classical' variation, 6 Bg5 is an interesting way for White to play, but both sides should remember Black's resource of ...Ng8.

Chapter Five

KIA Versus the ...Bf5 System

Introduction

In the next couple of chapters we're going to cover positions where Black brings out his queen's bishop very early and erects a solid pawn wall in the centre (c6, d5 and usually e6). These systems of development are popular amongst Black players because the problem of the light-squared bishop, so often a worry for Black in the KIA, is solved immediately, and in addition Black's centre is incredibly resilient against any attack.

In this chapter we'll deal with the bishop's development to f5 (Chapter 6 covers ...Bg4 systems). On f5 the bishop directly opposes the KIA plan of e2-e4, so this needs a bit more preparation than normal. However, White can still force through this pawn advance, and Black must be in a good position to react to this. Usually Black plays a quick ...h7-h6, giving the bishop an excellent resting place on h7. From this square it eyes White's central pawns (d3 and e4). Crucially, if these pawns advance, the influence of the h7-bishop is increased as its range extends into the heart of White's queenside.

 NOTE: Because both White and Black are playing opening 'systems', there is quite a bit of flexibility over move order. I will deal with the most common move orders, but bear in mind there are plenty of transpositional possibilities.

White Plays a Quick e2-e4

1 Nf3 d5 2 g3 Nf6 3 Bg2 c6 (Diagram 1)

The immediate 3...Bf5 is also possible, but most players prefer to play ...c7-c6 first because it makes White think twice about playing c2-c4.

4 0-0

After 4 c4!? the game enters the territory of the English Opening more than the KIA. It should be noted, though, that this is a real gambit because after 4...dxc4 there is no easy way for White to regain his pawn.

4...Bf5 5 d3

Again there is the possibility of transposing to the Réti/English via 5 c4.

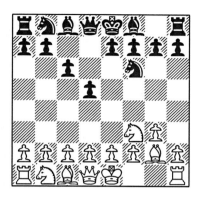

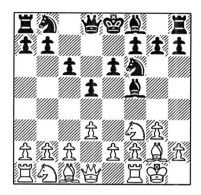

Diagram 1 (W)
Black plays 3...c6

Diagram 2 (W)
A solid black pawn triangle

5...e6 (Diagram 2)

Completing the super-solid triangle of pawns c6/d5/e6.

There's also the possibility to play for ...e7-e5 with 5...Nbd7, but this doesn't seem to be very popular. Perhaps one reason is 6 Nh4!?, when 6...Bg4 7 h3 Bh5 8 g4 Bg6 9 f4! is one idea (compare this to the next note).

6 Nbd2

6 Nh4 is not so effective now after 6...Bg4! 7 h3 Bh5 8 g4 Nfd7!. White has nothing better than 9 Nf3 but following 9...Bg6 White's knight sortie has achieved very little.

6...Be7

The most popular square for the bishop in this line.

6...Bd6?! is inaccurate because following 7 Qe1! (more about this in the next note) 7...Bg6 8 e4 Black has to expend another move with either the bishop or the knight in order to prevent a pawn fork on e5. However, developing the bishop on c5 is a reasonable alternative: 6...h6 7 Qe1 Bc5 8 e4 Bh7 9 Qe2 0-0 and here I would be tempted to continue with 10 b3 and Bb2, as in the next section.

7 Qe1! (Diagram 3)

Although slightly bizarre at first sight, there's a clear logic to this move. White wishes to force through e2-e4, but wants to keep the rook on f1 where it will be well placed if White decides to move the f3-knight and play f2-f4 (see Game 38). So White's idea is Qe1, e2-e4 and then Qe2 (the manoeuvre can be achieved in the same amount of time with e2-e3, Qe2 and then e3-e4).

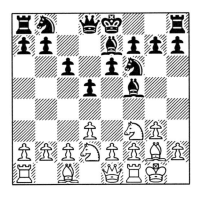

Diagram 3 (B)	Diagram 4 (W)
Forcing through e2-e4	The stage is set

There's also a practical difficulty in forcing through e2-e4 with Re1, which is seen in the variation 7 Re1 h6 8 e4? (b2-b3 and Bb2 should be played) 8...dxe4 9 dxe4 Nxe4! 10 Nxe4 Qxd1 11 Rxd1 Bxe4, winning a pawn.

7...h6!

 NOTE: Black nearly always plays ...h7-h6 at some point in the opening.

Black really wishes to maintain this bishop, so it is given a safe bolt-hole on h7 where it is out of range of the knight on f3 (on g6 the bishop could be harassed by Nh4 or Ne5).

8 e4 Bh7

It makes no real sense for Black to exchange on e4 so early and mess up his super-solid centre. Besides, as we've seen before, the e4-square becomes a handy post for White. For example, 8...dxe4 9 dxe4 Bh7 10 Qe2 Nbd7 11 e5! Nd5 12 Ne4 Nc5 13 Nxc5 Bxc5 14 Nd2! Qc7 (14...Bxc2? loses to 15 Qc4) 15 a3 0-0 (S.Reshevsky-V.Smyslov, Belgrade 1970) and now 16 Kh1! (Reshevsky), intending f2-f4 followed by

Ne4, looks pleasant for White.

9 Qe2

Virtually everyone improves the position of the queen here, but 9 Ne5!? is a promising alternative – see Game 38.

9...0-0! (Diagram 4)

9...Nbd7 is less accurate because after 10 e5 the queen's knight robs its partner of a natural retreat square.

Strategies

After 9...0-0 we have a position quite similar to the traditional main line of the KIA versus the French (see the first section of Chapter 1), the main difference being that Black's light-squared bishop is placed outside the pawn chain. I would say that this is clearly an advantage for Black because this bishop can be influential both in defence on the kingside and in counterattack on the queenside. Indeed, although in practice White usually plays a very quick e4-e5, there's certainly an argument for holding back on this move, thus limiting the presence of the h7-bishop (see Game 39 for further details).

Statistics

Black has scored well from Diagram 4 – 51% from over 200 games. Although only tested over 30 or so games, 9 Ne5 has scored much better for White (68%).

Game 38
□ R.Vaganian ■ Comp Centaur
The Hague 1996

1 Nf3 d5 2 g3 c6 3 Bg2 Nf6 4 0-0 Bf5 5 d3 h6 6 Nbd2 e6 7 Qe1 Bh7 8 e4 Be7 9 Ne5!? (Diagram 5)

White's knight clears the way for the f-pawn to advance. This is Vaganian's patent – he introduced it in a game against Sveshnikov in 1980.

9...Nbd7

9...0-0 10 f4 Nbd7 11 Nxd7 Nxd7 transposes to the main game.

10 Nxd7 Nxd7

The best recapture. After 10...Qxd7?! 11 e5 Black's knight is forced onto an unfortunate square.

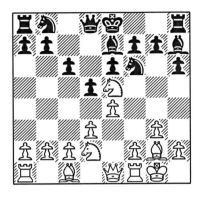

Diagram 5 (B)
Preparing f2-f4

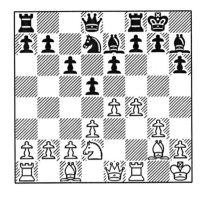

Diagram 6 (B)
How should Black react?

11 f4 0-0 12 Kh1 (Diagram 6) 12...a5

12...dxe4!? 13 dxe4 Nc5 is an idea first introduced by Karpov. The point is that Black's pressure against the e4-pawn restricts White's ambitions to some extent. The recent game R.Vaganian-L.Dominguez, Poikovsky 2005 continued 14 Qe3 Qd7 15 a4?! (this doesn't seem to help White; Marin's suggestion of the immediate 15 Nb3 makes more sense) 15...Rfd8 16 Nb3 Nxb3 17 Qxb3 Bc5 and the exchange of a pair of minor pieces had eased Black's task. White managed to block in the light-squared bishop with 18 g4 Qe7 19 f5 but this was only temporary: 19...h5! 20 fxe6 Qxe6 21 Qxe6 fxe6 22 gxh5 Rd4 23 Be3 Rc4 24 Bxc5 Rxc5 resulted in a level ending.

13 g4 a4?!

I suspect 13...dxe4 14 dxe4 Nc5 is still the way forward for Black.

14 a3!?

We've seen this idea of preventing ...a4-a3 more than once (see Chapter 1).

The stem game in this line continued 14 f5 a3 15 b3 Re8 16 Rb1 exf5 17 gxf5 Qa5 18 exd5 cxd5 19 Qg3 Bb4 20 Nf3 Kh8 21 f6! Nxf6 22 Bxh6! and White was doing very well in R.Vaganian-E.Sveshnikov, Sochi

1980 as 22...gxh6 23 Ne5 Re7 24 Rxf6 Rg8 25 Qh4! Rxe5 26 Rxh6 Rg7 27 Rxh7+ Rxh7 28 Qf6+ (Vaganian) is winning for White. Interestingly Vaganian diverges here. Did he suspect some computer-inspired improvement on Sveshnikov's play?

14...Bh4?

A typical computer move (from those days, of course; with the likes of *Hydra* around, no one would dare criticise a computer these days!). The bishop merely turns out to be vulnerable on this square. Even now it's not too late for 14...dxe4! 15 dxe4 Nc5.

15 Qe2 dxe4 16 dxe4 Nc5 17 Nc4! b5 18 Ne5 Qc7 19 g5! (Diagram 7)

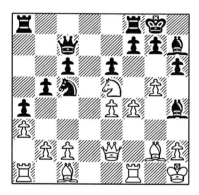

Diagram 7 (B)
Blocking out the bishop

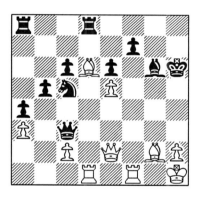

Diagram 8 (W)
Human interference?

A deep idea, which on the surface tries to exploit the offside position of Black's dark-squared bishop (19...hxg5 is met by 20 Nf3 f6 21 e5!). Black finds a tactical resource, but the resulting position is still favourable for White.

19...Bxg5 20 fxg5 Qxe5 21 Bf4! Qxb2 22 Bd6 Qc3 23 gxh6!

The bishop's a monster on d6 – there's no reason to give it up for a rook.

23...Rfd8 24 Rad1 Bg6 25 hxg7 Kxg7 26 e5! Kh6? (Diagram 8)

I can't explain this bizarre move at all – the computer must have short-circuited! Nevertheless, even after more stubborn defence White's position looks to be winning. For example, 26...Rac8 (meeting the threat of

Bxc6) 27 Qg4 Nb7 28 Be7! Rxd1 29 Bf6+ Kf8 30 Rxd1 Qxc2 31 Qd4! Bf5 32 Qd7 Rb8 33 Qe7+ Kg8 34 Rg1! Bg6 35 Qc7, winning the knight and retaining a massive attack.

27 Qf2!

Winning.

27...Ne4

Or 27...Nb7 28 Qh4+ Kg7 29 Be7 Rxd1 30 Bf6+ Kf8 31 Qh8 mate.

28 Qh4+ Kg7 29 Bxe4 Kg8 30 Bxg6 fxg6 31 Qf6 Qxc2 32 Qxe6+ Kh8 33 Rd4 1-0

Game 39
☐ **J.Kapischka** ■ **A.Goldberg**
Bundesliga 1999

1 Nf3 Nf6 2 g3 d5 3 Bg2 c6 4 0-0 Bf5 5 d3 h6 6 Nbd2 e6 7 Qe1 Be7 8 e4 Bh7 9 Qe2 0-0 10 Re1 (Diagram 9)

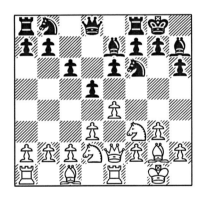
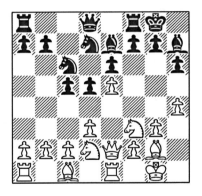

Diagram 9 (B)	**Diagram 10 (W)**
10 Re1 – the right move?	An improved French

This move has been played many times, but I'm not sure that I like it – why did White go to the bother of playing Qe1, e2-e4 and Qe2 if he was going to end up playing Re1 in any case? Instead playing à la Vaganian with 10 Ne5 and f2-f4 still makes considerable sense, while there's also the straightforward idea of b2-b3 followed by Bb2, with a likely transposition to the next section.

Lev Gutman is an expert on the white side of this line, so his games are always worth noting. In L.Gutman-G.Leinov, Israel 1980 he found an original way of playing on the kingside: 10 Kh1!? Nbd7?! (I prefer playing as in the main game with 10...c5 and ...Nc6) 11 e5 Ne8 12 Rg1! Nc7 13 g4! f6 14 exf6 Bxf6 15 Nf1 Qe7 16 g5!? hxg5 17 Bh3 Bf5 18 Nxg5 Bxg5 19 Bxg5 Qf7 20 Bxf5 Qxf5 21 f4 d4 22 Ng3 Qd5+ 23 Rg2 Rf7 24 Ne4 e5 25 f5! Rxf5 26 Bh6 Rf7 27 Rag1, when White had a very strong attack.

10...c5!?

This move is very rare in this actual position but its idea is well known. In general it's worth expending another tempo with this pawn so the queen's knight can develop more actively on c6 while leaving the d7-square free for the other knight, although Black usually waits for White to close the centre before doing this.

11 e5

Even though this move reaches a position that has been seen quite a few times, I believe it rather plays into Black's hands.

The disadvantage of Black's previous move was that it weakened the protection of the d5-pawn, so there's an argument for keeping the tension in the centre. Once more 11 Ne5!? followed by f2-f4 suggests itself.

11...Nfd7 12 h4 Nc6 (Diagram 10)

Now the position is looking very familiar indeed – the traditional main line of the KIA against the French but with Black's bishop placed on h7 rather than c8. This is a massive advantage for Black: his king is better defended and his queenside counterplay arrives much quicker than normal.

13 Nf1 b5 14 N1h2 c4!

Already the bishop's presence is felt down the long diagonal. White would love to keep the queenside closed with 15 d4?? but here that simply loses to 15...Nb4!.

15 Bf4 cxd3 16 cxd3 Nb4 17 Red1 Qb6 18 d4?

White wanted to prevent ...Nc5, but this move fully opens the bishop's diagonal and leaves White in big trouble on the queenside. Instead White could have slowed down Black's attack with 18 a3!.

18...Rfc8

Coveting the c2-square.

19 Bf1 a6 20 Ne1 Nc2! (Diagram 11)

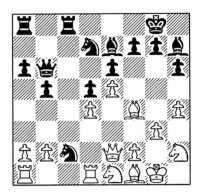

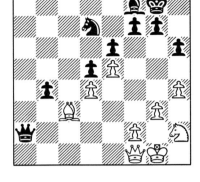

Diagram 11 (W)
It's all Black here

Diagram 12 (W)
The b-pawn decides

21 Nxc2

This was forced as the d4-pawn was hanging. It's all one-way traffic from here – White never has a chance to get things moving on the king-side.

21...Rxc2 22 Rd2 Rac8 23 a4 Bb4! 24 Rxc2 Rxc2 25 Qd1 Rxb2 26 axb5 axb5 27 Bd3

An unusual sight for the KIA – White is begging Black to exchange light-squared bishops! White gets his wish, but the damage on the queenside has already been done and Black has a healthy extra pawn.

27...Bxd3 28 Qxd3 Bf8 29 Bd2 Qc7 30 Rc1 Qa7 31 Bc3 Qa3 32 Qf1 Ra2 33 Ra1 b4 34 Rxa2 Qxa2 0-1 (Diagram 12)

The extra b-pawn is decisive, for example 35 Ba1 b3 36 Qc1 Ba3 37 Qc8+ Nf8 etc. With games such as this, it's little wonder the ...Bf5 system is so popular.

The Double Fianchetto

A popular way of playing the system for White is to slightly delay e2-e4 in favour of an early queenside fianchetto.

1 Nf3 d5 2 g3 Nf6 3 Bg2 c6 4 0-0 Bf5 5 b3 e6 6 Bb2 (Diagram 13)

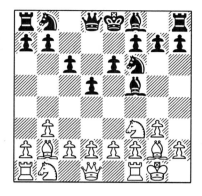

Diagram 13 (B)
Where does the bishop go?

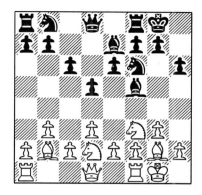

Diagram 14 (W)
Move order matters

6...Be7

As in the previous section, e7 seems to be the favourite place for this bishop, but both d6 and c5 are also possibilities:

a) 6...Bd6!? (usually this is a poor choice for the bishop as Black has to watch out for the e4-e5 fork, but here he has a specific idea in mind) 7 d3 Qe7! 8 Nbd2 Ba3! 9 Qc1 Bxb2 10 Qxb2 0-0. This idea has been played by the Russian grandmaster and theoretician Evgeny Sveshnikov, and it looks like a reasonable way to take some sting out of the position. In general White's bishop on b2 is more active than its counterpart, so this exchange should favour Black. Maybe White should consider avoiding it with 8 a3!?.

b) 6...h6 7 d3 Bc5 8 Nbd2 0-0 9 Qe1 Bh7 10 e4 a5 is identical to the main line except that Black's bishop is on c5 rather than e7. The bishop is more active on c5 and it prevents a very quick f2-f4. On the other hand, it sometimes obstructs Black's queenside counterplay because it blocks the c-pawn.

 TIP: If Black wishes to place his bishop on c5 then it's worth waiting for White to play d2-d3. The immediate 6...Bc5 might encourage White to gain a tempo and transform the position into a queen's pawn opening with 7 d4!? Bd6 8 c4.

7 d3

With the dark-squared bishop developed, White begins to prepare e2-e4.

7...h6 8 Nbd2 0-0! (Diagram 14)

> **WARNING: It may seem as if Black can play his moves in any order, but this is not always the case!**

If Black decided to get his queenside counterplay moving with 8...a5?! White would be able to play 9 e4! without the usual Qe1 preparation due to the vulnerability of the g7-pawn: 9...dxe4 10 dxe4 Nxe4 11 Bxg7 Rg8 12 Bb2 is clearly better for White as Black's king will have no safe place to hide. Instead Black should probably make do with 9...Bh7, but then White gains a tempo over normal lines because the queen can go to e2 in one go.

9 Qe1

If White wants his rook on e1 instead of f1 in the long run, then the way to force through e2-e4 is with 9 Re1 Bh7 10 e4. A very recent game worthy of note continued 10...a5 11 a3 Nbd7 12 Qe2 Nc5 13 Ne5 Ncd7 14 Ndf3 Re8 15 Nxf7!? **(Diagram 15)**

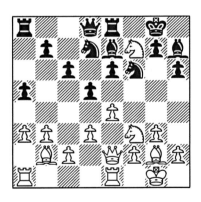

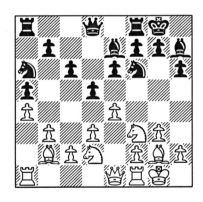

Diagram 15 (B)	Diagram 16 (W)
15 Nxf7!?	Planning ...Nb4

15...Kxf7 16 e5 Ng8 17 Nd4! Bc5 18 Qf3+ Ke7 19 Qg4 Kf7 20 Qf4+ Ke7 21 Qg4 Kf7 22 Qf4+ Ke7 with a draw by repetition, T.Petrosian-E.Ghaem Maghami, Tehran 2005 (White is not *the* Tigran Petrosian, of course, but another strong Armenian grandmaster nevertheless).

9...Bh7 10 e4 a5!

White's pawn on b3 is a slight target, so this is a good way of seeking some a-file action for the rook (White usually prevents this with his next move).

As in Game 39, 10...c5, intending ...Nc6, is certainly an option. Then 11 e5?! Nfd7 is the sort of position Black is after, so instead it makes sense for White to both keep the tension in the centre and the long diagonal open: 11 Ne5! followed by f2-f4 looks like the best way forward.

11 a4

White doesn't want to allow Black's a-pawn to a4, after which he would always have to consider both ...a4-a3 and ...a4xb3. The other way to deal with Black's positional threat is with 11 a3, preparing to meet ...a5-a4 with b3-b4 (see Game 40).

11...Na6! (Diagram 16)

A very clever move and the logical follow-up to ...a7-a5 and a2-a4. Black has spotted a weak point in White's camp – the c2-pawn – and the knight will sit very nicely on b4. The only way to get rid of the knight would be with c2-c3, but this blocks the b2-bishop and leaves the d3-pawn vulnerable.

The solid 11...Nbd7 is also possible, while 11...c5 should again be met by 12 Ne5!, preparing f2-f4. In the old game M.Vukic-V.Chekhov, Banja Luka 1976 Black added to his problems by blundering a pawn with 12...Nfd7?, allowing 13 Nxd7 Qxd7 14 exd5 exd5 15 Bxd5! Qxd5 16 Qxe7.

Strategies

Going back to 11...Na6, the stage is set for a typical battle where White attacks on the kingside and Black directs his counterplay on the other wing. The position is complicated somewhat by the fact that some tension remains in the centre, and White must be careful with his c2/d3/e4 pawns as any move by these three pawns gives Black's bishop on h7 greater influence on the position. See Game 41 for more details.

Statistics

White has scored 52% from around 280 games with 5 b3 (this doesn't count the many other games where White has played b2-b3 later on).

Game 40
□ H.Kallio ■ J.Nykopp
Vantaa 1999

1 Nf3 d5 2 g3 Nf6 3 Bg2 c6 4 0-0 Bf5 5 b3 e6 6 Bb2 Be7 7 d3 h6 8 Nbd2 0-0 9 Qe1 Bh7 10 e4 a5 11 a3

The plus point of this is that it eliminates the annoying ...Na6-b4 manoeuvre. The negative is that Black may well be able to arrange an effective ...a5-a4 push (played at once, White could react with b3-b4).

11...Na6

The automatic reaction to 11 a4, this move has also been seen quite a few times against 11 a3. However, without the possibility of ...Nb4 this move loses some of its effectiveness.

11...Nbd7 is sensible, while the most ambitious way of playing is with 11...c5!?, after which ...a5-a4 is firmly back on the agenda. Now using up another tempo with 12 a4 has been played a few times, but this looks extravagant; it's going to be difficult for White to use the b5-outpost and, after 12...Nc6 Black should be fine. Instead White should concentrate on kingside expansion with 12 Ne5 followed by f2-f4 etc.

12 Ne5!

Notice that with a bishop on b2 White is rightly more reluctant than normal to block things up with e4-e5. Instead, as usual, f2-f4 is coming.

12...Nd7 13 Nxd7 Qxd7 14 f4 dxe4 15 Nxe4! (Diagram 17)

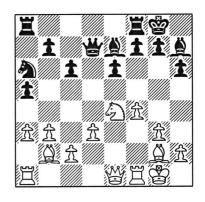

Diagram 17 (B)
15 Nxe4!

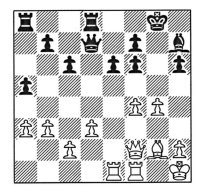

Diagram 18 (B)
The heavy mob are coming!

Showing good flexibility of thought. The 'normal' recapture would be 15 dxe4, but then 15...Bc5+! 16 Kh1 Bd4! looks okay for Black. After 15 Nxe4 White has excellent minor pieces including a very powerful bishop on b2. Meanwhile, Black must spend time getting his offside knight back into the game. It would be nice to be able to challenge White's knight with 15...Nc5??, but this loses a piece to the double attack 16 Qc3!.

15...Nc7 16 Kh1 Nd5 17 Qf2 Nf6?

Before this move Black was slightly passive but did still have a very solid position. It's understandable that he wishes to trade off White's knight and dark-squared bishop, but the kingside weaknesses he must accept to do so are pretty serious.

18 Nxf6+ Bxf6 19 Bxf6 gxf6 20 Rae1 Rfd8 21 g4! (Diagram 18)

Now Qh4 and Re3-h3 are real possibilities – it will be virtually impossible for Black to defend his weak pawns.

21...f5 22 Qh4 Qd6 23 Qxh6 fxg4 24 Re5 Bf5 25 Be4!

Easily breaking the attempted blockade. The rest is painful for Black.

25...Qf8 26 Qh4 Rd5 27 Bxd5 cxd5 28 h3! f6 29 Re2 gxh3 30 Rg1+ Kf7 31 Qh5+ Ke7 32 Qxf5! 1-0

Game 41
□ D.Norwood ■ J.Levitt
Amantea 1992

1 g3 d5 2 Bg2 Nf6 3 Nf3 c6 4 0-0 Bf5 5 d3 e6 6 Nbd2 Be7 7 b3 h6 8 Bb2 0-0 9 e3

This move followed by Qe2 and e3-e4 comes to the same thing as Qe1, e2-e4 and then Qe2.

9...a5 10 a4 Bh7 11 Qe2 Na6 12 e4 Nb4! (Diagram 19) 13 Ne1!

This appears a bit passive, but at least it allows the f-pawn to advance. In any case there was no better way to protect c2. The move 13 c3? is both positionally unjustifiable and tactically suspect: 13...Nxd3! 14 Qxd3 dxe4 and Black wins at least a pawn. 13 Rac1 has been played a few times, but even 13...Na2!? is playable here. After the rook moves the knight goes back to b4, asking the same questions. Of course if Black is playing for a win he must try something else!

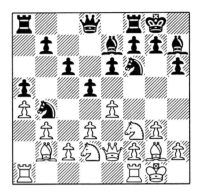

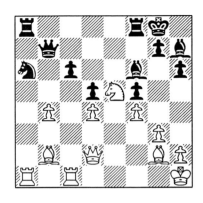

Diagram 19 (W)	**Diagram 20 (B)**
How to protect c2?	Spot the horrible piece!

13...b5!

There's no reason to delay counterplay on the queenside. The earliest known game from this position, L.Polugaevsky-W.Addison, Palma de Mallorca 1970, continued 13...Nd7 14 f4 Bf6!? (Black considers it worthwhile expending two tempi in order to force White to clarify the situation in the centre) 15 e5 Be7 16 g4 Re8 17 Kh1 f6? 18 Ndf fxe5 19 Nxe5 Nxe5 20 Bxe5 when White's strong dark-squared bishop and firm grip of the e5-square promised him a clear plus. Instead of the rather compliant 17...f6, Kotov suggested 17...c5!, intending ...Qc7 followed by ...d5-d4 and ...Nd5 when the knight eyes a juicy outpost on e3.

14 f4

Giving up the e4-spearhead with 14 exd5?! is inconsistent. In A.Miles-N.Short, London 1982 Black built up an edge: 14...exd5 15 Ndf3 Re8 16 Qd2 Bd6 17 Nd4 Qb6 18 Nef3 bxa4 19 bxa4 Nd7!.

14...bxa4 15 Rxa4 Nd7!?

Planning ...Nb6 or ...Nc5 followed by ...a5-a4.

16 Kh1 Nc5 17 Ra1 f5?

I don't think the bishop on h7 was consulted before this was played, and now it's stuck in the role of bystander for the rest of the game.

 TIP: As the Scottish grandmaster Jonathan Rowson would say, talk to your pieces!

For now, 17...a4 is well met by 18 c3! Nba6 19 b4!. Instead O.Hole-L.Ogaard, Oslo 2002 saw 17...Bf6!? 18 e5 (18 Bxf6 Qxf6 19 e5 may be stronger) 18...Be7 19 Ndf3 whereupon Black entered the complications of a knight sacrifice with 19...a4!? 20 d4 axb3! 21 Rxa8 Qxa8 22 dxc5 bxc2.

18 exd5 exd5 19 c3!

Now that there is no pressure on the h7-b1 diagonal, White is happy to move this pawn.

19...Nba6 20 Nef3 Bf6 21 d4 Ne4 22 Ne5 Qc7 23 b4! Nxd2 24 Qxd2 axb4 25 cxb4 Qb7 26 Rfc1! (Diagram 20)

The position has clarified but the bishop on h7 remains a shadow of its former self. Now the immediate 26...Nxb4 runs into 27 Rxa8 Rxa8 28 Nxc6! Nxc6 29 Bxd5+ so Black feels obliged to capture on e5.

26...Bxe5 27 dxe5 Nxb4 28 e6!

Giving Black a major headache on the long a1-h8 diagonal.

28...Bg6 29 Bd4 Rfb8?

Losing at once; Black's last chance was with 29...Rxa1 30 Rxa1 Na6.

30 Rxa8! Qxa8 31 Ra1 Na6

This loses a piece, but following 31...Qb7 32 Ra7! White would be crashing through on g7.

32 Bf1 c5 33 Rxa6 Qb7 34 Bxc5 Qb1 35 Qd3 Qc1 36 Be3 Qe1 37 Kg1 1-0

Points to Remember

1) Black must play an early ...h7-h6 in order to preserve his bishop.

2) White normally uses the idea of Qe1 (rather than Re1), d2-d3 and Nbd2 in order to force through e2-e4. This is because the rook is often better situated on f1, especially if White opts to play f2-f4.

3) White must be careful not to end up in a 'KIA versus the French' situation in which the bishop on h7 is a monster (see Game 39). Often White refrains from playing e4-e5 in favour of Ne5 and a quick f2-f4.

4) If White fianchettoes his c1-bishop, Black often reacts to b2-b3 with ...a7-a5. White usually responds to the positional threat of ...a5-a4 with a2-a3 or a2-a4.

KIA Versus the ...Bg4 System

Introduction

The ...Bg4 system, known as the Capablanca Variation, is very popular at all levels of chess. Unlike the ...Bf5 system of the previous chapter, White doesn't have to work so hard to achieve the e2-e4 advance, but when it comes he is exposed to an annoying pin on the h5-d1 diagonal. A practical advantage the ...Bg4 system has over ...Bf5 is that Black has more development options: he can play quietly with ...e7-e6 and ...Be7; he can play for an immediate ...e7-e5 with an early ...Nd7; he can exchange on e4 and play and early ...Bc5; he can even play a system with ...e7-e6, ...Bd6 and ...Ne7.

White Plays a Quick e2-e4

1 Nf3 d5 2 g3 Nf6 3 Bg2 c6

3...Bg4 can be played at once, but most players prefer 3...c6 for the reason outlined in the previous chapter – it discourages White to some extent from playing an immediate c2-c4.

4 0-0 Bg4 (Diagram 1)

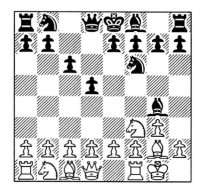

Diagram 1 (W)
Black plays ...Bg4

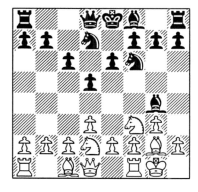

Diagram 2 (W)
Completing the triangle

5 d3

Immediately setting about preparing e2-e4, but there are some other options here:

a) 5 c4 transposes to the Réti/English.

b) Fianchettoing the c1-bishop with 5 b3 and Bb2 is the subject of the third section of this chapter.

c) 5 Ne5!? must be considered, whereupon Black's best bet is probably to keep the pressure on the h5-d1 diagonal with 5...Bh5. However, to make sense of 5 Ne5 White should probably transpose to a queen's pawn opening with 6 d4 e6 7 c4!, as playing in KIA fashion with 6 d3 Nbd7 7 Nxd7 Qxd7 doesn't really justify the early knight move.

5...Nbd7

It's possible to delay the development of this knight but it usually ends up going to d7 in any case. For example, 5...e6 6 Nbd2 Be7 7 h3 Bh5 8 e4 0-0 9 Qe2 Nbd7 transposes to the main line.

6 Nbd2 e6 (Diagram 2)

Completing the solid pawn triangle c6/d5/e6. Black's other main option here is 6...e5 – see the next section.

7 h3

White can ask the question of Black's light-squared bishop with h2-h3 at virtually any point in this opening, after which Black usually retreats with ...Bh5. Of course the immediate 7 e4 is also possible, while 7 b3 will transpose to positions covered in the third section.

 NOTE: As with the ...Bf5 system, there are many possible move orders to reach the same position.

7...Bh5

Exchanging on f3 with 7...Bxf3 is a solid if somewhat uninspiring option. The resulting positions are usually quiet in nature with White keeping a nagging pull. See Game 42 for further details.

8 e4

Unlike against the ...Bf5 system, White doesn't need any further preparation to play this move. However, White can still play in the same fashion as against ...Bf5 with 8 Qe1, which breaks the potential pin on the h5-d1 diagonal and has the advantage of avoiding the note to Black's next move. After, say, 8...Be7 9 e4 we have transposed to note 'c' to White's 10th move.

8...Be7 (Diagram 3)

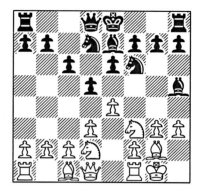

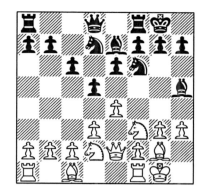

Diagram 3 (W)
Settling for e7

Diagram 4 (W)
How to proceed?

The bishop usually goes to e7 in this particular line, although c5 is also a reasonable square (Black usually exchanges on e4 first). Another possibility (after 8...dxe4 9 dxe4) is 9...Ne5!?, using the pin on the f3-knight in order to exchange a pair of minor pieces: 10 g4 Nxf3+ 11 Qxf3 Bg6 12 Qc3!? (preventing e4-e5) 12...Qb6 13 Nc4 Qb4 14 Qxb4 Bxb4 15 c3 Be7 16 Re1 Nd7 17 f4 f6 18 Be3 and White held a nice space advantage in the ending, Zhang Zhong-S.Solomon, Calvia Olympiad 2004.

9 Qe2

Certainly not the only move, for example:

a) It's not too late to transpose to b3 lines with 9 b3, which should reach positions discussed in the third section of this chapter.

b) Naturally White can play in typical 'KIA versus the French' fashion with 9 Re1 0-0 10 e5 Ne8, but we've already discovered in the previous chapter how the light-squared bishop being outside the pawn chain favours Black. S.Movsesian-P.Acs, FIDE World Championship, Tripoli 2004 continued 11 Nf1 c5! 12 Bf4 b5 13 g4 Bg6 14 Qd2 c4 15 Ng3 cxd3 16 cxd3 Nc5 with good counterplay for Black.

c) White's most common choice here has actually been 9 Qe1!?.

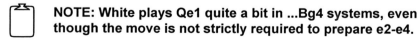

> **NOTE: White plays Qe1 quite a bit in ...Bg4 systems, even though the move is not strictly required to prepare e2-e4.**

The point is that now e2-e4 has been played, the knight on f3 is pinned.

By unpinning with Qe1, White is ready to move the knight and continue aggressively with f2-f4. A typical continuation is 9...0-0 10 Nh2!? e5 11 f4!? (very ambitious; White can also play more quietly with 11 Ndf3 followed by Nh4) 11...exf4 12 gxf4 dxe4 13 dxe4 Nc5 14 Kh1 Re8 15 Qf2 when White's pawns on e4 and f4 grant him considerable space, but he has to be careful as Black's active pieces offer him good counterplay. R.Hartoch-J.Waitzkin, Amsterdam 1996 continued 15...a5 16 e5 Nd5 17 Nc4 Ne6 18 f5 Bc5 19 Qg3 Nd4 with a very complex position.

9...0-0 (Diagram 4)

White must assess how to make progress on the kingside. The most obvious way seems to be g3-g4 followed by a knight move and f2-f4, but life is not that simple and White has to show some finesse. For more details, see Game 43.

Statistics

Taking the position after 5 d3, White has scored 51% from approximately 1500 games.

Game 42
□ **G.Barcza** ■ **J.Nun**
Decin 1975

1 Nf3 d5 2 g3 Nf6 3 Bg2 c6 4 0-0 Bg4 5 d3 Nbd7 6 Nbd2 e6 7 h3 Bxf3 8 Nxf3 (Diagram 5)

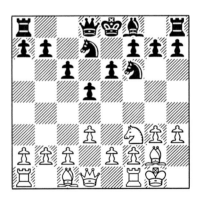

Diagram 5 (B)
Recapturing with the knight

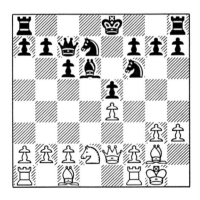

Diagram 6
Planning Nc4

This looks like the most natural recapture, and it's true that many experts prefer to give themselves this option by playing d2-d3 and Nbd2 before attacking the bishop with h2-h3. However, 8 Bxf3 has also been played a few times. The advantage of this move is that White is in a better position to force through e2-e4; the disadvantage is that White's king is not so well defended. In the game M.Yabiansky-M.Tempone, Buenos Aires 1991 Black attempted to take advantage of this with some imaginative play: 8...Bd6 9 e4 Qc7 10 Qe2 h5! 11 d4 dxe4 12 Nxe4 Nxe4 13 Bxe4 h4! 14 g4 Bf4 15 Bxf4 Qxf4 16 Qe3 and now if Black exchanges queens his position looks okay. Instead the game continued 16...Qd6 17 c4 Nf6 18 Bg2 0-0-0 19 Rfd1 when the long-range power of White's bishop promises some sort of edge.

8...Bd6 9 e4!?

Offering a pawn sacrifice. If White wishes to force e2-e4 without offering a pawn then either 9 Qe1 or 9 Re1 is the move to play.

9...Qc7?!

Black is planning to castle queenside, but I don't think that this is the right idea. Instead Black should choose one of the following:

a) 9...dxe4 10 dxe4 Nxe4 11 Ng5! Nxg5 12 Qxd6 (threatening to trap the knight with f2-f4 or h3-h4) 12...h6 and now White has a promising initiative for the pawn after either 13 Be3 or 13 f4.

b) The simple 9...0-0 is Black's most solid option. White was only slightly better after 10 Re1 e5 11 Nh4 Re8 12 Nf5 Bf8 in L.Ljubojevic-Z.Polgar, Monaco (blindfold) 1994.

 NOTE: A white knight often heads for the f5-square in this variation.

10 Qe2 dxe4 11 dxe4 e5 12 Nd2 (Diagram 6)

With the intention of Nc4. Instead 12 Nh4, planning Nf5, is an enticing alternative, but Black would be happy to weaken his kingside with ...g7-g6 to prevent this given that he is castling long.

12...0-0-0!?

Following 12...0-0 13 Nc4 Be7 14 b3 and Bb2 White has a small but long-lasting advantage based on the bishop pair and greater control of the light squares.

NOTE: One way the light-squared bishop can re-enter the action is with h3-h4 and Bh3.

13 Nc4 Bc5?

This only helps White because the bishop proves to be a target on c5 – White will gain time in his pursuit of a queenside attack.

14 c3! a5

Preventing b2-b4 for the moment but at a cost of weakening the queenside. Black's already in big trouble here.

15 b3 Ba7 16 a4 Rhe8 17 Rb1 Nc5 18 Be3 Kb8 19 b4! (Diagram 7)

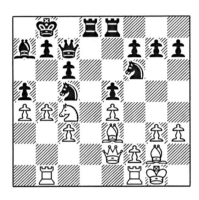
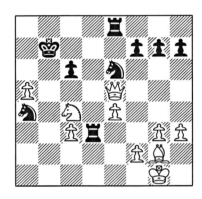

Diagram 7 (B)
Opening up the queenside

Diagram 8 (B)
Cleaning up

19...Nxa4

Or 19...axb4 20 cxb4 Nxa4 21 Bxa7+ Kxa7 22 Ra1 b5 23 Nb2 when the queenside opens up completely, much to the irritation of Black's king.

20 Bxa7+ Kxa7 21 Qe3+ Kb8 22 bxa5

Now White has a ready-made attack and a straightforward plan of doubling rooks on the half-open b-file.

22...Nd7 23 Rb4! Ndc5 24 Rfb1 Rd3

Otherwise White plays Bf1 followed by Nb2, but now White has a winning combination.

25 Rxb7+! Qxb7 26 Rxb7+ Kxb7 27 Qg5 Ne6 28 Qxe5 (Diagram 8)

With White's queen hovering around, Black's king is far too exposed to have any chance of survival.

28...Ka7 29 Qf5 Re7 30 e5 Rxc3 31 Qe4 Rc7 32 Nd6! Nec5 33 Qxh7 Ka6 34 Qg8 Rc1+ 35 Bf1+ Nd3 36 Kg2 Nac5 37 Qa8+ 1-0

Forcing mate after 37...Ra7 38 Qxc6+ Kxa5 39 Qb5. Not a good advert for the exchange on f3, although it's true that Black's play could be improved at various stages.

Game 43
□ **A.Roizman** ■ **W.Uhlmann**
USSR 1966

---

1 Nf3 d5 2 g3 Nf6 3 Bg2 c6 4 0-0 Bg4 5 d3 Nbd7 6 Nbd2 e6 7 h3 Bh5 8 e4 Be7 9 Qe2 0-0 10 g4 (Diagram 9)

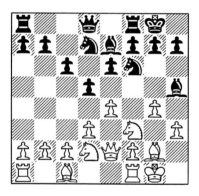 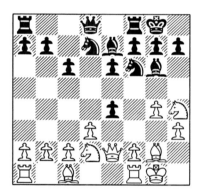

Diagram 9 (B)	Diagram 10 (W)
Lunging with g3-g4	Careful!

This is the most obvious way to continue the attack, but there are other options for White. 10 e5 Ne8 is possible although, as we've noted before, White is often reluctant to release the tension in this way. 10 b3 followed by Bb2 remains an option, while in A.Karpov-V.Anand, Lausanne (7th matchgame) 1998, the ex-world champion kept his options open by playing 10 Re1, the game continuing 10...dxe4 11 dxe4 e5 12 b3 Qc7 13 Bb2 Rfe8 14 Qf1 (to release the f3-knight) 14...Rad8 15 a3 b5 16 Bc3 Bf8 17 Nh4 Nc5 with a roughly level position.

10...Bg6

Black can also flick in 10...dxe4!? 11 dxe4 (11 Nxe4!?) before retreating with 11...Bg6 because now the plausible 12 Nh4? loses a pawn to the trick 12...Bxe4! 13 Nxe4 Nxe4 14 Qxe4 Bxh4. Instead in B.Damljanovic-E.Geller, Vrsac 1987, White continued with 12 Rd1 Qc7 and only now did he play 13 Nh4. With the insertion of Rd1 and ...Qc7, the 'trick' 13...Bxe4? fails after 14 Nxe4 Nxe4 15 Qxe4! Bxh4 16 g5! when the bishop is trapped on h4. So the game continued 13...Rad8 14 Nxg6 hxg6 15 Nf3 e5 16 b3 Nc5! when White had successfully traded off Black's bishop but the plan of ...Ne6-f4 gave Black good counterplay.

11 Nh4

11 Nh2?! plans f2-f4 but 11...e5! is a good reply. Now 12 f4?! exf4 13 Rxf4 Bd6 14 Rf1 Qc7 15 Nhf3 Rfe8 leaves White in some trouble.

11...dxe4 (Diagram 10) 12 Nxg6!

WARNING: The careless capture 12 dxe4? loses a pawn after 12...Bxe4!.

12...hxg6 13 Nxe4!

It's to White's advantage to open up the structure for his two bishops. After 13 dxe4 Black plays 13...e5 and follows up with ...Nc5-e6 à la Geller.

13...Nxe4 14 Qxe4 e5 15 b4?

This move, preparing Bb2, gives Black an easy hook on which to base his counterplay. Suetin suggested opening the position further with 15 d4, which looks sensible, while V.Savon-I.Farago, Kiev 1978 was agreed drawn after 15 f4 exf4 16 Bxf4 Nc5 17 Qc4. This second line also looks a bit better for White – the bishops are beginning to enjoy the open spaces.

15...a5!

Obvious and good.

16 b5

Otherwise White would have to capture on a5, leaving him with clear pawn weaknesses. That said, his structure doesn't look too clever in the game either.

16...cxb5 17 Qxb7 Rb8 18 Qd5 Qc7 19 a4

Or 19 c4 b4! and Black will follow up with ...Nc5 and ...Rfd8, targeting d3.

19...b4 20 f4? (Diagram 11)

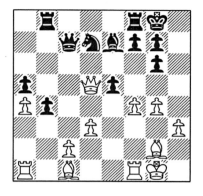

Diagram 11 (B)
Too rash

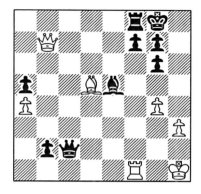

Diagram 12 (W)
Touchdown is imminent

Desperately trying to keep the initiative, but in truth it was time to hunker down with 20 Be3 Rfd8 21 Rfc1, even if this does look depressing for White.

20...Qxc2!

Spotting a vulnerability in the a1-rook.

21 Qxd7 Bc5+ 22 Kh1 Bd4 23 fxe5

23 Be3 loses to 23...Bxa1! 24 Rxa1 b3 and ...b2.

23...Bxa1 24 Bg5 Bxe5 25 Be7 b3!

Nothing's going to stop this pawn.

26 Bxf8 Rxf8 27 d4 b2! 28 Qb7 Bxd4 29 Bd5 Be5 0-1 (Diagram 12)

Threatening mate on h2. The game could finish 30 Bxf7+ Kh8 31 Qg2 b1Q.

Black Plays ...e5

Playing ...e7-e5 over ...e7-e6 is a double-edged sword. On one hand Black obtains more space and freedom of movement for his pieces; on the other hand, his centre is less secure and White may also be able to use the f5-square to his advantage.

1 Nf3 d5 2 g3 Nf6

Another possible move order to reach the main line position after six moves is 2...c6 3 Bg2 Bg4 4 0-0 Nd7 5 d3 Ngf6 6 Nbd2 e5, although even here White could play 4 b3 – compare with the note to White's 5th move.

3 Bg2 c6 4 0-0 Bg4 5 d3

> NOTE: If White decides on a double fianchetto here then Black has more difficulties arranging ...e7-e5.

After 5 b3 Nbd7 6 Bb2 **(Diagram 13)**

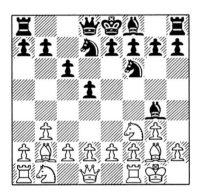

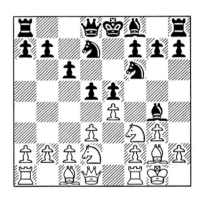

Diagram 13 (B)	Diagram 14 (B)
Preventing ...e7-e5	White plays e2-e4

the only way for Black to force through ...e7-e5 is with 6...Qc7, but this is not necessarily a move that Black would freely play otherwise.

5...Nbd7 6 Nbd2 e5 7 e4 (Diagram 14)

The main move here, although of course many players opt for 7 h3 first.

7...dxe4

Black releases the tension in the centre before placing his bishop on its most active square. 7...Bd6 is Black's most common alternative (see Game 44), while 7...Bc5!? is less common but also looks reasonable – I'm not 100% sure why Black is meant to capture on e4 so quickly. Perhaps it's because of the possibility of 8 h3 Bh5 9 exd5 cxd5 10 d4!.

8 dxe4 Bc5 9 h3 Bh5

9...Bxf3 10 Qxf3 gives the sort of position we've seen before. Black's position is solid but he hasn't any real active prospects, and White can massage his small advantages, which include the bishop pair. The game R.Vaganian-J.Piket, Bundesliga 1996 is worth quoting in full because it demonstrates how White can create serious winning chances from seemingly simple positions: 10...Qe7 11 a4 a5 12 Nc4 Qe6 13 b3 Nb6 14 Nxb6 Bxb6 15 Ba3 0-0-0 16 Rfd1 Rxd1+ 17 Rxd1 Rd8 18 Rxd8+ Kxd8 19 Bf1! (a typical way to reactivate this bishop) 19...Ke8 20 Kg2 Nd7 21 Bc4 Qf6 22 Qxf6 Nxf6 **(Diagram 15)**

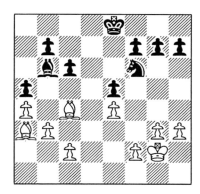

Diagram 15 (W)
Utilising the bishop pair

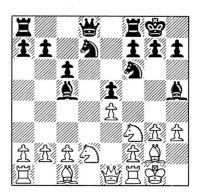

Diagram 16 (W)
Play on both sides

23 f3 Nd7 24 f4 Bc5 25 Bc1 (of course White wants to keep both bishops on the board) 25...Ke7 26 Kf3 h6 27 h4 Bb4 28 Bb2 Bd6 29 Bf1 f6 30 h5 Nc5 31 Bc4 Nd7 32 Kg4 (the king infiltrates the weak light squares) 32...Bb4 33 Kf5 b6 34 Ba6 Be1 35 Bc8! exf4 (or 35...Bxg3 36 Bxd7 Kxd7 37 fxe5 fxe5 38 Bxe5 Bxe5 39 Kxe5 Ke7 40 Kf5 Kf7 41 e5 with a winning pawn ending) 36 Bxd7! (finally giving up the bishop pair to simplify to a winning ending) 36...Kxd7 37 gxf4 Ke7 38 Kg6 Bd2 39 f5 Kf8 40 e5 fxe5 41 Bxe5 and Black resigned. Excellent technique from Vaganian, who is a real fan of this KIA line.

10 Qe1!

Releasing the pin on the f3-knight so that it can move (probably to h4 and then to f5).

10 Qe2 is clearly also possible, but after 10...0-0 White has fewer possi-

bilities if he wishes to play solely on the kingside. One idea is 11 g4 Bg6 12 Nh4, but then Black will reply with 12...Re8! followed by ...Nf8-e6, eyeing that f4-outpost.

 NOTE: The 'trick' 12...Bxe4 doesn't work here: 13 Bxe4! Nxe4 14 Nxe4 Qxh4 15 Bg5! Qxh3 16 Rad1 with the double threat of Rxd7 and Rd3, trapping the queen.

10...0-0 (Diagram 16)

Strategies

White has quite a few opportunities here to play on both sides of the board. The plan of Nh4-f5, a king move and a timely f2-f4 is one option, while there are also expansion ideas on the queenside, including Nc4, a2-a4 and perhaps b2-b4 and Bb2. Black's plans are less clear – he tends to play a more reactive role. See Game 45 for further details.

Statistics

Taking the position after 6...e5, White has only scored 48% from around 1000 games. The success rate climbs a little if we only take games from the position after 10 Qe1 (51% from 130 games).

Game 44
□ R.Tibensky ■ F.Berkes
Austria 2003

1 Nf3 d5 2 g3 Nf6 3 Bg2 c6 4 0-0 Bg4 5 d3 Nbd7 6 Nbd2 e5 7 e4 Bd6

With this move Black prefers to keep the tension in the centre, at least for the moment. In this case the bishop is usually better off on d6 because on c5 it could be hit by a timely d3-d4.

8 h3 Bh5 (Diagram 17) 9 Qe1

Sticking to the traditional way of handling the position, White prepares Nh4. In recent years White has also been trying a completely different approach starting with 9 exd5!? cxd5 10 c4!, directly attacking Black's centre.

There are two main options for Black here. The first is to advance in the centre with 10...d4 leading to a Modern Benoni structure. Now the continuation 11 Qe2 0-0 12 g4! Bg6 13 Nh4! has occurred in more than one game; White will exchange Black's danger bishop on g6 and then try to expand on the queenside with a2-a3 and b2-b4.

Black's second option is to ignore the attack by playing 10...0-0 when a few games have continued 11 cxd5 Nxd5 12 Qb3; White has given up the centre but has quite a few active possibilities – Nc4 or Ne4 is coming up next.

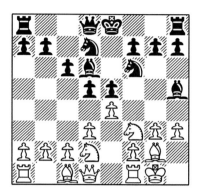

Diagram 17 (W)
Tradition or fashion?

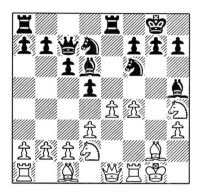

Diagram 18 (W)
Inviting a fork

9...0-0 10 Nh4 Re8

Discouraging White from playing f2-f4 by putting his rook on the same file as White's queen...

11 f4?

But White goes ahead anyway! To be fair to Tibensky, this move had been played quite a few times previously without it being severely punished as in this game. In hindsight White should probably opt for a quieter continuation like 11 Nf5! Bf8 and now perhaps 12 b3 followed by Bb2 or 12 Nf3 followed by N3h4.

11...exf4 12 gxf4 Qc7! (Diagram 18)

A major improvement over the line given by *ECO*: 12...dxe4 13 dxe4 Nd5 14 Nc4! Bc5+ 15 Kh1 N7b6 16 Ne5 Nb4 17 Nf5! Bg6 18 Qc3 Bf8 19 Ng3 with an edge for White, Ki.Georgiev-E.Torre, Saint John 1988.

13 e5

What else?

13...Nxe5! 14 fxe5 Rxe5! 15 Qf2!

The right choice; 15 Qg3? Re2 16 Qg5 h6! 17 Qf5 Be5! (Berkes) leaves White in big trouble as it's difficult to see a good answer to the threat of ...g7-g6, trapping the queen.

15...Re2 16 Qf5 Bc5+!

There's already a draw by repetition on offer with 16...Re5 17 Qf2 Re2 18 Qf5 Re5, but not surprisingly Black is after more.

17 Kh1 Qg3 18 Ndf3?

Erring in a very difficult position. White had to force a trade of queens at any cost. After 18 Qf4! Qxf4 19 Rxf4 Black can regain material with 19...Be3!, but 20 Rxf6! gxf6 21 Ndf3 Bb6 22 Bd2 Rae8 (Berkes) still leaves White well in the game.

18...Bd6! (Diagram 19)

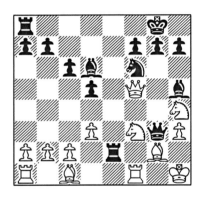
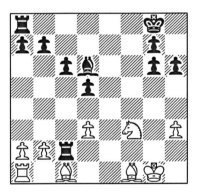

Diagram 19 (W)
Trouble on board

Diagram 20 (W)
No survival hopes

Threatening simply to capture on f3 followed by mate on either g2 or h2. The move 19 Qg5 is no good on account of 19...Rxg2! 20 Nxg2 Qxh3+ 21 Kg1 Bxf3.

19 Rg1 19...Bg6! 20 Qg5 Nh5 21 Rf1!

The only move, as Black was threatening mate with 21...Qxg5! 22 Bxg5 Ng3+ 23 Kh2 Ne4+ 24 Kh1 Nf2.

21...h6 22 Qxg3 Nxg3+ 23 Kg1 Nxf1 24 Bxf1 Rxc2 25 Nxg6 fxg6

(Diagram 20)

Somehow White has managed survive to the endgame, but Black's attack continues and he is even material ahead.

26 d4 Rf8 27 Bg2 g5 28 Ne1 Re2 29 Nd3 Bg3 30 a4 Rc2 31 b4 Rc3 0-1

One possible finish is 32 Nc5 Rf2! 33 Nxb7 Rcc2!. On the basis of this game it seems that 11 f4 is premature.

Game 45
□ **L.Aronian** ■ **K.Asrian**
World Junior Championship, Yerevan 1999

---

1 Nf3 Nf6 2 g3 d5 3 Bg2 c6 4 0-0 Bg4 5 d3 Nbd7 6 Nbd2 e5 7 e4 dxe4 8 dxe4 Bc5 9 h3 Bh5 10 Qe1 0-0 11 Nc4

The immediate 11 Nh4 is also playable, but White prefers to organise his queenside first. In any case, White is certainly not afraid of an exchange on f3.

11...Re8 12 a4 Qc7

Challenging White's c4-knight with 12...Nb6 is a serious alternative because an exchange on b6 frees Black's position and 13 Ne3? drops a pawn to 13...Nxe4. Instead in S.Movsesian-Z.Gyimesi, Ohrid 2001 White continued with 13 Na5! Qc7 14 Nh4 Nfd7 15 b4! Bf8 16 c4 c5 17 b5 and he enjoyed some extra space on the queenside.

13 Nh4 Rad8 14 Bg5 Bg6?! (Diagram 21)

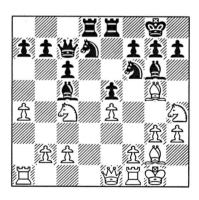
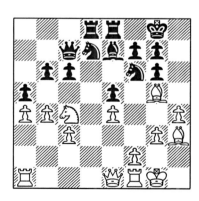

Diagram 21 (W)
Too accommodating

Diagram 22 (B)
Taking control

This is too accommodating. One of Aronian's later opponents showed the way forward for Black here: 14...h6! 15 Bd2 Nh7! (again a black knight heads for e6) 16 Kh1 Nb6 17 Ne3 Ng5 18 Ba5 Ne6 with a level position, L.Aronian-Z.Hracek, Bundesliga 2001. Black doesn't have to be worried by the possibility of 19 g4 Bg6 20 Nxg6 fxg6 – Black's pawns have been split, but there is a wonderful outpost on f4 and Black may be able to use the half-open f-file.

15 Nxg6 hxg6 16 c3 a5 17 h4!

Planning to activate the light-squared bishop via h3.

17...b6 18 Bh3 Be7 19 b4! (Diagram 22)

White has the initiative on both sides of the board. Understandably Black tries to liquidate the pawns on the queenside, but he's not totally successful.

19...axb4 20 cxb4 b5 21 axb5 cxb5 22 Na5 Nb6 23 Qe2! Nc4

Black would love to eliminate White's b4-pawn with 23...Bxb4 but he is living on the edge after 24 Rfc1, for example 24...Qd6 25 Nc6! Ra8 26 Qxb5 Rxa1 27 Rxa1 Bc3 28 Ra6! and the pressure is becoming unbearable.

24 Rfc1 Rd4!

24...Bxb4 leads to a trade of the queenside pawns with 25 Nxc4 bxc4 26 Rxc4 Qe7, but White's initiative persists with 27 h5 when 27...gxh5?! 28 Bxf6! gxf6 29 Qxh5 gives Black a real headache over his king.

25 Be3!

A deep temporary pawn sacrifice, which dramatically brings the bishop on h3 to life.

25...Rxe4 26 Bg2 Rg4

26...Rxe3 27 fxe3 e4! 28 Nxc4 bxc4 29 Rxc4 Qxg3 gives Black good compensation for the small material deficit as White's king is shaky. However, White can improve with 27 Qxe3! Nxe3 28 Rxc7 Nxg2, and now the clever 29 Nc6! Bd6 30 Rb7 leaves the knight on g2 trapped – this ending should be winning for White.

27 Bc6 Rb8 28 Nxc4 Rxc4 29 Rxc4 bxc4 30 b5! (Diagram 23)

Aronian must have seen this idea when he played his 25th move. Now the b-pawn is a long-term danger for Black, and White will restore material equality by picking up the doomed c-pawn.

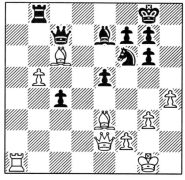

Diagram 23 (B)
The point

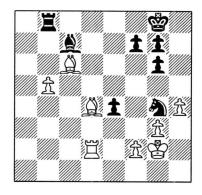

Diagram 24 (B)
A powerful b-pawn

30...c3 31 Qc4 c2 32 Rc1 e4 33 Qe2 Bd6 34 Kg2 Qa5 35 Rxc2 Bc7 36 Qd2

White is happy to trade queens. The b-pawn combined with the bishop pair should be enough to force a winning position.

36...Ng4 37 Bd4 Qxd2 38 Rxd2 (Diagram 24) 38...e3

Or 38...f5 39 Ba7! Rf8 40 b6 Bb8 41 Bd5+ Kh7 42 Bxb8 Rxb8 43 b7 Ne5 44 Rc2 Nd7 45 Rc8 followed by Bc6.

39 fxe3 Ne5 40 Rc2 Nxc6 41 Rxc6 Ba5 42 b6 Kf8 43 Kf3 1-0

Black could struggle on for a few more moves, but with White's king marching up the board the ending is hopeless for Black; e.g. 43 Kf3 Ke8 44 Ke4 Kd7 45 Kd5 Rb7 46 Rd6+ Kc8 47 Kc6 etc.

The Double Fianchetto

Just as against ...Bf5 systems, White often fianchettoes his queen's bishop early on. One advantage of this is that it makes it more difficult for Black to play ...e5.

1 Nf3 d5 2 g3 Nf6 3 Bg2 c6 4 0-0 Bg4 5 b3 (Diagram 25) 5...Nbd7 6 Bb2 e6

Black can force through ...e7-e5 by playing ...Qc7 or by trading on f3 without any provocation. Following 6...Bxf3!? 7 Bxf3 e5 8 d3 Bc5 9 e4 dxe4 10 dxe4 0-0 11 Nd2 we reach the type of quiet position that has been discussed before, with White enjoying a small but long-term advantage.

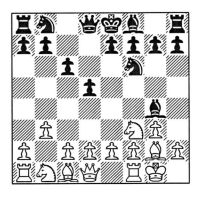

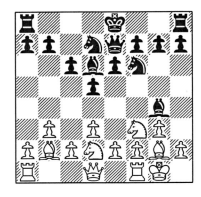

Diagram 25 (B)	Diagram 26 (W)
White plays 5 b3	Intending ...Ba3

7 d3 Bd6

The more active 7...Bc5 is covered in Game 46, while 7...Be7 has also been played many times. A typical continuation is 8 Nbd2 0-0 9 h3 Bh5 10 e4 a5 11 a4 (or 11 a3) when White's basic plan is Qe1, a knight move from f3 and then f2-f4 etc.

8 Nbd2 0-0

8...Qe7!? **(Diagram 26)**, intending to offer an exchange of bishops with ...Ba3, has been played quite a few times.

In the game M.Gundlach-J.Wegerle, Dresden 2003 Black succeeded in 'killing' the position after 9 e4 Ba3! 10 Qc1 Bxb2 11 Qxb2 dxe4 12 dxe4 Bxf3!? 13 Nxf3 e5; this type of position is nothing for White unless he has the bishop pair.

With this in mind, it makes sense to avoid the exchange of bishops by playing 9 a3. The very recent game Art.Minasian-M.Grabarczyk, European Championship, Warsaw 2005 is worth seeing because it highlights a problem with having the queen on e7 together with the bishop on d6: 9...0-0 10 h3 Bh5 11 Qe1! a5 12 e4 (threatening e4-e5) 12...dxe4 13 dxe4 Bxf3 (or 13...e5 14 Nh4! with the idea of Nf5) 14 Nxf3 e5 15

Nh4! g6 16 f4! b5 17 f5 a4 18 b4 c5 19 c3 Nb6 20 Bc1! Nfd7 21 Ra2 cxb4 22 cxb4 Nc4 23 Raf2 Bc7 24 Kh2 Bb6 25 Rf3 Rfd8 26 g4 and White had built up a very promising attack on the kingside.

9 h3 Bh5 (Diagram 27)

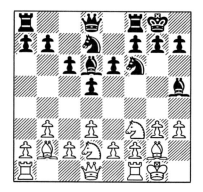

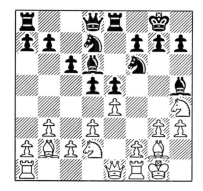

Diagram 27 (W)
10 e4 or 10 Qe1?

Diagram 28 (B)
White shows his hand

10 e4

If White for some reason wishes to avoid the next note then he can play 10 Qe1 followed by e2-e4.

10...e5

Black was forced to do something as White was threatening to play g3-g4 followed by a fork with e4-e5.

The other option was 10...dxe4 11 dxe4 and now after 11...Be5 White should decline the offer of the exchange with 12 c3!. At first sight this looks a bit ugly, but Black's bishop is vulnerable on e5 as White has g3-g4 in his locker. V.Akopian-A.Beliavsky, Linares 1995 continued 12...Bc7 13 Ba3! Re8 14 Qc2 a5 15 Nd4 Qb8 16 Rae1 with a better position for White.

11 Qe1!

This move should be second nature by now!

11...Re8

Defending the e-pawn, which was becoming a concern. It certainly makes sense to place the rook on the same file as White's queen because this may well help Black in the tactics if the position opens up.

12 Nh4 (Diagram 28)

Strategies

White's plan is quite clear – he is preparing to attack on the kingside with Nf5 and f2-f4, which will bring the b2-bishop right into the game. On the other hand, Black is reasonably well placed to meet this onslaught, and a kingside attack by White does carry some risk as the position will undoubtedly open up. If Black trades on e4 in the near future White will obtain the c4-square for his knight and he may explore queenside possibilities with Nc4 and a2-a4 etc. However, it's more difficult for White to do anything constructive on the queenside if Black keeps the tension in the centre. See Game 47 for further details.

Statistics

From the position after 5 b3, White has scored 54% from around 300 games, and from Diagram 28 White has scored 51% from just over 100 games.

Game 46
□ **B.Chatalbashev** ■ **M.Palac**
Bled Olympiad 2002

1 b3

You can even reach the KIA from 1 b3!

1...d5 2 Bb2 Bg4 3 g3 Nd7 4 Bg2 c6 5 Nf3 Ngf6 6 0-0 e6 7 d3 Bc5 8 Nbd2

Continuing in KIA fashion. Black must also be ready for White to transpose to a queen's pawn opening with 8 d4 Bd6 9 c4.

8...0-0 9 e4 (Diagram 29) 9...dxe4

Following the traditional plan when having a bishop on c5: trading on e4 and then playing a quick ...e6-e5. However, there's also a case for keeping the status quo in the centre. Of course Black must be ready for White's e4-e5, but we've already seen how effective Black's light-squared bishop may become in this scenario. The only problem Black experiences is that the bishop on c5 sometimes obstructs his queenside counterattack. An example: 10 a3 b5 11 h3 Bh5 12 Qe1 Ne8 13 Kh1 Nc7 14 e5!? Bb6 (Black wants to push the c-pawn so the bishop is forced to move again) 15 Nh2 c5 16 g4 Bg6 17 f4 f5 18 exf6 Nxf6 19 Nhf3 with a very complex middlegame, M.Bezold-J.Kipper, Münster 1996.

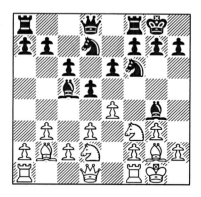

Diagram 29 (B)
To capture or not?

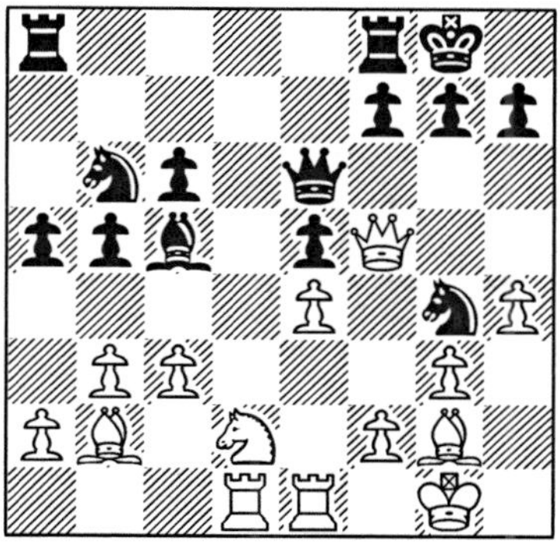

Diagram 30 (W)
Ideal for Black

10 dxe4 e5 11 h3 Bxf3

Even though every game I have found has continued with this trade, it's not entirely forced. After 11...Bh5 White can grab the e5-pawn with 12 g4?! Bg6 13 Nxe5 Nxe5 14 Bxe5, but following 14...Re8! White must either return the pawn immediately or give Black all the dark squares in the position with the very ugly 15 Bxf6 Qxf6 – not to be recommended!

Instead of 12 g4, White should continue with the familiar 12 Qe1! when both Nh4-f5 and Nc4 followed by a2-a4 come into the equation.

12 Qxf3 a5

The game Z.Ribli-M.Tal, Montpellier 1985 is worth giving because it illustrates some model play on Black's part: 12...Qe7 13 Rad1?! b5! 14 h4 a5! (Black wants to play ...a5-a4, exchange on b3 and then annoy White with ...Ra2) 15 c3 (blocking the bishop, but at least now 15...a4 can be met by 16 b4, keeping things blocked) 15...Nb6 16 Rfe1?! (16 Bh3!) 16...Qe6! 17 Qf5 Ng4! **(Diagram 30)** when White was suddenly in real trouble. The rest of the game witnesses some typical Tal fireworks: 18 Re2 Rad8 19 Bf3 Rd3! 20 Kg2 (or 20 Bxg4 Rxg3+!) 20...Nxf2! 21 Rxf2 Bxf2 22 Kxf2 Qd6 23 Bc1 g6 24 Qg5 f6 25 Qh6 f5! 26 Kg2 Rxf3! 27 Nxf3 (27 Kxf3 loses to 27...Qd3+ 28 Kg2 Qe2+) 27...Qxd1 28 Ng5 and White resigned before Black could play 28...Qh5.

In this game 13 Rad1?! was the culprit that allowed Black to seize the initiative on the queenside. A much better example from White's point of view is 13 a4! Rfd8 14 Nc4 Ne8?! 15 Rfd1 f6?! 16 Bf1! (moving to a better diagonal) 16...Nf8 17 Ne3 Ne6 18 Nf5 Qf7 19 Bc4 and White's light-squared bishop was really beginning to show its influence, J.Urban-B.Lengyel, Budapest 1993.

13 Nc4 Qc7 14 a4!

Making sure that Black cannot play ...a5-a4 after ...b7-b5 as in the Tal game.

14...b5 15 Ne3 Rfe8 16 Rfd1 bxa4

Temporarily giving White the stronger structure on the queenside, but Black's plan is to exchange pawns with ...Nb6 and ...a5-a4.

17 Rxa4 Nb6 18 Raa1 a4 19 Nf5 Bf8 20 Nh6+! Kh8 21 bxa4 (Diagram 31)

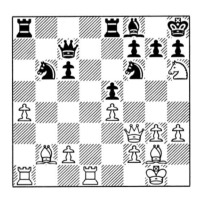

Diagram 31 (B)
The a-pawn is taboo

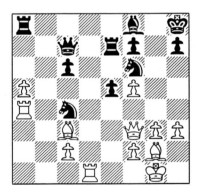

Diagram 32 (B)
26 Ra4!

21...Re6

Recapturing on a4 runs into tactical problems after 21...Nxa4 22 Qb3! Reb8 (or 22...Nxb2 23 Nxf7+ Kg8 24 Nxe5+ Kh8 25 Nf7+ Kg8 26 Nd6+

Kh8 27 Nxe8) 23 Qxf7! Qxf7 (23...Qb6 allows a nice smothered mate after 24 Qg8+!! Nxg8 25 Nf7) 24 Nxf7+ Kg8 25 Bxe5 when White has two extra pawns.

22 Nf5 g6

Trying to chase away the annoying knight, but Black is in for a shock. 22...Nxa4 is undesirable as it leaves Black in a self-pin, so perhaps the safest is 22...Rxa4, even if White still keeps some advantage here.

23 a5! Nc4

Now Black is attacking two pieces...

24 Bc3!

So White simply sacrifices one in order to unleash his bishop on g2!

24...gxf5 25 exf5 Re7?

Black has much better chances of holding on after 25...Rd6! 26 Rxd6 Bxd6 27 Qxc6 Ra7.

26 Ra4! (Diagram 32)

I imagine Black missed the strength of this move. After 26...Nxa5 27 Rda1! White regains his piece, so Black's knight is forced back to d6 and his position falls apart.

26...Nd6 27 Qxc6 Qxc6 28 Bxc6 Rd8 29 a6 Ra7

Otherwise White would play a6-a7, but now Black's e5-pawn drops too.

30 Bxe5 Be7 31 g4!

White's pawns are unrelenting!

31...Kg8 32 g5 Nfe8 33 f6 Bf8 34 Bxe8 Rxe8 35 Bxd6 Rd8 36 Rad4 Rxa6 37 Be7! 1-0

Game 47
□ **V.Akopian** ■ **S.Ionov**
El Vendrell 1996

---

1 Nf3 Nf6 2 g3 d5 3 Bg2 c6 4 0-0 Bg4 5 b3 Nbd7 6 Bb2 e6 7 d3 Bd6 8 Nbd2 0-0 9 h3 Bh5 10 e4 e5 11 Qe1 Re8 12 Nh4 Nc5

Black has tried quite a few different moves in this position. Here are a couple:

a) 12...dxe4 13 dxe4 Bf8 14 Nf5 Qc7 15 a4 Nc5 16 f4?! (16 Nc4 is probably more sensible here) 16...exf4 17 Bxf6 gxf6 18 gxf4 (perhaps 18

Rxf4!?) 18...Bg6 19 Qg3 Rad8 20 Rf2 Rxd2! 21 Rxd2 Nxe4 22 Bxe4 Rxe4 23 Rad1 Qxf4 24 Qxf4 Rxf4 when Black's bishop pair and two extra pawns provided him with more than enough compensation for the exchange, V.Akopian-S.Shipov, Berlin 1996.

b) 12...a5 13 a3 Bc5 14 Kh1! Nf8 15 f4!? (15 Nf5 is the more solid option) 15...exf4 16 gxf4 dxe4 17 Nxe4!? (17 dxe4 Bd4 18 Bxd4 Qxd4 19 e5 Bg6 20 Qf2 Qxf2 21 Rxf2 Nd5 22 Nc4 looks a bit better for White, S.Bjarnason-E.Mednis, Reykjavik 1982) 17...Nxe4 18 dxe4 f6 19 Qg3 Bg6 20 f5 Bh5 21 e5 with a promising attack for White, B.Damljanovic-J.Hodgson, Belgrade 1993.

> **NOTE: As these previous two variations illustrate, the assessment of the position often depends on the success of White's f2-f4 advance.**

13 Nf5 Bc7!?

13...Bf8 is the normal retreat for the bishop, against which Akopian suggests 14 f4!? exf4 15 Rxf4.

14 f4!? (Diagram 33)

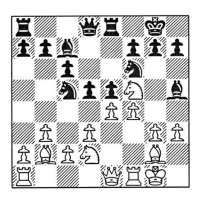

Diagram 33 (B)
Showing no fear

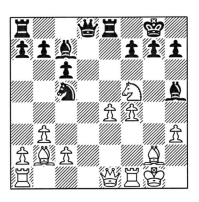

Diagram 34 (B)
Targeting g7

The complications begin...

14...exf4 15 gxf4 dxe4?

In his notes to the game Akopian identified this move as a mistake, after which White obtains an irresistible attack. He suggested the sensible 15...Bg6 as an improvement, and eight years later it got an over-the-board testing: 16 Ng3 dxe4 17 Ndxe4 Nfxe4 18 dxe4 Qh4 19 Qc3 Ne6 20 Kh1 f6 (20...Bxf4? 21 Nf5! gives Black problems) 21 e5 Bb6 22 Rad1 fxe5 23 f5! Bd4 24 Rxd4! exd4 25 Qd3 Rad8 26 fxg6 with a plus for White, Z.Rahman-H.Stefansson, Calvia Olympiad 2004, although there could well be improvements for both sides here.

16 Nxe4!

It's a good decision to trade a pair of knights. After 16 dxe4? Bg6!, with ...Ba5 coming too, White's centre is under considerable pressure.

16...Nfxe4 17 dxe4 (Diagram 34) 17...Ne6

White's attack runs very smoothly, with the fianchettoed bishop on b2 playing a major role. The difficulties Black faces are illustrated very well in the simple variation 17...f6? 18 Qh4 Bg6 19 Rad1! Qc8 20 Nxg7!, when White crashes through on f6.

18 Qg3 Bg6 19 Rad1 Qb8?

Up to here this game had actually all been played before in V.Jansa-R.Keene, Aarhus 1983. That encounter had continued 19...Nxf4 20 Qxf4! Bxf4 21 Rxd8 Raxd8 22 Rxf4 Rd1+ 23 Rf1 when White's two minor pieces outweighed the rook in the ending. Akopian had obviously done his homework, even improving on some of Jansa's original analysis later on.

20 Qc3! Bxf4

After 20...f6 21 Nxg7! Nxg7 22 Qxf6 Nh5 23 Qc3 Black's king has little or no chance of surviving down the long diagonal, while following Jansa's 21...Nxf4, *Fritz* ignores the threat of ...Ne2+ and wins with 22 Nxe8! Ne2+ 23 Kh1 Nxc3 24 Nxf6+ Kg7 25 Bxc3 Be5 26 Nd7.

21 Rxf4! Qxf4 22 Rf1! (Diagram 35)

Jansa had dismissed this line on account of 22 Nxg7? Red8 23 Rf1 Qd2, which is unclear, but 22 Rf1 answers all the questions.

22...f6

Or 22...Qg5 23 h4! when White wins after 23...Qg4 24 Nh6+! and 23...Qh5 24 Bf3 (Akopian).

23 Rxf4 Nxf4 24 Qf3

With a queen and minor piece against two rooks, White has a decisive material advantage. Akopian finishes the game in pleasing fashion.

24...Nxg2 25 Nh6+! Kh8

25...gxh6 26 Qxf6 and there's no avoiding the mate on the diagonal.

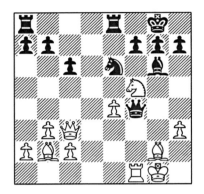

Diagram 35	Diagram 36
An improvement	Finishing in style

26 Qxf6! (Diagram 36)

Inviting Black to allow a finish in style after 26...gxf6 27 Bxf6 mate.

26...Rg8 27 Qf2 Rge8 28 Qf6 Rg8 29 Qf2 Rge8 30 Kxg2 Rxe4 31 Qf6! Rg8 32 Qc3 Re2+ 33 Kg3 1-0

Following 33...Rxc2 White has one more trick up his sleeve with 34 Qxc2! Bxc2 35 Nf7 mate. A fine game by Akopian/Jansa(!) which illustrates the depth of White's attacking chances with the f2-f4 plan.

Black Plays ...Bd6 and ...Ne7

Another way for Black to play this system is to develop the bishop to d6 and the knight to e7. On e7 the knight has less influence on the central squares, but there are certainly some positives for Black too. For one thing, on e7 the knight isn't such a target in White's kingside attack, while Black also has the option of moving his f-pawn. This line reminds me of Black's set-up with ...Bd6 and ...Ne7 in the 'KIA versus the French' and there are many positional similarities.

1 Nf3 d5 2 g3 c6 3 Bg2 Bg4 4 0-0 Nd7 5 d3

NOTE: White can avoid the ...Bd6/...Ne7 system by employing the double fianchetto with 5 b3 e6 6 Bb2.

Unless Black is willing to play the ugly ...f7-f6, there's no way for him to reach his desired set-up with ...Bd6 and ...Ne7 without leaving the g-pawn en prise.

 WARNING: If White plays in this manner, he should be aware of Black's option of playing a caveman-style attack with 6...h5!? (Diagram 37).

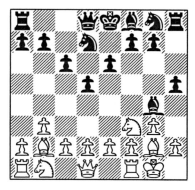

Diagram 37 (W)
Caveman chess

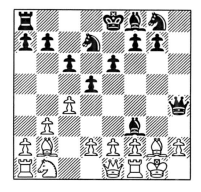

Diagram 38 (W)
10...Bg4-f3!!

There's certainly an argument here for White to stop any nonsense on the kingside with 7 h4, as allowing Black to play ...h5-h5 could lead to some alarms. Strictly speaking, it's not really KIA territory, but I can't resist quoting some analysis from the correspondence database *MegaCorr 3*: 7 c4 h4! 8 Nxh4 Rxh4! 9 gxh4 Qxh4 10 Qe1? (preparing to meet 10...Bd6 with 11 f4) 10...Bf3!! **(Diagram 38)** and suddenly White has no defence to the threat of ...Bd6, for example 11 h3 Bd6 (threatening ...Qf4) 12 Ba3 c5 13 e3 Qg5 and White will be mated on g2.

Another miniature that will serve to put White players off this line continued 7 d3 h4! 8 e4? (8 Nxh4 Rxh4 9 gxh4 Qxh4 gives Black obvious compensation, but this is still probably White's best course) 8...hxg3 9 hxg3 dxe4 10 dxe4 Qa5! 11 Nbd2 Qh5 12 Re1 0-0-0 13 Qe2 Bb4 14 c3 Ne5! 15 Qe3 (or 15 cxb4 Rxd2!) 15...Nxf3+ 16 Nxf3 Bc5 17 Qf4 g5! 18 Nxg5 f6 and White resigned in K.Zolnierowicz-A.Stripunsky, Pardubice

1994 on account of 19 Nf3 e5!. There's no finesse to 6...h5!? but it certainly looks very effective!

5...e6 6 Nbd2 Bd6 7 e4

Another typical continuation is 7 b3 Ne7 8 Bb2 0-0 9 h3 Bh5 10 e4 a5! when White must decide whether to play a3 or a4. The encounter E.Kengis-S.Smagin, USSR 1988 continued 11 a3 b5 12 g4 Bg6 13 e5 Bc7 14 Qe2 c5! 15 Ne1 a4 16 f4 with a complicated middlegame.

7...Ne7 (Diagram 39)

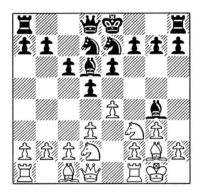

Diagram 39 (W)
The desired set-up

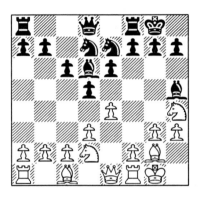

Diagram 40 (B)
The usual story

8 h3 Bh5 9 Qe1

Even against ...Ne7, this move is still the main way forward for White, although another way for White to continue is with 9 d4 0-0 10 c3, making use of the fact that without ...Nf6 there is no pressure on e4.

9...0-0 10 Nh4 (Diagram 40)

The usual story – White is preparing for kingside expansion with f2-f4. With no knight blocking the f-pawn, Black is ready to meet f2-f4 with the challenging ...f7-f5 or the restraining ...f7-f6. Play from this position is covered in Game 48. Alternatives for White include:

a) 10 e5 Bc7 11 b3 c5! 12 Bb2 Nc6 13 g4 Bg6 14 Qe2 Qb8! 15 Rfe1 Nb4 16 Nf1 d4! 17 Bc1 Nc6 18 Bf4 f6!, R.Eidelson-Y.Marrero, Calvia (Women's Olympiad) 2004, is a graphic illustration of what can happen to White if the e-pawn is pushed too early.

b) 10 Nh2!? is similar to 10 Nh4 in spirit, with White aiming for a quick f2-f4. For example, 10...e5 11 f4 exf4 12 gxf4 dxe4 13 dxe4 f6 14 Nc4 Bc7 15 a4 Ng6 16 Be3 Re8 with a roughly level position, G.Vujadinovic-B.Damljanovic, Cetinje 1993.

Statistics

White has scored only 46% in around 150 games from the position after 7...Ne7, but on average Black was rated quite a bit higher. Black's score with 5 b3 e6 6 Bb2 h5!? is a very impressive 72%.

Game 48
□ **M.Lazic** ■ **M.Dzevlan**
Kladovo 1991

1 Nf3 d5 2 g3 c6 3 Bg2 Bg4 4 0-0 Nd7 5 d3 e6 6 Nbd2 Bd6 7 e4 Ne7 8 h3 Bh5 9 Qe1 0-0 10 Nh4 Qb8?! (Diagram 41)

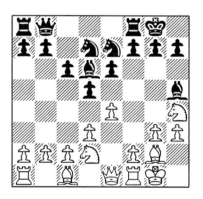

Diagram 41 (W)
Too clever

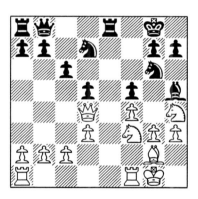

Diagram 42 (B)
Dark-squared control

An over-finesse – there's no reason not to put the queen on c7, which is a much better square than b8. After 10...Qc7! we have:

a) 11 d4!? Ng6 12 Nhf3 Bxf3 13 Nxf3 dxe4 14 Qxe4 e5 was equal in K.Langeweg-P.Keres, Amsterdam 1971.

b) 11 f4 f6 (11...f5 is also possible, meeting 12 e5 with 12...Bc5+ 13 Kh1 Bb6) 12 Nhf3 c5 13 Rf2 Nc6 14 Nf1 Bf7 15 Ne3 Rfe8 16 h4 b5 17 Bd2 a5 18 Qf1 a4 19 exd5 exd5 20 Nf5 Bf8 21 g4 when both sides were making gradual progress in their attacks, A.Akhmetov-A.Stripunsky, Orel 1996.

11 f4 f5!

After 11...f6? we see a problem with putting the queen on b8: 12 exd5 exd5 13 Qe6+! and White picks up the knight on d7.

12 exd5 exd5 13 Ndf3!

Beginning a plan of dark-squared control, especially on the squares e5 and d4. Note that the enticing 13 Qe6+? Bf7 14 Qxd7? now fails to 14...Rd8!, trapping the queen.

13...Re8 14 Qf2 Bc5 15 Be3 Bxe3 16 Qxe3 Ng6 17 Qd4! (Diagram 42) 17...Bxf3?

Allowing a simple intermezzo. Black must play 17...Nxh4 18 Nxh4 Rf8, although after 19 Rae1 White has a pleasant advantage.

18 Nxf5! Nf6 19 Bxf3 Qc7 20 Nh6+! Kf8 21 Ng4 Nxg4 22 Bxg4 Qd6 23 Rae1 b6 24 Kg2 Re7 25 Rxe7 Qxe7 26 Qc3 Qd6 27 Re1 d4 28 Qc4 b5 29 Re6! bxc4 30 Rxd6 Rb8 31 b3 cxd3 32 cxd3 c5 33 Rc6 Rb5 34 Rc8+ Kf7 35 Bh5 Kf6 36 Rc6+ 1-0

36...Kf5 saves material but allows mate in one with 37 Bg4.

Points to Remember

1) After an early h2-h3 by White, most of the time it pays for Black to retain his bishop with ...Bh5. The positions after an exchange on f3 are usually quiet in nature, with White having a small but stable advantage based on possessing the bishop pair.

2) The move Qd1-e1 is usually an important part of White's strategy. By unpinning on the h5-d1 diagonal, the knight on f3 is free to move, after which White is free to play f2-f4.

3) If Black plays his pawn to e5, this leaves a slight weakness on the f5-square, which White often exploits with Qe1 followed by Nh4-f5. If White chases the light-squared bishop away with h2-h3 and g3-g4, he must be wary of the new weakness created on f4. Black can often utilise this outpost by playing the manoeuvre ...Nd7-f8-e6.

4) When White employs a queenside fianchetto, Black sometimes plays an early ...Bd6 and ...Qe7 with the intention of offering a trade with ...Ba3. This exchange usually eases Black's position, so White will often prevent it by playing a2-a3.

Chapter Seven

The Queen's Indian and The Dutch

Introduction

I've covered most black set-ups against the KIA, but there are a couple more worth mentioning that Black can play against the 1 Nf3 move order: the Queen's Indian and the Dutch.

KIA versus the Queen's Indian

The Queen's Indian (3...b6) is a very respectable defence to 1 d4 Nf6 2 c4 e6 3 Nf3, and many Queen's Indian practitioners also look to play a queenside fianchetto against Réti, English and KIA systems.

Game 49
□ J.Kaplan ■ A.Pomar Salamanca
Madrid 1973

1 Nf3 Nf6 2 g3 b6 (Diagram 1)

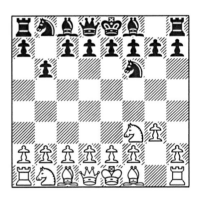
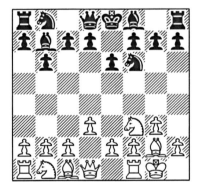

Diagram 1 (W)
Black plays 2...b6

Diagram 2 (B)
White plays d2-d3

Black can also play more aggressively on the queenside with 2...b5, the point of which is to avoid systems where White plays an early c2-c4. Of course this doesn't make any real difference to a KIA player, and a typical continuation from here would be 3 Bg2 Bb7 4 0-0 e6 5 d3 d5 6 Nbd2 Be7 7 e4! c5 8 Re1 0-0 9 e5 Nfd7 10 Nf1 leading to a position very similar to ones discussed in Chapter 1.

NOTE: 7...dxe4 8 dxe4 Nxe4? 9 Ne5! leaves Black in big trouble on the long diagonal.

Black can also play in a more restrained way with 5...Be7 6 e4 d6 7 Nbd2 c5 when one logical way for White to continue is 8 Nh4, preparing to expand on the kingside with f2-f4.

3 Bg2 Bb7 4 0-0 e6 5 d3 (Diagram 2)

Keeping the KIA flavour. 5 d4 is likely to transpose to the main line of the Queen's Indian.

5...d5

Forcing White to work to achieve e2-e4. Another option for Black is to move into Sicilian territory with 5...c5 6 e4 d6, reaching positions similar to the ones discussed in Chapter 2.

6 Nbd2 Nbd7!

Unlike the traditional main line in the French (see Chapter 1), Black refrains from playing ...c7-c5 as he hopes to use that square for either a knight or a bishop. The line 6...c5 7 e4 will probably transpose to Chapter 1 (7...dxe4?! 8 dxe4 Nxe4? 9 Ne5! again leaves Black in trouble).

7 Qe1!?

Not the most natural-looking move to play, but the logic behind it becomes apparent once the alternatives are examined:

a) After the logical 7 Re1 Black's idea is to play actively with 7...Bc5! **(Diagram 3)**.

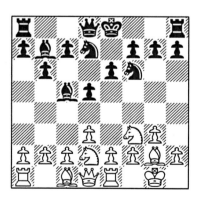

Diagram 3 (W)
Alarm bells should ring!

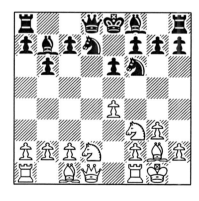

Diagram 4 (B)
Offering a gambit

WARNING: Black threatens 8...Bxf2+! 9 Kxf2 Ng4+! and ...Ne3, trapping the queen!

The point is that after the automatic 8 e4 dxe4 9 dxe4 Black has 9...Ng4!, rather justifying his 7th move. Instead of 8 e4, White should perhaps play the preparatory 8 h3, a typical continuation being 8...0-0 9 e4 dxe4 10 dxe4 e5 and now 11 Nh4, or 11 a3 a5 12 b3 followed by Bb2.

b) 7 e4 dxe4 8 Ng5 Nc5! can lead to dull equality after 9 Ngxe4 Nfxe4 10 Nxe4 Nxe4 11 Bxe4 Bxe4 12 dxe4 Qxd1 13 Rxd1. Instead, 8 dxe4!? **(Diagram 4)** is more ambitious. This time it really is a proper pawn sacrifice because after 8...Nxe4 White doesn't have the move Ne5 available. Instead the game A.Murariu-D.Stellwagen, Oropesa del Mar 2000 continued 9 Ng5!? Qxg5! (9...Nd6? 10 Bxb7 Nxb7 11 Nxf7! Kxf7 12 Qf3+ is good for White) 10 Nxe4 Qf5 11 Nf6+! Nxf6 12 Bxb7 Rd8 13 Bc6+ Nd7 14 c3 Bd6 15 Qa4 h5. Now after 16 h4!, preventing Black from playing ...h5-h4, White has some compensation for the pawn.

7...g6!?

7...Be7 would be more typical, after which play could continue with 8 e4 dxe4 9 dxe4 (9 Ng5!? 0-0 10 Ngxe4 Nxe4 11 Nxe4 looks fairly even) 9...Ba6 (or 9...0-0 10 e5 Nd5 11 a3! preventing ...Nb4 and threatening to win a piece with c2-c4) 10 e5! Nd5 (10...Bxf1 11 exf6!) 11 c4 Nb4 12 Qe4! Nc5 13 Qg4 with a very double-edged position. Black's pieces are very active on the queenside, but White's queen has reached a good square and Black may experience problems down the h1-a8 diagonal.

8 e4 dxe4 9 Nxe4!? Nxe4

9...Bg7 looks sensible.

10 dxe4 Ba6?

Is it possible Black simply missed White's reply? 10...Bg7! has to be played.

11 Qc3! (Diagram 5) 11...Bxf1

This is forced as 11...Qf6? 12 Qc6! leaves Black in a real mess.

12 Qxh8 Bxg2 13 Kxg2 Qf6 14 Qxh7 0-0-0?

Here I think Black must have missed the strength of White's 17th move. 14...Ne5 is relatively best, although after 15 Nxe5 Qxe5 16 Qh4 White is a safe pawn ahead.

15 Bg5! Qxb2 16 Bxd8 Qxa1

Black was probably banking on 17 Bg5 Qg7! but he was in for a nasty shock!

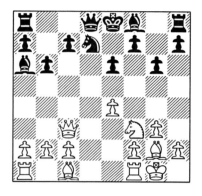

Diagram 5 (B)
Both rooks attacked

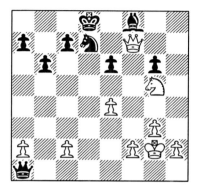

Diagram 6 (B)
Winning back the piece

17 Qxf7! Kxd8 18 Ng5! (Diagram 6)

Regaining the piece with a couple of pawns to boot.

18...Qxa2 19 Nxe6+ Kc8 20 Qe8+ Kb7 21 Qxd7 Bd6 22 Nd8+! Ka6 23 Qc6 Qa5 24 c4! Qc5 25 Qa4+ Qa5 26 Qd7! b5

Or 26...Qh5 27 e5! Qxe5 28 Qc8+ Ka5 29 Nc6+ (Minic).

27 Qc8+ Kb6 28 Qb7+ Kc5 29 Qd5+ 1-0

29...Kb6 allows mate on c6, while 29...Kb4 30 Nc6+ picks up the queen.

KIA versus the Dutch

The Dutch (1...f5) is one of the most uncompromising defences to 1 d4, and it's not surprising that many Dutch players try ...f7-f5 against other non-1 e4 openings such as the English and 1 Nf3. The advantage that 1 Nf3 has over 1 d4 is that, without the d-pawn committed to d4, White is in a much better position to force through an early e2-e4. Given that one of the main goals of the Dutch is to prevent this move, this must be good news for White. Nevertheless, the Dutch is certainly a viable option against the KIA.

Game 50
□ **M.Tal** ■ **H.Pohla**
Tallinn 1977

1 Nf3 f5 2 g3

Although they are not strictly in KIA territory, it's worth mentioning a couple of aggressive options that Black players must be ready to face here:

a) 2 e4!? is the Lisitsin Gambit, the main idea of which is seen in the variation 2...fxe4 3 Ng5 Nf6 4 d3 exd3 5 Bxd3 when White has a strong attack against Black's weakened king (capturing on h7 is already a threat). Of course Black doesn't have to be so obliging, and one recommended way to play is to give back the pawn with 3...Nc6 4 d3 e3! 5 Bxe3 e5.

b) 2 d3!? **(Diagram 7)**, aiming for a very quick e2-e4, is an interesting sideline that has received some attention recently.

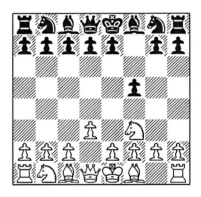

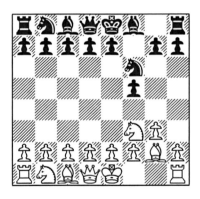

Diagram 7 (B)	Diagram 8 (B)
An accelerated KIA?	A choice of lines

One point is that after 2...Nf6 3 e4! fxe4 4 dxe4 Nxe4 5 Bd3 Nf6 6 Ng5! we have reached a favourable variation of the Lisitsin. In fact, 2 d3 has been causing Black some problems, and this was graphically illustrated in the miniature M.Carlsen-S.Dolmatov Moscow 2004, where the experienced Russian grandmaster, an expert on 1...f5, was downed in just 19 moves by the Norwegian prodigy: 2...d6 3 e4 e5 4 Nc3 Nc6 5 exf5! Bxf5 6 d4! Nxd4 7 Nxd4 exd4 8 Qxd4 Nf6 9 Bc4! c6 10 Bg5 b5?! 11 Bb3

Be7 12 0-0-0 Qd7 13 Rhe1 Kd8 14 Rxe7! Qxe7 15 Qf4 Bd7 16 Ne4 d5 17 Nxf6 h6 18 Bh4 g5 19 Qd4! and Black resigned, not wishing to continue in a hopeless position after 19...Rf8 20 Nxd7 Qxd7 21 Bg3. I imagine that there will be some more developments in this line, but it certainly looks worth a punt from White's point of view.

2...Nf6 3 Bg2 (Diagram 8) 3...g6

Black's other mode of development is with 3...e6 4 d3 and now:

a) 4...Be7 5 0-0 0-0 6 Nbd2 d6 7 e4 fxe4 8 dxe4 e5 is a typical set-up. The game A.Vaisser-F.Ochoa de Echaguen, Palma de Mallorca 1989 continued 9 c3 Qe8 10 Nh4 Nc6 11 Nc4 Qh5 12 Qxh5 Nxh5 13 Nf5 Bd8 (13...Bxf5 14 exf5 Rxf5? loses material after 15 g4) 14 a4 Nf6 15 Nfe3 Be6 16 b4 and White was slowly building up pressure on the queenside (the grip on d5 certainly helps here). I'm not sure I like Black's decision to offer an exchange of queens with 11...Qh5, as this seemed to kill his play on the kingside. Perhaps 11...Kh8, intending ...Bg4 is a stronger way to play.

b) The 'Stonewall' is not very effective against the KIA because, contrary to d2-d4 lines, Black cannot prevent White from achieving the e2-e4 advance: 4...d5 5 0-0 Bd6 6 Nc3! 0-0 7 e4! and already White has a nice position. In R.McKay-P.Giulian, Scottish Championship 1988 it turned from 'nice' to 'winning' in just a few moves: 7...fxe4 8 dxe4 dxe4?! 9 Ng5! Nc6 10 Ncxe4 e5? 11 Nxf6+ gxf6 12 Nxh7! (Diagram 9) and Black decided to throw in the towel due to 12...Kxh7 13 Qh5+ Kg8 14 Bd5+ Kg7 15 Qh6 mate.

4 0-0 Bg7 5 d3

5 d4 will reach regular Dutch Leningrad lines.

5...0-0 6 e4 d6

Taking advantage of the fact that 6...fxe4 7 dxe4 Nxe4? drops a piece to 8 Qd5+ to play e2-e4 without the usual preparation. Now White's queen's knight can be developed more actively.

7 Nc3 fxe4 8 dxe4 e5 9 Be3

Alternatively:

a) 9 Bg5 h6 10 Bxf6 Bxf6 11 Nd5 Be6 12 c3 Nd7 13 Nd2 Bg7 14 Qe2 Rf7 15 Rad1 Nb6 16 Nb3 with a roughly level position, I. Ivanov-Y.Seirawan, Denver 1998.

b) 9 h3 Nbd7 10 Be3 b6 11 Ne1!? Bb7 12 Nd3 Qe7 13 Kh2 a5 14 Qd2 again with approximate equality, L.Barczay-Z.Polgar, Lillafured 1989.

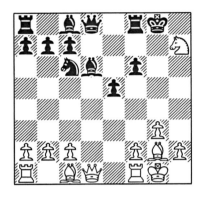

Diagram 9 (B)
Winning for White

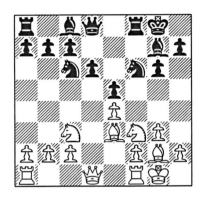

Diagram 10 (W)
The typical structure

9...Nc6 (Diagram 10)

Black can pin the knight with 9...Bg4, but following 10 Qd2 the idea 10...Nxe4?? has a major flaw in 11 Qd5+!.

10 Qd2 Kh8 11 h3 Be6 12 Rad1 Qd7 13 Ng5 Bc4 14 Rfe1 h6 15 Nf3 g5 16 h4!

White forces Black to compromise his kingside structure before he has a chance to regroup with ...Ne7-g6.

16...g4 17 Nh2 Ng8 18 Nd5 Nd4 19 Bxd4!?

Giving up the bishop pair, but winning the f4-square for the knight.

19...exd4 20 Nf4 Bf7?

Missing White's very sneaky idea. The best way to prevent Ng6+ was with 20...Ne7!.

21 Qa5! c5

Preventing Qf5, but...

22 Nxg4! (Diagram 11)

Now 22...Qxg4 allows 23 Bh3! Qf3 24 Rd3!, trapping the queen, so White has simply won a crucial pawn.

22...b6 23 Qa3 Be5 24 Nxe5 dxe5 25 Nd3 Rae8 26 c3

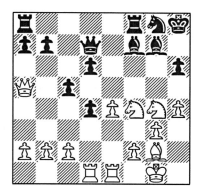

Diagram 11 (B)
The knight is poisoned

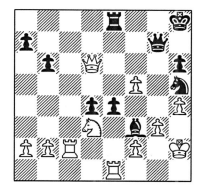

Diagram 12 (B)
The refutation

Black's only compensation for the pawn is in the shape of his central pawns, so White begins to nibble at them. Now 26...c4? is met by 27 Nxe5! as 27...Rxe5 leaves the rook hanging on f8.

26...Bh5 27 Rd2 Qg7 28 cxd4 cxd4 29 Rc2! Bf3 30 Bh3 Nf6 31 Bf5 Nh5 32 Kh2!

Black's next move is a final desperate attempt to mix things up.

32...Rxf5 33 exf5 e4 34 Qd6! (Diagram 12)

...which Tal refutes easily.

34...Nf6 35 Rc7 exd3 36 Rxg7 Kxg7

36...Rxe1 threatens mate in one, but White gets in first with 37 Qf8+!

37 Rxe8 1-0

Points to Remember

1) Against the Queen's Indian, d2-d3 followed by e2-e4 will block out Black's bishop on b7, so Black often plays a quick ...d7-d5. Sometimes White can force through e2-e4 without much preparation due to tactical tricks on the h1-a8 diagonal.

2) The Dutch is certainly playable against the KIA and leads to different pawn structures to those examined in previous chapters. However, 1 Nf3 f5 2 d3!? followed by 3 e4 is an enticing way for White to play.

Index of Variations

KIA versus the French

KIA versus the Sicilian

KIA versus the Caro-Kann

The Reversed King's Indian

KIA versus the ...Bf5 System

1 Nf3 d5 2 g3 Nf6 3 Bg2 c6 4 0-0 Bf5 5 d3
 5 b3 e6 6 Bb2 Be7 7 d3 h6 8 Nbd2 0-0 9 Qe1 Bh7 10 e4 a5
  11 a4 *177*; 11 a3 *176*
5...e6 6 Nbd2 Be7 7 Qe1 h6 8 e4 Bh7 9 Qe2 *170*
 9 Ne5 *167*

KIA versus the ...Bg4 System

1 Nf3 d5 2 g3 Nf6
 2...c6 3 Bg2 Bg4 4 0-0 Nd7 5 d3 e6 6 Nbd2 Bd6 7 e4 Ne7 *208*
3 Bg2 c6 4 0-0 Bg4 5 d3
 5 b3 Nbd7 6 Bb2 e6 7 d3
  7...Bd6 *198*; 7...Bc5 *200*
5...Nbd7 6 Nbd2 e6
 6...e5 7 e4
  7...dxe4 *190*; 7...Bd6 *192*
7 h3 Bh5 *182*
 7...Bxf3 *184*

The Queen's Indian and the Dutch

1 Nf3 Nf6
 1...f5
  2 g3 *216*; 2 d3 *216*; 2 e4 *216*
2 g3 b6 *212*
 2...b5 *212*

Index of Complete Games

LaVergne, TN USA
20 November 2010
205725LV00003B/4/P